About the author

Born in 1951 in the city of Ahvaz, Iran, Hamid Dabashi received his college education in Tehran before moving to the United States, where he received a dual Ph.D. in Sociology of Culture and Islamic Studies from the University of Pennsylvania, followed by a postdoctoral fellowship at Harvard University. He is currently Hagop Kevorkian Professor of Iranian Studies and Comparative Literature at Columbia University in the City of New York.

Dabashi has written twenty books, edited four, and contributed chapters to many others, in addition to authoring more than a hundred essays, articles and book reviews. He is an internationally renowned cultural critic and award-winning author whose writings have been translated into numerous languages.

A committed teacher for nearly three decades, Hamid Dabashi is also a public speaker, a current affairs essayist, a staunch anti-war activist, and founder of Dreams of a Nation, a Palestinian film project dedicated to preserving Palestinian cinema. He has four children, and lives in New York with his wife and colleague, the Iranian-Swedish feminist Golbarg Bashi.

Iran, the Green Movement and the USA

The Fox and the Paradox

HAMID DABASHI

Zed Books

LONDON & NEW YORK

Iran, the Green Movement and the USA: The Fox and the Paradox was first published in 2010 by Zed Books Ltd, 7 Cynthia Street, London N1 9JF, UK and Room 400, 175 Fifth Avenue, New York, NY 10010, USA

www.zedbooks.co.uk

Copyright © Hamid Dabashi 2010

The right of Hamid Dabashi to be identified as the author of this work has been asserted by him in accordance with the Copyright, Designs and Patents Act, 1988

Designed and typeset in Monotype Joanna
by illuminati, Grosmont
Index by John Barker
Cover design by www.alice-marwick.co.uk
Printed and bound in in Great Britain
by CPI Antony Rowe, Chippenham and Eastbourne

Distributed in the USA exclusively by Palgrave Macmillan, a division of St Martin's Press, LLC, 175 Fifth Avenue, New York, NY 10010, USA

A catalogue record for this book is available from the British Library
Library of Congress Cataloging in Publication Data available

ISBN 978 1 84813 815 5 hb
ISBN 978 1 84813 816 2 pb
ISBN 978 1 84813 818 6 eb

Contents

Acknowledgments

I AM GRATEFUL to three anonymous readers who recommended the publication of my book to Zed and gave me caring guidance to develop my initial ideas in more accessible and timely form. To my editor at Zed, Tamsine O'Riordan, I owe a special note of gratitude for her diligence in seeing this book through publication. I am also indebted to illuminati for their excellent typesetting and editorial skills during the final stages of production. I thank Mina Khanlarzadeh for reading carefully through the final proofs fishing for typos and other infelicities. I am equally grateful to 'Termeh' (the pseudonym of an Iranian poet, painter, and civil rights activist) for allowing her powerful and endearing illustrations to accompany my text in this book. Termeh's tireless work has emerged as perhaps the most compelling visual register of the Green Movement in Iran. I have followed her work closely and consider it the visual memory of a civil rights movement that has given birth to her powerful and memorable art. Termeh was a young Tehran-based poet and artist long before the commencement of the Green Movement in June 2009. But something happened between her relentless creative urges and the occasion of that momentous uprising that opened in her creative soul an entire gallery of loving visual tableaux that have best captured the urban disposition of a civil rights movement in which she is a participant observer. She represents an entire generation of young Iranian artists whose magnificent work the world at large is yet to discover. I feel privileged to have discovered their work on the ground zero of a seismic change in the habitual politics of despair they are determined to change. On her Facebook page Termeh has written a poem, 'Without a Vista of Oneself,' in which she says (my translation):

> My name is Termeh/Paisley and the name of all I paint –
> The Termeh that is everywhere, has been everywhere, for as
>   long as I remember:
> Under the New Year ceremonial objects, over the dead people's
>   corpse...
> Termeh is my story
> From here, from this elongated memory, from the days
> When I have feared...
> With all the sorrow and the ecstasy of what has happened
> I was born to tell.

This book is dedicated to this generation of visionary recitals (of facts, fictions, and vistas of a whole new march to liberty) and of storytellers bent on putting a different spin on their own destiny.

In loving memory of
Neda Agha Soltan, Kianoush Asa, Sohrab A'rabi,
Somayyeh Jafargholi, Amir Javadifar, Mohsen Ruhol-amini...
and countless other young men and women
cold-bloodedly murdered by the officials of the Islamic Republic
— may their untimely and cruel deaths not be in vain!

PROLOGUE

A Parable

ONCE UPON A TIME, and what a wondrous and strange time it was, in a faraway jungle there was a Lion under whose majestic shadow and extended benevolence a shrewd and enterprising Fox was making quite a lucrative living. For years the Lion and the Fox had quite a cozy arrangement. The Lion hunted down and feasted on large and small prey, and whatever was left of his meals was more than sufficient for a luxurious leftover for the weak but wily Fox living off his might and majesty. In exchange for that sumptuous meal, the Fox would periodically sing the praise or else mark the authorial deficiencies of the Lion (in an ever more conniving language of course) just enough to keep the egomaniacal vanity of the Lion King on the sharp edge of his hunting prowess. After a long and prosperous life, old age and frailty finally overcame the Lion King and he eventually lost the physical force and agile facility with which he used to hunt his prey, and he was soon afflicted (and was thus clinically diagnosed) with a common balding disease and lost much of his mass of magisterial hair. The old Fox was quite obviously not so happy with this sight and state of affairs, for if the Lion King could not and would not hunt and thus did not succeed in feasting on fat and lazy prey, so would the Fox lose his daily (quite sumptuous, one might add) livelihood.

'Your Majesty,' the wily Fox finally turned one day to his benefactor and said solemnly (with an air of sustained gratitude), 'does His Majesty not think that he ought to do something about his illness – this simply cannot be. You cannot just go for days on end without a single worthy hunt to Your Majesty's name. It is unbecoming of your powerful position and royal name and honor.' The Lion King agreed. 'If there were a cure for our illness,' he royally consented, with a majestic 'we' that declared to the whole jungle who was in charge, 'we,' he cleared his drying throat and said, 'would gladly resume our hunting habits and dispense our magnanimity as we have in the past. We have in fact heard, and indeed we have been thus advised by our own royal physicians, that the heart and ears of an ass are the only cures for our sort of illness. But where in this jungle, our most royal realm, are we to find an ass?'

'No problem, Your Majesty,' the eager Fox said assuredly. 'If that is Your Majesty's wish and that is what it takes to cure your most unfortunate illness, your most humble servant will happily oblige and readily produce an ass on whose heart and ears Your Royal Appetite can feast, get well, and resume Your most auspicious hunting, for after this misfortune Your gracious hair has all fallen down and Your Majesty, if you pardon your most obedient and humble servant for saying so, lacks that stately awe with which you roamed our realm. Your royal subjects scarce recognize you, Sire, these days. You do still have that in your countenance that I would fain call master (the wily Fox had read this phrase once in an ancient book and instantly

memorized it to use it on such opportune occasions as this) but
it is increasingly less authoritative than it used to be.' The Lion,
now coming to terms with his aging weakness, listened intently,
not without a little tinge of disgust towards the wily Fox. 'In a
nearby wood,' the Fox offered ever so meticulously, 'there is a
small spring where a textile manufacturer comes every day to
dye his wools and the Ass that carries his merchandise, Sire,
seems to me to be the perfect candidate for Your Royal Highness's cure. I can procure that ass henceforth and momentarily
so that Your Majesty can have his heart and ears and dispense
with the rest to your most humble servant, if your royal will
were thus ever so graciously to deign and condescend.'

The Lion listened quite leisurely but still attentively and
agreed, and it was thus that one fine morning the scheming Fox
went straight to that most unfortunate Ass, as his owner was
busy dying his wools at the spring, and asked him how was
he doing and why was it that he looked so skinny and seemed
so utterly afflicted with labor abuse and malnutrition. 'This
master I have,' the donkey readily complained, 'works me really
hard and scarce gives me anything to eat.' The devious Fox
assured the attentive Ass that this was his lucky day for he had
the perfect solution for him. 'Not to worry,' the Fox said, and
strange not a single sign of a conniving creature was evident
about him when he thus plotted his treacherous scheme, 'there
is a wondrous prairie nearby where you can have a wonderful
life, eat as much grass as you wish, and there would be not a
single savage soul to harass or bother you. Just a while ago I
invited another ass, looking very much weak and feeble like
you, to this prairie and you should see how happy, fat, and
prosperous he now looks.' The Fox went on and on about the
paradisiacal properties of this fictive prairie until finally the
poor Ass was deceived and lured towards the ailing but still

quite ferocious Lion King. At the Fox's signal the Lion King ever so abruptly attacked the Ass and aimed for his throat, but much to his own surprise and the disappointment of the Fox he could not overcome the wretched creature. Though slightly wounded the Ass managed to run away.

The Fox turned to the Lion King in utter disappointment and with an air of condescending bewilderment (he was rather good at exuding these twin emotive sentiments that came quite naturally to him without appearing malicious or wicked), wondering what had happened to his hitherto mighty benefactor — now incapable of handling even a foolish Ass. The Lion King, quite frazzled by now, used whatever was left of his royal aura to send the Fox back to the Ass to convince him to return. The Fox agreed and went back to the Ass and saw him visibly shaken and frightened out of his wits, and of course (and quite obviously) exceedingly angry. 'Where did you take me and what was that,' the poor Ass asked in bitter disappointment. 'Obviously providence has not seen fit yet for your misery to come to an end,' the Fox offered with a certain air of detached incredulity, 'otherwise,' he went on, 'you would not have run away so fast without giving the poor creature who had come to embrace and welcome you a chance to express his friendship and solidarity with you. All the poor thing was trying to do was to greet you warmly and hug and kiss you in a gesture of asinine solidarity — that's all. Though in his excitement, I admit, he may have appeared a bit rough and quite obviously uncouth.' Not having ever seen a lion, the gullible Ass was thus easily convinced that what he saw was in fact none other than a fellow ass, happy and excited to have seen him. The Fox thus used and abused every conceivable device in the arsenal of his smooth-talking trickery to bring the poor and unfortunate Ass back to the Lion King.

This time around the Lion took his sweet time and approached the Ass very cautiously and gently and spent some time attending to his injured ego, with smooth talking and gentle gestures, and then suddenly at an opportune moment jumped on him and tore him to pieces, before the wretched creature had a chance even to notice what was happening to him. The Lion King then turned to the Fox and said, with the solemnity of his former magisterial self suddenly evident in his voice, 'I am now going to do my ablutions, for I am told this is what I need to do before I eat his heart and ears for them to be effective in curing my illness.' The Lion said that and went to do his ablutions, but as soon as he left the scene of the incident, the Fox swiftly ate both the heart and the ears of the Ass — and he thought they were quite delicious, though he had to gobble them down hurriedly before the Lion returned. 'Where are his heart and ears?' the anxious Lion asked the instant he returned to his prepared feast. 'My most Honored Majesty,' the Fox said, as he ever so slowly downed the very last bite of the heart and ears of the forsaken Ass, 'if the wretched thing had a heart and a pair of ears, one the seat of reason and the other the instrument of sense perception, would he, I ask Your Majesty, come back here after Your Exalted Highness first sought to slaughter him?'[1]

ONE

The Paradox

THERE IS A NOT SO HIDDEN POLITICS to the prose and purpose of old Persian animal fables, deeply rooted as they are in even more ancient Indian and Mesopotamian wisdom literatures. Today scarce anyone reads these old animal fables except in useless academic and scholastic circles. But the enduring wisdom they contain and the allusions they happily sustain are deeply evident in the collective subconscious of a political culture that claims them and speaks their language in sublated disguises and colorful camouflages. If in the current geopolitics of the region, Iran were to be offered here as the wily Fox of the fable and the United States as that slumbering Lion, who or what would be the gullible Ass? This thing they call 'the Middle East'? There need not be a one-to-one correspondence in such parables that anticipate our collective fate and that always run ahead of any allusion or application one might ask them to offer. The moral of the story is the superiority of visionary wit (of course predicated on a politics of desperation) over the might and majesty of a hapless superpower, afflicted with an illness that it is clueless how else to cure. The key, the wily Fox had learned in his long and adventurous life, was to get the fat and balding Lion do for him what he could not do himself – like eliminating Saddam Hussein and his massive military apparatus on one of its hostile fronts, or amassing a mighty military prowess to dismantle the nuisance of the Taliban on another. This is not to attribute to the ruling Iranian clerical clique a political wit or ancient wisdom they so obviously lack in many other respects, but simply to offer a parabolic leitmotif hidden under how things have unfolded in a region so vital to world peace and yet so afflicted with chronic diseases of domestic tyranny and foreign domination.

My principal thesis in this book, which I write under the playful light of the parable of the Lion King, the Wily Fox, and the Gullible Ass, and exactly at the moment when President Obama is weighing his options vis-à-vis the Islamic Republic, is that prior to the rise of the Green Movement in Iran in June 2009 the resourceful clerics in Iran had turned themselves into the key strategic factor in any move that he may make in the region – and that in an age of asymmetric warfare, whatever the US president may opt to do he will make Iran, perforce, even more powerful than it is. If President Obama proceeds to negotiate with Iran (over the nuclear stalemate, Iraq, Afghanistan, Lebanon, or the Palestinian predicament – in a so-called Grand Bargain) he will strengthen its hand; and if alternatively he opts for a combination of military and diplomatic pressures on Iran he will lose even more spectacularly. Accommodating the Islamic Republic will give it even more regional power and prestige; attacking it will instantly bring out its scarcely hidden nature as basically a guerrilla operation and a garrison state. This paradox is not an indication of how diplomatically savvy or politically shrewd the Islamic Republic (the Fox of the fable) is; but how catastrophic is the enduring legacy of George W. Bush's presidency (the balding Lion King with his tail on fire and yet scarce anyone around him dared to tell). That this paradox has now assumed a new twist after the rise of the civil rights (Green) movement in Iran in the aftermath of the June 2009 presidential election will first have to be bracketed for a moment so we will get a full picture of the lay of the land before we factor in the all-important weight of that potentially groundbreaking event.

One of the major promises of President Barack Obama during his presidential campaign (2007–08) was to withdraw American forces from Iraq. His timely speech against the US-led invasion of Iraq in October 2002 had in fact emerged as a principal touchstone of his victory first over Senator Hillary Rodham Clinton during the Democratic primaries, and later against his Republican rival Senator John McCain. 'We ought to be as careful getting out,' Obama repeatedly stipulated during his presidential campaign, 'as we were careless getting in.' But how careful can he be in pulling the American forces out of Iraq – and what does he need to be careful about? There is only so much that a crippled Lion afflicted with an economic meltdown of unfathomable proportions (the result of generations of greedy mismanagement and deregulation) can do. With any scenario where the US and its allies pull out of Iraq, the Islamic Republic will be even more powerful than it is in the region – and yet if the US opts to stay its current course in Iraq, it will make the custodians of the belligerent theocracy even more crucial in the region.

In order to deliver on that defining promise of his campaign, perhaps the defining issue of his presidency, Barack Obama will have to solicit, one way or another, the active support of the Islamic Republic of Iran – and in achieving that end he will have to concede their regional share of power, which might include accepting a nuclear dot on an 'axis of evil.' The alternative, a combination of economic sanctions and covert operations that could ultimately culminate in a military strike against Iran (by the US and/or Israel), would be in fact even more beneficial to the clerical custodians of the Islamic Republic and strengthen their militarized state apparatus even more than the Israeli invasion of Lebanon did to Hezbollah in 2006, or Hamas in December 2008–January 2009. The reigning clergy in Iran has played its cards – though playing cards is prohibited in Shi'i law – so masterfully that if Obama opts to attack the Islamic Republic militarily in order to neutralize its influence in Iraq it will exponentially strengthen its power in the region, even more than what it is now – and if conversely, and as he promised during his campaign, he were to sit down to talk with them he will equally legitimize the domestically beleaguered and brutal mullarchy and strengthen them regionally even more. It is just like the predicament of the old and balding Lion King – if he concedes to the wily Fox helping him out, he is totally at his mercy and the conniving creature will end up eating the heart and ears of the poor Ass, and if the weakened monarch of the jungle refuses the Fox's offer he will have no power or glory to show and stage in order to sustain his authority. You feel rather sorry for the aging Lion King, so forced as he is in his old age to attack and slaughter a poor Ass just to convince the wily Fox he is still in charge. For the devious and sly Fox it is a win–win situation; as for the wretched Lion King it is a lose–lose scenario. The abused Ass is just a ploy – his fatal end a foregone conclusion.

The force of this paradox, which empowers the Islamic Republic no matter what Obama does, is in part because of the sheer stupidity of George W. Bush and the Middle East map of power Obama has inherited from him, and in part because of the historic unfolding of events in the region even before Bush became the president in 2000. In either of those two scenarios, and whatever the causes that have occasioned them, Obama in Iran faces a see-saw game that will raise the Islamic Republic if he raises his stick, and paradoxically give the Shi'i clergy even more momentum if he were to offer the few carrots he has in his bag that the mullahs covet — and thus the tired old cliché of 'carrots and sticks' is by now entirely useless. The Shi'i clergy will eat those carrots and use those sticks to drum up even more support for itself in the region — so we need to change the metaphors and come up with different parables to read the present circumstances and the future unfolding.

The reason for the unique position of power Iran now holds is very simple. Over the last eight years, the Islamic Republic has strengthened its relations with three major national liberation movements in the region, the Hezbollah in Lebanon, Hamas in Palestine, and the Mahdi Army in Iraq. That the Islamic Republic abuses these relations — and the battle that these three revolutionary movements wage against Israel and the United States — in order to strengthen its domestic tyranny and regional power has so far remained the least of the issues in the global configuration of power. What has been eminently more consequential is that the factual miseries that the United States and Israel have left behind in the wake of their colonial and imperial projects have exponentially strengthened the hand of the Islamic Republic in the region. This is the age of asymmetric warfare, and the senseless flaunting of raw power both by the Bush administration and by Israel has lost its military logic and become entirely counterproductive. From this asymmetric battle, articulated and defined by weaker nations during George W. Bush's presidency (2000–2008), Iran has emerged even more powerful than it has ever been — no matter what Obama opts to do. The fact that he presides over the deadliest military machinery in human history, or that his chief regional ally Israel is in command of an equally deadly military prowess, means absolutely nothing in this age of asymmetric warfare, when a single Hezbollah fighter in southern Lebanon can outlast an entire platoon of the Israeli army. This is the age of weak but wily foxes outmaneuvering mighty but outdated lions for good. Decades of billions of dollars' worth of military aid that the pro-Israeli lobbies procured for Israel from American taxpayers' money have come to naught. Nothing could defeat Zionism. Zionism is defeating Zionism. The moral and military meltdown of Israel, and by extension the US, have ushered in the age of asymmetric warfare.

The Iranian presidential election of June 2009 gave a sudden and dramatic jolt to the whole geopolitics of the region by throwing a monkey wrench at it. Everything may appear to have stayed the same, but it is not. Whatever the end result of the current electoral crisis in Iran, the dramatic commencement of a civil rights movement and the rise of national politics have already cast a long shadow.

Prior to the June 2009 presidential election, the realpolitik of the region had placed Iran, Syria, the Palestinian Hamas, the Lebanese Hezbollah, and the Iraqi Mahdi Army on one side of the geopolitical divide, and the US and its regional allies (Israel, Pakistan, Saudi Arabia, and Egypt in particular) on the other. With an extended foot in Venezuela, Iran even had a claim on the backyard of the United States. In this precarious condition, the Islamic Republic had emerged not out of its own capacities, but by virtue of serious follies that President Bush had committed in its neighborhood, as a regional 'superpower.' The presidential election of June 2009 has suddenly made of that geopolitics something of an archeological relic.

With the commencement of the civil rights movement in Iran in earnest in June 2009, the moral map of the Middle East is being changed before our eyes, with the democratic will of one nation, in their millions and whomever they voted for, disrupting the geopolitics of the region. The moving pictures of Iranians flooding colorfully into their city landscape have forever altered the visual vocabulary of the global perception of 'the Middle East.' As a major cosmopolis, Tehran is now the ground zero of a civil rights movement that will leave no Muslim or Arab country, or even Israel, untouched. 'The unrest in Iran,' said the prominent Israeli columnist Gideon Levy of *Haaretz*, soon after it stated, 'makes me green with envy.'

However things may turn out in the near future, Ahmadinejad has returned to the global scene with a lame duck presidency that may indeed last to a full term, but the constitutional foregrounding of the belligerent theocracy has forever changed. There is a domino effect to Ahmadinejad's weakened second-term presidency in the region. The Syrian position in its immediate regional context, from Lebanon, through Israel, to Palestine, is now seriously compromised. The rushed and injudicious siding of Hasan Nasrallah, secretary general of the Lebanese Islamist party and paramilitary organization Hezbollah, with Ahmadinejad has wedded the fate of the Lebanese Hezbollah with that of the discredited Iranian president. The Palestinian Hamas would now be infinitely more inclined to strike a deal with Fatah and join President Obama's renewed peace process; as the Iraqi Mahdi Army now has to fend for itself in more pronouncedly Iraqi (even nationalist) terms, and make it more urgent for the US military to leave. The fundamental domestic challenge to the very legitimacy of the Islamic Republic puts all its regional allies under strategic and logistic pressure.

The domino effect, however, is not limited to the allies of the Islamic Republic and extends well into the domains of its nemesis, for now the options available to both the US and its regional allies regarding the Iranian nuclear project have also become categorically compromised. The feasibility of economic sanctions or blockade, or a military strike, in the future unfolding of the nuclear stalemate has become increasingly difficult to sell to the international community at large. The heroic fate of millions of young Iranian men and women has now become a global concern. How can you starve Neda Aqa Soltan's soulmates, or, even worse, bomb them?

The democratic will of Iranians has changed the moral map of the Middle East, and the civil rights movement that they have started will have a domino effect that will leave no nation in the region unaffected. We have to start thinking of a new term for 'the Middle East.' It is central, but to no one's East or West. As a civil rights movement, demanding the most fundamental constitutional guarantees of civil liberties, in a region and political culture that has never had them, the Green Movement has recentered the world.

As President Obama wisely keeps Ahmadinejad at arm's length, and as his task in securing a just and lasting peace between Palestinians and Israelis has been made much easier for him, the gift that millions of young and old Iranian men and women have just handed him and the cause of peace and justice in region is set to change the very nature of politics as usual in the region. By the fall of 2009, a severe crackdown had dampened the spirit of the civil rights movement in Iran; scores of peaceful demonstrators were killed or injured; hundreds of civic leaders and public intellectuals arrested; the leaders of the Green Movement were being accused of treason and threatened with execution; human rights organizations were deeply troubled; and, even worse, ominous news was still in the offing. But the morning had broken, and the whole world was now witness to something extraordinary.

Any dealing with the Islamic Republic must now begin with acknowledging this grassroots civil rights movement and continue with a reconsideration of the geopolitics of the region, particularly the Israeli–Palestinian issue. In this book I argue that what Ahmadinejad/Khamenei are now doing is playing high power politics with P5+1 (the five permanent UN Security Council members – Britain, China, France, Russia, and the United States – plus Germany) in order to pull the theater of operation and the focus of global attention away from their domestic troubles and into the geopolitics of the region. The weakness of the Islamic Republic is in its domestic affairs; its strength is in regional geo-politics. It is now playing the nuclear issue against its weakness and towards its strength. Signs of this strategy include: accepting the sending of uranium enrichment to Russia, then changing their mind on that issue; being taken aback by the discovery of a new nuclear site near Qom, and declaring enrichment in ten additional sites soon after; reaching agreement in Geneva during the difficult months of summer, then reneging during the quieter months of fall. Everything that Ahmadinejad's government does now, I argue, is under domestic pressure, with a massive civil rights movement rattling his security apparatus and with it the legitimacy of the regime in general. The military apparatus of the Islamic Republic would love to go the North Korean way or else engage in a Tiananmen Square crackdown the Chinese way – but the highly agitated (youth-driven) opposition does not relent. Meanwhile, the Islamic Republic would welcome additional economic sanctions, because: (1) they are ineffective; (2) they will be a greater source of illegal trade in the Persian Gulf and thus of more income for the military–security–commercial conglomerate of the Revolutionary Guards; (3) they represent an opportunity to blame the regime's economic woes on 'the enemy'; and (4) they will provide them with the perfect excuse to crack down on the growing opposition even more violently. Addressing the larger regional politics – pulling out of Iraq, not exacerbating the situation in Afghanistan, letting the brewing tribal conflicts in the Swat area of the North-West Frontier Province (NWFP) be addressed without US interference, disallowing further Israeli settlements, and pushing towards Palestinians statehood – will rob the Islamic republic of its regional strength and, ipso facto, help the civil rights movement in Iran.

The presiding paradox that defines the US–Iran relationship and endangers the ever-fragile peace of the region has now assumed wider geopolitical significance. Old and tiresome clichés like 'carrot and stick' no longer mean anything in this context; for the United States is no longer the active agent it used to think it was, and is unable to offer any carrots, let alone raise any threatening stick – given the quagmire of Iraq, Afghanistan, and northern Pakistan, all the way down to Somalia and Yemen, that Neoconservative warmongering has left for President Obama to measure or manage. We need a new language, newer readings of forgotten fables, to fathom the world. The aging Lion is incapable of manhandling the gullible Ass of regional dominance, while the wily Fox had been well poised to manipulate the region for its own benefits, before the Green Movement loudly declared to the whole world that its tail was fast on fire. If people ever thought this was anything but a Christian empire facing an Islamic republic on the premiss of a Jewish state, the eight-year crusade of the Bush–Cheney administration put an end to that. 'And if a sparrow cannot fall to the ground without His notice,' Mr and Mrs Cheney declared in their infamous Christmas card in 2003, quoting Benjamin Franklin more than two hundred years earlier, 'is it probable that an Empire can rise without His aid?' Cheney was, of course, not alone in that Christian conviction. 'George sees this as a religious war,' so said a friend of the president's family, 'he doesn't have a PC view of this war. His view of this is that they are trying to kill the Christians. And we Christians will strike back with more force and more ferocity than they will ever now.'[1] Let's change the language, but keep the facts on the ground what they are, for literature is an infinitely more wholesome guide than the level of literacy afforded this perilous planet.

TWO

Jammed in a Jungle and Nowhere to Go

JUST A BIT, NOT TOO MUCH, of history and a bit more of a changing political culture are what we need in order to see how this perhaps peculiar (and perhaps not so peculiar) paradox was set in motion during the last quarter of the twentieth century. What we witnessed during the closing decades of the century was the aggressive resurgence of a politics of despair predicated on a nativist provincialism of unsurpassed dimensions – all at the heavy cost of dismantling a vast cosmopolitan culture. How an Islamic republic, a Jewish state, and a Christian empire devoured their own and each other's innately worldly disposition and degenerated into a provincial nativism (one pitted against the other) is at the root of the predicament we face together. What I mean by the 'politics of despair' now common to all of these provincialized political cultures is a desperation in accepting reality as it is, not as it should be. That pervasive culture of defeatism delegates to the ephemeral domain of 'idealism' (now used as a derogatory term) any alternative vision of reality that seeks to suspend the here and now in order to cultivate an emancipatory vision of there and then.

The story of this aggressive nativism can be told from the late 1940s with the partition of the Indian subcontinent along sectarian lines and the separation of Pakistan from India, or even more emphatically with the formation of a Jewish state in Palestine. But with that immediate background, the current state of affairs and the radical nativization of otherwise cosmopolitan cultures was in full formation in the preparatory stages of an 'Islamized' revolution in Iran when that wiliest of all wily foxes Ayatollah Khomeini outmaneuvered President Jimmy Carter and deposed that ass of a monarch, the Shah of all Shahs, in the course of the 1977–79 revolution. The origin of the current paradox involving the US and the Islamic Republic must be traced back to the Islamic Revolution, when a massively popular social uprising managed to outmaneuver the Carter administration, rob it of one of its major regional allies, and depose Mohammad Reza Shah. The event created a major political vacuum in the region, and tipped the balance of power against the United States and its Arab, Muslim, Jewish, and Hindu allies from India, to Pakistan, through Israel, and all the way to Morocco. The Islamic Revolution of Iran had massive popular support, sympathy, and appeal in the rest of the Arab and Muslim world, with the potential to set the entire region on fire. Since it coincided with the Sandinista Revolution in Nicaragua, the two events had even more ominous implications for the United States in particular.

The Islamic Revolution in Iran most probably cost President Carter his second term and resulted in the recuperative era of Ronald Reagan (1980–88) – overcompensating for Carter's failures and salvaging American militarism from its Vietnam Syndrome. Reagan outlived Ayatollah Khomeini, who died in 1989, and skillfully managed to construct two mighty firewalls around Iran: one in Iraq in the figure of Saddam Hussein and the other in Afghanistan in the formation of the Mujahideen/Taliban. 'The loss of Iran' was a major factor in the presidential election of 1979/80 in the US and resulted in the spectacular victory of Ronald Reagan, who commenced the prolonged process of shifting American politics to the right. This move ultimately culminated in the ascendency of the American neoconservative movement in the early twenty-first century – and the rapid degeneration of the US into a nativist militarism. Soon after his election, President Reagan moved to curtail the damage of the Islamic Revolution in the region: (1) by heavily arming Iraq to its west and encouraging Saddam Hussein to invade Iran – a war that lasted eight long and bloody years and exhausted both countries' resources; and (2) by creating and arming the Mujahideen/Taliban in Afghanistan both to repel the Soviets and to resist the Shi'a-inspired revolutionary zeal of the Islamic Republic via the Wahabi-inspired ideology of the Taliban. The dual strategy was effective and successful. The Islamic Revolution was contained within the confines of the Islamic Republic itself and degenerated into a terrifying theocracy for its own citizens – women, students, and the labor unions in particular. The calamitous degeneration of the Iranian Revolution of 1979 into an Islamic republic now mirrored the Jewish state and became its arch nemesis, the flip side of its coin.

The happiness of the Reagan doctrine was short-lived and was not meant to last, for Reagan's chickens came home to roost soon after he left office in 1988, and the crescendo of violence it had set in motion was all but evident long before the events of 9/11 in 2001. The two monsters that the Reagan administration had created to contain the Islamic Republic – Saddam Hussein on one side and the Taliban on the other – came back to bite their creator. Soon after the end of the Iran–Iraq war (1980–88), Saddam Hussein invaded and occupied Kuwait on 2 August 1990; and soon after that the Taliban helped expel the Russians from Afghanistan. In 1988 the world learned of the existence of al-Qaeda (established some time between 1988 and 1990), and identified with Osama bin Laden), and soon after that a wide range of terrorist attacks against American targets were attributed to them. Military and diplomatic targets were hit by al-Qaeda in Nairobi, Kenya, in August 1998, in Dar es Salaam, Tanzania, in August 1998, and in Aden, Yemen, in October 2000. The Islamic Republic could not have been any happier. It had protected itself against these two monsters by becoming a monster like them and remained steadily in power, and by 1986 had managed either to silence or else to slaughter all its internal opposition forces – ranging from anticolonial nationalists to Third World socialists to human rights activists. As al-Qaeda was out on a rampage against American targets, and the fanatical Taliban became the legacy of US Afghan involvement during the Soviet occupation, we were witness to the aggressive Talibanization of any political culture that came close to Afghanistan.

By now the events of 9/11 in 2001 had put an entirely different spin on world events. Iran had nothing to do with the events of 9/11, and in fact was a staunch enemy of both the Taliban and al-Qaeda, and almost went to war with Afghanistan in 1997. As the US first led an invasion of Afghanistan in October 2001 and then of Iraq in March 2003, on the pretext of destroying those who had perpetrated the events of 9/11, Iran watched patiently and quietly, and at times even collaborated with the US, as its two arch nemeses were knocked down by a mighty superpower. The wily Fox would happily let the old Lion have both the heart and the ears of these particular asses.

As the US was busy destroying the enemies of the Islamic Republic left and right, Israel was hard at work creating new allies for it. During the eight years of George W. Bush's presidency, as the American military went after the Taliban and al-Qaeda in Afghanistan and against Saddam Hussein in Iraq, the Islamic Republic just sat there quietly and did not do anything other than consolidating its own position of regional power while the US destroyed its two principal opponents in Afghanistan and Iraq. Having just concluded a UN-facilitated peace treaty with Iraq in 1988, it could not be happier to see the might of the American army on Saddam Hussein's trail as early as in 1990. Having almost gone to war with the Taliban in 1997, it was equally pleased to see the US wipe them off the map of Afghanistan in 2001 (they would of course resurface again later). Iran even offered strategic help and airspace to American forces on their way to Taliban targets in Afghanistan.

Meanwhile the Israeli slaughter of Palestinian and Lebanese civilians and the stealing of even more of their land created two major regional allies for the Islamic Republic – Hamas in Palestine and Hezbollah in Lebanon. The creation of the Mahdi Army (a Shi'i militia in southern Iraq) soon after the US-led invasion in March 2003 generated yet another mass-based guerrilla movement in the region in alliance with the Islamic Republic. With the Taliban on the run, Saddam Hussein out of the way, Hezbollah empowered after defeating Israel yet again in 2006, Hamas even more entrenched in Gaza after the Israeli massacre of Palestinians in 2008–09, and the Mahdi Army perfectly poised to reap the benefits of the US occupation and/or withdrawal from Iraq, the Islamic Republic emerged not just as the most popular hero of the Arab and Muslim masses in the region (this is all before the Green Movement of course), but also strategically positioned as the most powerful political force, in an asymmetrically superior position to the military might of the US and Israel combined. The Lion (the US), the Fox (the Islamic Republic), and the Ass (the Middle East) had of course completely stripped each other of their worldly demeanor and were reduced to absolutist tribalism and survivalist instincts; but the persona in a position of power was the wily Fox, and there was very little that the neocon disciples of Leo Strauss at the Washington Institute for Near East Policy (WINEP) could do about the matter.

In the midst of this regional see-saw of power politics, Iranian nuclear ambitions surfaced as the principal site of contestation between the Islamic Republic and its nemesis. The origin of Iranian nuclear projects, now all but forgotten in the thicket of immediate urgency, dates back to the 1950s with the full knowledge and support of the US and even Israel. The late Shah's ambitious project to turn Iran into 'the Japan of the Middle East' was not satisfied with keeping Iran a merely petroleum-producing country. In the aftermath of the CIA-engineered coup of 1953, and under President Eisenhower's Atoms for Peace program, Iran received direct assistance from the US to develop a peaceful nuclear project. In 1968, Iran signed the Nuclear Nonproliferation Treaty (NPT), and in 1974 concluded its Safeguards Agreement with the International Atomic Energy Agency (IAEA). Throughout 1970s Europeans had joined Americans in providing the Shah with advanced nuclear technology. It was a lucrative business. But when in 1974, India tested its first atom bomb, American concern about the Shah going after the Bomb was now shared by Europeans.

The Iranian nuclear program came to a sudden halt in the immediate aftermath of the Islamic Revolution of 1979, with all US and European assistance obviously ceasing. Soon after the Iran–Iraq war (1980–88), Iran resumed its nuclear project, which it now kept secret because of the active opposition of the US to the Islamic Republic's acquisition of that technology. By the mid-1990s Iran had turned to Russia, China, North Korea, and Pakistan to acquire and advance its nuclear technology. It was only in the aftermath of the events of 9/11 in 2001 that Iranian nuclear capabilities became a matter of grave concern to Israel and its American supporters. As of 2003, according to a US intelligence report published in November 2007, the purposes of the Iranian nuclear project was limited to its NPT obligations, and as such entirely peaceful. But Israel, neither a NPT signatory nor even admitting to its massive stockpile of nuclear weapons, used its AIPAC (American Israel Public Affairs Committee) driven propaganda machinery to focus on the non-existent Iranian nuclear threat. The hypocrisy worked to the advantage of the Islamic Republic, the scandal of the Jewish state (if it needed any more), and the embarrassment of the Christian empire. The more Israel protested about the non-existent 'Iranian nuclear threat,' as it remained the singularly most dangerous menace to regional peace, the wider stretched the smile on the Fox's face. The Islamic Republic and the Jewish state were now staring each other down, gnarling with their fangs out, all under the watchful eyes of the Christian empire.

The concern of the US and its European and regional allies has continued to mount that the Islamic Republic will use its various known and unknown sites to produce enough weapons-grade uranium to build one or two bombs a year. It was first in 2002 that the Iranian Mujahideen-e Khalq Organization (MKO) joined Israel in providing the US with detailed maps of heavy-water production and uranium-enrichment facilities in Arak and Natanz, raising international alarm about the intentions of Iran to go nuclear. While such hawks as the former US ambassador to the UN John R. Bolton encouraged military action against the Islamic Republic, President Obama was following a more diplomatic course. Either way, the Islamic Republic seemed solidly in a position to define the terms of engagement with the international community. Iran was surrounded by four nuclear powers – Pakistan, Russia, Israel, and the United States (in the Persian Gulf) – and none of them was in a moral or even a military position to tell the ruling clergy in Iran that it could not even have nuclear technology. If the dream of peace in the Middle East remained as elusive as the illusions of that gullible Ass, the Lion King seemed solidly trapped, and the wily Fox triumphant – unless it were to turn and look at its own tail. It was on fire. But more of that fire, esteemed and learned reader, will come later.

How is it that this myopic vision of our parabolic predicament, three fabulous creatures at each other's mercy, has come about and defined and distorted our worldly dispositions?[1] Unless and until we come to terms with the particularities of this globalized provincialism we will never see the fuller picture in which the Islamic Republic, the Jewish state, the Christian empire, and by extension Hindu fundamentalism, have now come to define the terms of engagement in the geopolitics of the region.

To begin with the Lion King, perhaps the most striking aspect of the contemporary United States – from Ronald Reagan to the George W. Bush era – compared even with the 1970s, let alone with the era of the Civil Rights Movement in the 1960s, is its recalcitrant provincialism. That belligerent parochialism is today even beyond the pale of what the great American historian Richard Hofstadter diagnosed and theorized in his Pulitzer Prize-winning landmark study *Anti-Intellectualism in American Life* (1964),[2] with its theoretical roots extended all the way back to Alexis de Tocqueville's prophetic work *Democracy in America* (1835–40).[3] An alarming combination of religious fanaticism, political fascism, and unbridled corporate greed has emerged as the defining moment of a potentially cosmopolitan culture now at the thither end of its own worst nightmares. Xenophobia of the most racist disposition, fear of foreigners of all colors and climes (as perhaps best captured in *300*, Zack Snyder's phantasmagoric film of 2006[4]), and above all the frightened and captured imagination of an entire nation are now all in full display, and perhaps nowhere better evident than in an anti-immigration and anti-immigrant mentality that is diametrically at odds with the very fabric of a nation of immigrants. What the colorful rainbow of recent and arriving immigrants (legal and illegal) seem to remind this culture of cruelty and intolerance is the factual promise of its own worldly and cosmopolitan character, now blindfolded and hijacked by a band of religious zealots and ideological fanatics of the Christian imperialist persuasion. Underlying this frightful gathering of political absolutism, religious fanaticism, and global warmongering is the calamity of a corporate culture that breeds career opportunists who aspire to become 'public servants' only to amass more than $100 million in private wealth (in just eight years) in a country in which some 50 million of its inhabitants live under the poverty line, and even more millions can scarce hold themselves above it − with up to 30 million of them depending on food stamps if they are not to starve to death.[5]

Nothing is more definitional of this frightful picture of globalized provincialism than a rampant religious fanaticism that is eating into the very moral and normative fabric of a civil society constitutionally at odds with the theocratic tendencies that are now endangering its historic fate. It is not just the Islamic Republic and its arch nemesis the Jewish state that endanger the world. The Christian empire is at the heart of the perilous planet. More than four decades ago, Robert Bellah proposed the idea of 'civil religion' in America by way of suggesting a normative morality that was irreducible to any particular religion or organized church.[6] Today that idea (and practice) is categorically eclipsed under the calamity of very powerful evangelical zeal with an absolutist and triumphalist writ written into the fabric of its fanaticism. What we are witnessing today in the United States − and by extension the countries and cultures it opts to invade, destroy, occupy, and leave in ruins − is the active transmutation of a variety of cosmopolitan cultures around the globe − *cosmopolitan* not by virtue of an outdated and meaningless proposition colonially codenamed *Westernization*, but *cosmopolitan* by virtue of the historical worldliness of all human conditions and the living cultures they create – into xenophobic tribalism of one sort or another. That fanatical tribalism today in the United States spells out the particulars of Christian fundamentalism in general, Christian Zionism in particular, and thus the active invocation of the idea of a Christian empire, in strategic alliance with a Jewish State, now targeted most immediately against a belligerent Islamic republic, and in a more distant relation with a Hindu fundamentalism in India and a Buddhist separatism extending from Sri Lanka to Tibet.

What today seems to obscure a clear recognition of the fact of this overriding parochialism is an endemic historical amnesia in the United States, where the rapid succession of news – of one calamity in Iraq succeeding another in Afghanistan, and yet another in Palestine – is commensurate with a chronic attention deficit disorder. Consider an exchange between senators McCain and Obama in the course of the US presidential campaign of 2008. On Tuesday 26 February 2008, in a debate with Senator Clinton, Senator Obama had stated that if after he withdrew US forces from Iraq (should he be the next president of the United States) he were to find out that 'al-Qaeda is forming a base' there, he would not hesitate to send the US military back into Iraq. On Wednesday, 27 February 2008, Senator McCain, seeking to portray Obama as naive and ill-informed on international affairs (particularly on the so-called 'War on Terror'), said: 'I have some news – al-Qaeda is in Iraq. It's called: "Al-Qaeda in Iraq." The following day, Senator Obama retorted: 'I have some news for John McCain ... there was no Al-Qaeda in Iraq until George Bush and John McCain invaded Iraq.'[7]

In the same spirit of remembering and reminding, one could also offer an additional piece of news for both Senator McCain and now President Obama: that there was no al-Qaeda, or Taliban, or a bellicose Saddam Hussein armed to the teeth with US- and

EU-supplied chemical, biological, and other weapons, until the United States government created these monsters in collaboration with the Pakistani intelligence, Saudi money, and Israeli strategic support – this only by way of a small dosage of historical record and remembrance, of course.

This chronic attention deficit disorder, along with the absolutist fanaticism it (perhaps inadvertently) serves, requires a relentless, repeated, and critical rearticulation of recent history – and that task will always have to begin by an active decoding of the events of 11 September 2001, which have now assumed iconic and sacerdotal significance, beyond the reach of any critical reading. One reason that there is now an overabundance of rather outlandish conspiracy theories about 9/11 attracting increasing attention in the United States[8] is precisely because the official story that the Bush administration and its neocon chicanery has crafted is itself the supreme conspiracy theory and leaves much room and hope for critical reconsideration – a legitimate criticism of that official reading that does not degenerate into conspiracy theories (that 9/11 was an inside job) but that places the United States' role as an imperial source of menace, mayhem, and degenerate imperialism in proper historical context, a matter irreducible to the so-called critique of American 'foreign policy.' If anything, the post-9/11 era is the end of foreign policy, for there is, as Amy Kaplan (and before her W.E.B. DuBois) has aptly demonstrated in her exquisite book *The Anarchy of Empire in the Making of U.S. Culture* (2005), an active correspondence between US domestic and foreign affairs, local and globalized cultures.[9] The retelling of the American imperial tale around the globe is one crucial way of articulating its own cosmopolitan manner of resisting and overcoming it. The historical fact is that American culture goes imperial in its worst parochial denomination, and resists it with its own most cosmopolitan disposition. It's not just Bush, Cheney, and Rumsfeld that are American. Countless millions of anti-war demonstrators who brave the streets are American too.

To state the obvious (and to refresh the historical memory): there is no structural, causal, or thematic correspondence between the criminal events of 9/11 by a band of militant adventurists and a massive US-led army descending upon the people of Afghanistan in October 2001 and Iraq in March 2003. It is imperative to link these two wars together and see them both as part and parcel of the American imperial project, and by way of correcting the assumption of those who thought the Afghan War was the case of a 'just war.'[10] The liberal bravura that takes issue with the Bush administration on the grounds that there was no link between Iraq and 9/11, or between Iraq and al-Qaeda, detracts attention from the more fundamental fact that there was no link between 9/11 and the US-led invasion of Afghanistan, even if indeed Osama bin Laden and his al-Qaeda operation were responsible for the atrocities of 9/11 (to this day a mere military and propaganda conjecture – on the part of both the US and Osama bin Laden – that has assumed iconic sanctity and thus is beyond the realm of reasonable doubt).

The re-emergence of US militarism after the so-called 'Vietnam Syndrome' of the 1970s was well under way long before the events of 9/11; it began soon after the end of President Jimmy Carter's administration (1976–80) and his military fiasco in the Tabas during the Operation Eagle Claw (or Operation Evening Light) on 24 April 1980, when the US military tried in vain to rescue the American hostages in Tehran. Beginning with the US invasion of Granada on 25 October 1983, and continuing with the criminal involvement of the US (according to the International Court of Justice) in Nicaragua in the mid-1980s, this development kept a steady pace for the rest of the Reagan administration (1980–88), until it came to full fruition during the First Gulf War under George Herbert

Walker Bush in 1990–91. The Clinton administration's military thuggery around the globe (in Afghanistan, Iraq, Libya, and Sudan – including the bombing of an aspirin factory in Sudan on 20 August 1998) continued on the same path of military recovery from the Vietnam Syndrome – and it is to that 'recovery' that the events of post-9/11 will have to be linked. The events of 9/11 may have anachronistically and *ex post facto* assumed iconic significance, but they did nothing but exacerbate the aggressive re-militarization of America's foreign/domestic disposition.

The Islamic Revolution in Iran (1977–79) and the Soviet invasion and occupation of Afghanistan (1978–89) are the most immediate points of departure for our understanding of the current cycle of post-Vietnam Syndrome US military adventurism, all entirely independent of the events of 9/11. The widespread regional appeal of the Iranian Revolution deeply troubled the Washington Middle East establishment.[11] The US-sponsored creation of the Afghan Mujahideen/Taliban (with the assistance of Saudi money and Pakistani intelligence) on the Western frontiers of the Iranian Revolution sought (1) to create a Sunni Wahabi barrier against the spread of the Shi'i radicalism embedded in that revolution, and (2) to use the same fervent Sunni militancy to expel the Soviets from Afghanistan. The massive arming of Saddam Hossein by the US and its European allies during the eight brutal years of the Iran–Iraq war (1980–88) sought to do the same on the Eastern borders of that militantly Islamized revolution. The strategy worked, the Soviets were expelled, and the multifaceted cosmopolitan disposition of the Iranian Revolution could not spread its revolutionary wings, and thus soon degenerated into an Islamist theocracy and commenced a fiercely fanatical reign of terror systematically destroying all its non-Islamist (both nationalist and socialist) rivals. But the strategic victory of the US/Israel and their European allies was not to last. The two monsters they had created – Osama bin

Laden and his al-Qaeda and the Taliban that embraced them, on one side, and Saddam Hussein, on the other – now came back to haunt their creators.

No sooner had the Soviets left Afghanistan and the Soviet Union collapsed than the first American sites in and out of the country were targeted by the combined forces of the Taliban and the al-Qaeda – in New York in 1993, in Saudi Arabia in 1996, in East Africa in 1998, and in Yemen in 2000. No sooner had the Iran–Iraq war ended in 1988 that Saddam Hussein, emboldened by US support throughout the war, invaded Kuwait in August 1990. Forcing Saddam Hussein to leave Kuwait in the First Gulf War (1990–91) was the easy part of the US's conundrum in the region. It was Osama bin Laden and his al-Qaeda terror organization that proved to be the more shadowy reflection of the US imperial imagination. The events of 9/11 were subsequently narrated officially in a manner that linked them to that shadowy organization, and yet remained nothing but the blowback consequences of the US military adventurism in the region since the Islamic Revolution in Iran and the commencement of the Reagan administration.

This is so far as the most immediate short-term memory of our current predicament is concerned. But the more enduring question remains whether this renewed post-Vietnam Syndrome resurrection of US militancy will amount to a full-fledged imperial project. The combined calamity of neoconservatism and neoliberalism makes one thing clear: if anything, this is an empire with no commanding ideology, an empire with no hegemony; and a constellation of provincial doctrines and dogma do not make a legitimizing ideology of domination. Francis Fukuyama and Samuel Huntington protest too much: the period of civilizational thinking is over; the aggressive provincialism of the United States has in fact acted as the catalyst for all other cosmopolitan cultures around the globe and at the mercy of American parochialism to degenerate equally into provincialism. The *Islamic* republic and the *Jewish* state mirror and reflect the *Christian* predilection of this empire they alternately oppose or befriend, and they all wish to clone themselves around the globe – and thus the fundamental problem of Israel with Lebanon, or the long-term project of the Islamic Republic of Iran for Iraq. The same is true about the possibility of a cross-sectional coalition in Palestine. Iraq, Lebanon, and Palestine can potentially be the site of a cosmopolitan political culture in which Islam (the Mahdi Army in Iraq, Hezbollah in Lebanon, Hamas in Palestine) remains integral but not definitive. And that mere possibility is precisely the mutual nightmare of both the Islamic Republic and the Jewish state, and above all of the Christian imperialism of the United States they oppose or befriend: all of them have degenerated into fanatical religious states seeking to clone themselves around the region.[12]

As a potential ideology of domination, neoconservatism (à la William Kristol's Project for the New American Century)[13] has done nothing but in fact make Americans detested the world over, and along with Israel considered (global poll after global poll) the chief sources of menace and mayhem around the globe.[14] Destroying cosmopolitan cultures, nourishing tribalism and religious fanaticism, American imperialism in general and the Israeli colonization of Palestine in particular are universalizing the most provincial aspects of American culture and Zionist tribalism, two aspects of a militant triumphalism running amuck – squarely embedded in the heartbeat of Christian (and Christian Zionist in particular) fundamentalism.[15]

If the bankrupt, shallow, and provincial hallucinations of the Project for the New American Century make no sense and do nothing but increase global fear and loathing of the United States, how else are we to understand the American empire and the victory of a nativist triumphalism it has occasioned all over the world? Any discussion of the American imperial project today will have to begin with Antonio Negri and Michael Hardt's pathbreaking book on the subject. In their *Empire* (2000) they have argued that the period of classical imperialism has in fact ended and the time of Empire (as the new political order of globalization) has begun: *Empire without Imperialism*.[16] Negri and Hardt have further elaborated that this new Empire draws from US constitutionalism, from hybrid identities, and also from expanding frontiers. Notions such as sovereignty, they have argued, as well as the boundaries of the nation-state and the institutions of civil society, have all transformed, as have the modalities of racism, gender politics, labor migration, transnational corporations, and post-industrial forms of labor. Paramount in Negri and Hardt's conception of Empire is the absence of an active imperial agency, for this for them is a *condition* of world dis/order, with militant and powerful economies and militaries seeking to take advantage of their heavy weights and control the flow of military power and economic prowess. 'Globalization' as such is the ideology of this Empire.

Both the Afghan (since 2001) and the Iraq (since 2003) wars have obviously challenged Negri and Hardt's proposition, for what we are witnessing here is a blatant and full-throttle imperial agency at work. One may consider the fact that Negri and Hardt's book was published in 2000, having been written between the First Persian Gulf War (1990–91) and the Kosovo War (1996–99), when the world was still in a state of post-two-superpower limbo. As such their ideas were formed in the period right after the collapse of the Soviet Union in the late 1980s and the commencement of George Herbert Walker Bush's 'New World Order,' (which as a proposition was in fact rooted in the early 1900 Cecil Rhodes idea, but resuscitated in the early 1990s by President Bush to suggest a new vision of world power relations). The events of 9/11 and after have indeed changed many of those conditions and require a rereading of the ideas of empire and imperialism.

Of more immediate and detailed concern would be the extraordinary work of Chalmers Johnson in his *Blowback* trilogy (2000–2008), in which he, speaking as a courageous US patriot, seems deeply frightened and concerned about his country's foreign policy disasters – of successive US administrations – which have *ipso facto* resulted in the formation of a globalized empire, and in the process endangered American civil liberties.[17] The problem with Chalmers Johnson's heartfelt and persuasive argument is that he is fixated with the CIA and its clandestine activities that have invariably resulted in catastrophic blowbacks; thus for him this form of blatant imperialism is an aberration from American republicanism. Johnson's diagnosis is predicated on a very limited vision of the economic and political machinery – and in turn the normative ethos it occasions – behind the imperial design. Chalmers' fetishization of the CIA as the main culprit is at the expense of a more universal perspective that includes CIA covert operations but is not limited to them. Despite its notorious covert activities, the CIA (or at least most of its operations) is still very much an organ of the US government and pretty much under the oversight of the US Congress.

Niall Ferguson's *Colossus: The Price of America's Empire* (2004), meanwhile, goes for the most obvious evidence, and lists the American military, economic, and even popular cultural domination of the globe and calls the US version of the phenomenon 'the Imperialism of anti-Imperialism.'[18] Ferguson looks at the history of the US and demonstrates how the L word (liberty) has stood for the E word (Empire), and concludes that the US should in fact come out of this narrative closet and declare itself an Empire – for Ferguson believes empires are actually good for the world. What Ferguson

is reformulating is in fact the gist of the argument provided much
earlier by the great Scottish historian of empire V.G. Kiernan
in his 1978 masterpiece *America: The New Imperialism* – minus, of
course, Kiernan's unflinching solidarity with scattered manners
of opposing the predatory monster.[19] The same argument is also
made by Michael Mann in his *Incoherent Empire* (2003), in which he
demonstrates that the emerging American imperialism amounts
to nothing more than a new militarism, without the necessary
ideological wherewithal of sustaining an enduring or convincing
empire.[20] It can easily destroy, but can never conquer; so it is in
fact a closet empire, with all the incumbent terrors of an inner
urge to come out and flex its military muscles, but with perhaps
a Protestant inhibition to admit to its follies.

To be an empire despite itself, or a reluctant empire, or an
empire caught in the delusion of spreading 'the good word' – in
this case 'liberty' – all point to a fundamental fact about American
imperialism: its strategic asceticism, a perhaps Protestant (Calvin-
ist) predilection to avoid admission of wealth through ostentatious
living, mixed with a Spartan proclivity towards brevity of immediate purpose. In this case, American imperialism stands in exact
contradiction with, say, the Persian, the Roman, or even the British
Empire – empires that thrived on putting up spectacular shows of
their military wherewithal. Consider the fact that contrary even
to the Soviets, there is no military parade (say on the Fourth of
July) in the United States. US imperialism, one can also suggest,
is different from its European predecessor in very much the
way American football is different from European soccer. Just
like soccer, European imperialism worked through gradual and
systematic territorial conquest, while the US version works on
the model of a quarterback surgically throwing the ball to a wide
receiver far into the enemy's territory, without physically having
the control of the land in between the quarterback and the wide

receiver – with, say, the New York Giants Eli Manning managing to avoid a sack and while still scrambling managing to complete a rather awkward pass to the wide receiver. The predominance of football metaphors in American warfare is, of course, very obvious – best used by General Norman Schwarzkopf in the First Persian Gulf War (1990–91) when explaining to reporters his strategies of forcing the Iraqi army out of Kuwait.

Another way of looking at US empire-building is through the lens of John Ford's lifetime achievement as an epic filmmaker, in which we see the Homeric projection of a European dream of an ideal empire yet to come, informed by an Irish boy's memories of his parents' formative destitution – the Monument Valley as Ford's uncharted territories of the world to conquer, a *terra incognita* of an empire to build – with John Wayne as his contemporary Ulysses. John Ford's vision of the American empire is in sharp contrast to David Lean's portrayal of the British Empire, in which – from *Lawrence of Arabia* (1962) to *Ryan's Daughter* (1970) to *A Passage to India* (1984) – he is reflecting back on and totally preoccupied with the pathologies of an empire that is forever lost: with Arabia, Ireland, and India as the sites of his nostalgic reflections. As much as Ford's vision of the coming American empire is bright, wide-angled, and hopeful, David Lean's vision of the lost British Empire is sad, seditious, pathological, and contorted. Both Ford's and Lean's respective visions of empire are yet again sharply different from Akira Kurosawa's and his post-nuclear holocaust contemplation on the inner terrors of violence at the heart of any imperial project. When we compare these three great visionaries of epic power, John Ford's stands out as the festive celebration of an emancipatory mission to liberate, civilize, and set the course of history aright.

As much as Ford's vision of the American empire is life-affirming, broad-chested, and bright, the contemporary grasp of the American empire is deeply dire, dark, and apprehensive.

There is no understanding the American imperial project without simultaneously coming to terms with the transmutation of
American politics, state apparatus, economy, and society in effectively imperial terms – a fact that will be totally eclipsed if our
analysis of US imperialism is limited to a critique of so-called
'American foreign policy.' American foreign policy is American
domestic policy and vice versa – as from W.E.B. DuBois to Amy
Kaplan the most perceptive observers of American imperialism
have agreed.

The specter of fascism was fast upon the United States during the
eight terrifying years of the Bush administration, and signs of its
recognition were evident in the most insightful studies that have
come out since the apocalyptic reading of the events of 9/11 commenced by Christian fundamentalists. Consider a groundbreaking
(but scarcely noted) short volume: Heinrich Meier, *Carl Schmitt and
Leo Strauss: The Hidden Dialogue* (1988), which exposes the degree to
which the Nazi political theologian Carl Schmitt's seminal work,
The Concept of the Political (1927), particularly in its categorical opposition to liberalism, is in fact indebted to Leo Strauss, the guru
of the neoconservatives, who had come to the same anti-liberal
conclusions though through philosophical reasoning rather than
theological speculation.[21] If you are still not quite sure who is this
Leo Strauss and what is his connection to the neoconservative
cabal that has brought this nightmare upon the United States, then
you should take a look at the revelatory pages of Anne Norton's
Leo Strauss and the Politics of American Empire (2005),[22] or at least read
Earl Shorris's 'Ignoble Liars: Leo Strauss, George Bush, and the
Philosophy of Mass Deception' (2004).[23]

If you think the comparison between Nazi Germany and Bush's
America is too outlandish, or perhaps the feverish nightmares of
a recent immigrant American with a first name not too dissimilar
to Barack Obama's (hidden and denied) middle name, then I draw

your attention to Naomi Wolf's text *The End of America: Letter of Warning to a Young Patriot* (2007), in which we read a judicious warning.[24] By shifting her bone of contention away from women's rights and towards civil rights, Wolf goes through a sustained course of argument documenting what she calls the 'fascist shift' initiated during the eight nightmarish years of the Bush administration. Pointedly addressed to a young Vietnamese American, Wolf's daring argument outlines the 'Ten Steps to Fascism' that are already fast upon us. She speaks bravely of the fragility of democracy as an ideal, and then reads like the roadmap of a descent to fascism: invoke an external and internal enemy; establish secret prisons, develop a paramilitary force; surveil ordinary citizens, infiltrate citizens' group, arbitrarily detain and release citizens, target key individuals, restrict the press, cast criticism as 'espionage' and dissent as 'treason'; subvert the rule of law. Of *The End of America*, Michael Ratner of the Center for Constitutional Rights, has said:

> You will be shocked and disturbed by this book. Most Americans reject outright any comparison of post 9/11 America with the fascism and totalitarianism of Nazi Germany or Pinochet's Chile. Sadly, the parallels and similarities, what Wolf calls the 'echoes' between those societies and America today, are all too compelling.[25]

What is perhaps most frightful is the fact that the evident parameters and emerging institutions of this potential fascism are being woven into the fabric of American capitalism. 'The war on terror' sells, and it sells well. Consider Solomon Hughes's *War on Terror, Inc.: Corporate Profiteering from the Politics of Fear* (2007), in which he demonstrates how the war on terror has expanded the role of private enterprise, extending market thinking and market forces into the domains of public policy.[26] Supplying the additional private army that made the invasion of Iraq plausible and possible, establishing a database of people deemed national security threats, providing frontline mercenaries, security services guarding key installations and VIPs, prison, torture, and law enforcement, media management, intelligence gathering at home and aboard, blanket surveillance of the civilian population, providing Psy-Op[27] scholarship (as perhaps best represented by Seyyed Vali Reza Nasr and Abbas Milani), Propaganda War (again best represented by Fouad Ajami, Azar Nafisi, Hirsi Ayaan Ali, Irshad Manji, etc.[28]): this is no longer just a country whose economic fore-structure is capitalist. This is capitalism running amuck and eating into the heart of the civil society that once harbored it.

Equally compelling in the rising specter of American fascism was the structural link between Christian Zionism (widely embraced by the pro-Israel industry) and the right wing of the Republican Party. In his *American Fascists: The Christian Right and the War on America* (2006), Chris Hedges's point of departure is Pat Robertson's pronouncement almost a quarter of a century ago that the US was a Christian nation that should be at the center of a vast (global) Christian empire.[29] Chris Hedges is unrelenting in his cry against the terror of Christian fundamentalism, which in his judgment is poised to transform American society into a closed and hermetically sealed web of unbridled fanaticism and xenophobia. He narrows in on hundreds of US senators and members of Congress who have received 80 to 100 percent rates of approval from extremely influential Christian Right advocacy groups, on the curriculum of Christian schools, on myriad radio and television stations, all giving rise to a chorus of apocalyptic violence in anticipation of the Second Coming. Hedges compares the Christian Right movement to the fascist movements in Italy and Germany in the 1920s and 1930s. All it will take, Chris Hedges is convinced, is one more national crisis like 9/11, and the Christian Right is well placed to destroy American democracy.

One need not look around too much to see the justification for Chris Hedges's concerns. John Hagee, the founder and senior pastor of Cornerstone Church in San Antonio, Texas, and one such Christian fundamentalist (a devout Christian Zionist) has said of Hurricane Katrina that it was an act of God, punishing New Orleans for 'a level of sin that was offensive to God' – with particular reference to a 'homosexual parade.' Next to homosexuals comes Islam, of which John Hagee has said: 'those who live by the Qur'an have a scriptural mandate to kill Christians and Jews.' He has then proceeded to characterize the military threat posed by Muslims:

> There are 1.3 billion people who follow the Islamic faith, so if you're saying there's only 15 percent that want to come to America or invade Israel to crush it, you're only talking about 200 million people. That's far more than Hitler and Japan and Italy and all of the Axis powers in World War II had under arms.

As for Catholicism, it is, for Reverend John Hagee, 'the Great Whore,' the 'apostate church,' the 'anti-Christ' and a 'false cult system.' As a Christian imperialist, John Hagee is a fierce supporter of the Jewish state, and in common with many American evangelicals he believes that God gave the land to the Jewish people and that Christians have a Biblical duty to support it and the Jews.[30] Hagee's latest book, *Jerusalem Countdown: A Warning to the World*, interprets the Bible to predict that Russian and Arab armies will invade Israel and be destroyed by God. This will set up a confrontation over Israel between China and the West, led by the Antichrist, who will be the head of the European Union, Pastor Hagee writes. That final battle between East and West – at Armageddon, as the actual Israeli location of Megiddo is known in English – will precipitate the second coming of Christ, he concludes.[31]

These are not merely the outlandish figments of a demented imagination. These hallucinations represent a much wider political constituency. Kevin Philips's *American Theocracy: The Perils and Politics of Radical Religion, Oil, and Borrowed Money in the 21st Century* (2006), which focuses on three concurrent crisis of oil supply, religious fanaticism, and national debt, gives a frightful picture of the power of Christian messianism in the making of the American imperial imagination.[32] In Kevin Phillips's estimation, the Republican Party has been transformed into 'the first religious party in U.S. history.' His examination of the relationship between oil and religious fanaticism very much presages Paul Thomas Anderson's film masterpiece *There Will Be Blood* (2007). Based on Upton Sinclair's *Oil* (1927), *There Will Be Blood* matches Daniel Day-Lewis's hard-headed capitalist entrepreneurial Daniel Plainview against Paul Dano's fanatical Eli.

How does this frightful combination of gargantuan military power and religious fanaticism of the most delirious sort come together? Answer: in the metamorphosis of humanity into insects. In an interview with Thomas P.M. Barnett for *Squire* magazine, Admiral William 'Fox' Fallon, the head of US Central Command, was asked what if there is a war between the US and Iran: 'And if it comes to war? 'Get serious,' the admiral said. 'These guys are ants. When the time comes, you crush them.'[33] Animal fables from Aesop's to *Panchatantra* to *Kalilah and Dimnah* may help us see something otherwise invisible about world politics. But perhaps with a bit more literary grace than what Admiral 'Fox' Fallon has managed to muster here.

Such iniquitous comments can be dismissed as 'exceptions' in the same way that instances of torturing people in Abu Ghraib, Guantánamo Bay, Bagram Airbase, and in an entire subterranean labyrinth run by the CIA in Europe have been passed off as 'exceptions.' Likewise 'exceptional' are those legal theorists like

Alan M. Dershowitz who have sought to legalize heinous act of torture. 'Exceptional,' in this sense, too is the massacre of Iraqis at Hadithah, or the rape and murder of Abeer Qasim Hamza al-Janabi by American soldiers in the village of Yusufiyah. These are all exceptions, ordinary and decent Americans might say to themselves by way of washing their hands of and cleansing their soul of these stains on their national character – and it is indeed as states of exception that they ought to be read, and have been read, by the great Italian legal philosopher Giorgio Agamben. It is not the rule and the condition of normalcy that demand attention, but precisely those fragile moments when nations go tribal, and humanity descends to bestiality. 'In every case,' Agamben believes, 'the state of exception marks a threshold at which logic and praxis blur with each other and a pure violence without logos claims to realize an enunciation without any real reference.... The entire Third Reich can be considered a state of exception that lasted twelve years.'[34]

THREE

The Fox in the Hen House

WITH THE INCREASED INTERNATIONAL SIGNIFICANCE of the Islamic Republic, its domestic affairs have been – until very recently – powerfully overshadowed by the regional geopolitics of its strength. An anatomy of the internal (domestic) strength and weakness of the regime shows that the more it has become regionally powerful the less its domestic policies have mattered, until lately, to the world at large. Iran is assuming unprecedented significance not just in its immediate region, but also as far away as in Latin America, the US's backyard; at the same time, its internal affairs have very much taken a back seat. As recently as May 2009, US Secretary of State Hillary Clinton drew attention to emerging Iranian influence in Latin America, equating it with that of China in terms of significance and magnitude. 'If you look at the gains, particularly in Latin America,' she said, 'that Iran is making, that China is making, it's quite disturbing.'[1] Iran in Latin America? Now that is quite a novelty, which speaks volumes about where the world stands today in terms of the extended logic of asymmetric warfare that now defines the world that George Bush has left behind.

The behavior of Mahmoud Ahmadinejad, traveling all the way to Gabon in Africa, and from there to Brazil in South America, to pose and have his picture taken as president[2] while his own country cannot stand him, is reminiscent of a wondrous story in the thirteenth-century Persian poet Sa'di's *Golestan* about an astronomer who comes home one day to find a man in bed with his wife. He kicks and screams, neighbors gather and someone tells him: *To bar ouj falak cheh dani chist, chon nadani dar sarayat kist,* 'How would you know what's happening in the heavens when you have no clue who is in your home?' Ahmadinejad's trip to Africa and Latin America, as indeed his government's pronouncements on Iraq, Afghanistan, Pakistan, or Palestine, are all indices of a preference to shift global attention away from his domestic woes to a place where he can play hardball. He, and with him the Islamic Republic, is well positioned to look as stately and omnipotent regionally, and even globally, as he is weak and wobbly domestically. Under any other circumstances, the formation of south-to-south alliances, away from the East–West binary, would have been plausible and positive developments, but not when one of the two parties to such an alliance is a fundamentally fraudulent president of a deeply flawed and tyrannical republic.[3]

To be sure, with the legitimate outcry against the Islamic Republic by its internal and external critics and foes, the fact is that it has a fairly stable state apparatus, however beleaguered it might be in claiming legitimate authority over its defiant citizens. Having successfully outmaneuvered all real and potential alternatives early in the course of the Islamic Revolution (1977–79), the Muslim revolutionaries concocted a bizarre and brutal theocratic republic, a contradiction in terms that only reveals the overriding paradox in which the Islamic Republic now finds itself.

The roots of the internal stability of the regime (against all odds) must be traced back to the nascent revolutionary phase, to the period between 1977 and 1979, when the Islamist forces led by Ayatollah Khomeini were integral to but not definitive of the revolutionary uprising. After the June 1963 revolt against the Pahlavi regime, also led by Ayatollah Khomeini, the militant Islamism that he best represented had to share the collective memory of national liberation with both nationalist and socialist forces. At the wake of the 1977–79 revolution all these forces were evident and present – albeit to varying degrees. During the crucial year of 1979–80, however, when the Shah's regime collapsed, Ayatollah Khomeini returned to Iran, and the various revolutionary factions vied for power, the Islamist forces took full advantage of the American hostage crisis, outmaneuvering all their rivals and rapidly ratifying an Islamic constitution. By the time the hostages were released in January 1980, as President Reagan was being inaugurated in Washington DC, all the major institutions of an Islamic Republic were established, the military was either neutralized or incorporated into the Muslim militia, and the most important rival revolutionary forces were either forced into exile or else brutally suppressed and silenced. The violently Islamized revolution, the Islamic Republic, and the constitution that it drafted were all militant distortions of the multifaceted Iranian cosmopolitan culture. That forced twisting of a worldly cosmopolitanism, which had been in the making for millennia, was the original sin and the foundational folly of the Islamic Republic. From its very inception, as a result, the Islamic Republic has been kept in power by crisis management, and not predicated on any sustained body of doctrinal, ideological, or institutional legitimacy.[4] The Islamic Republic is systematically and consistently in the business of either taking advantage of crises that come its way (the militant student takeover of the US embassy in 1979–80 and the Iran–Iraq war of 1980–88 being the chief examples), doing the same with the crises that have flared up in its neighborhood (the Israeli atrocities in

Palestine and Lebanon; the US-led invasions of Afghanistan and Iraq), or else helping create its own crises in troubled parts of the world (anywhere from Iraq to Yemen).

The Iran–Iraq War was by far the most critical period in the life of the young Islamic Republic, when behind the smokescreen of a deadly and prolonged war the clerical clique consolidated its power and destroyed all its political and ideological enemies. Soon after the war ended in 1988 and Khomeini's death in 1989, a period of massive post-war reconstruction commenced, which lasted from 1989 to 1997. This created a new middle class that was heavily invested in the internal stability of the regime. This was the time of the Ali Akbar Hashemi Rafsanjani presidency, a truly wily fox of unsurpassed Machiavellian tenacity. Rafsanjani's post-war reconstruction presidency witnessed the rise of the Reagan doctrine in the 1980s; its repercussions into the 1990s made the Islamic Republic the direct beneficiary of US involvement in anti-Soviet engagements in Afghanistan;[5] at the same time, the successive rise of the two Palestinian intifadas and Israeli military adventurism in Lebanon and Gaza also strengthened the geopolitical position of the regime.

In part due to the geopolitics of the region, by now all internal and external opposition to the Islamist regime was either brutally eliminated or neutralized – but the seeds of opposition and strife were now evident in the hearts and minds of the children of the revolution. Abdolkarim Soroush now emerged as by far the most eloquent public intellectual of his time, at odds with the totalitarian policies of the Islamic Republic; and around him a whole movement of 'religious intellectuals' (*Roshanfekran-e Dini*, as they now called themselves) began to challenge the status quo. A devout and practicing Muslim, a committed revolutionary, a dedicated activist who had served the Islamic Revolution ardently by systematically seeking to cleanse the higher education system of what he deemed non-Islamist elements and 'Islamize' this sector, Soroush was a force to recognize and contend with. He could not be easily dismissed on a pretext or with an excuse. Soroush thus emerged as the bête noire of the clerical establishment – both of them and against them. He was also, *ipso facto* and quite paradoxically, a safety valve. All legitimate (that is, considered to be legitimate) opposition to the Islamic Republic was now expressed in Islamic terms. Soroush shook the ideological foundation of the regime and made it stronger. He even, and again paradoxically, gave the belligerent and fragile regime an aura of intellectual legitimacy.[6]

All the pent-up frustrations of the emerging religious intellectuals and, even more important, the rising expectations of the younger generation and the new middle class were released during the presidential election of 1997 when a popular Muslim cleric, Mohammad Khatami, attracted the love and attention of most of the oppositional forces. Khatami's election as president in June 1997 was a transformative catharsis in the history of the Islamic Republic.[7] It (once again, paradoxically) placated its enemies and solidified its claim to legitimacy. The Khatami election was so vastly popular that it could have either killed or cured the Islamic Republic. It did not kill it; nor did it completely cure it. It gave the fragile state apparatus a strong popular basis of legitimacy, as it became abundantly clear that there was enormous dissatisfaction with the status quo. A period of relative ease – some even called it glasnost and perestroika – emerged between the election of Khatami in June 1997 and the end of his second terms in June 2005.[8] But by now the events of 9/11 and after and the American designation of Iran as part of an 'axis of evil' completely changed the scene, and in part contributed to the election of the belligerent Mahmoud Ahmadinejad as president in June 2005, and subsequent re-election in a massively disputed vote in June 2009. As Khatami's two-term presidency gave a simulacrum of implicit popular legitimacy to the regime (which barely lasted for two years before the July 1999 student uprising, which Khatami categorically condemned, instantly puncturing it), the warmongering presidency of George W. Bush and his Israeli counterparts in the region provided further, external, buttresses to the Islamic Republic.

At the threshold of a new presidential election in 2009, the Islamic Republic remained as unpopular with significant segments of its constituency as ever. But no viable opposition, in or out of the country, was threatening its stability. The late Shah's son was wasting his father's money on useless courtiers; the Mujahideen-e Khalq Organization was entirely discredited after it collaborated both with Saddam Hussein and with the American army; and the panoply of other oppositional forces were blowing into a wayward wind. The most serious challenges to the regime came from inside the country, and yet again the Islamic Republic was facing a massive internal opposition – though with a peculiar twist: it was no longer ideologically driven. A page had turned, perhaps a chapter ended, maybe even a whole book was about to be written on Iranian political culture. The nature of the opposition that was now unfolding and the mode of suppression that the Islamic Republic was mounting against it were of two different dispositions.

Nowhere are the rising sentiments of the youth against the Islamic Republic better evident than in the underground music of the 1990s and 2000s, categorically defying the status quo, not in ideological but in fact in lyrical terms. The career of Shahin Najafi (born in 1980 in Bandar Anzali in Northern Iran) as a leading rapper is the case in point. Najafi had abandoned any formal education early and, with a creative command over Persian poetry of the preceding generation and a gifted affinity with the guitar, opted for a rebellious musical career. He began working with underground music groups, but because of the uncompromising political message of his music he was soon forced into exile and by 2005 had immigrated to Germany, where he joined the group Tapesh 2012. Early in 2009 he left that group and continued his widely popular career independently. His music and lyrics are a perfect mirror of the sentiments and anger of his generation. Here is a translation of the opening lines of his song 'Taraf-e Ma' (Our Side):

> When I opened my eyes I was fed up with living –
> I have no clue when my youth turned into old age.
>
> They told me you are a leftie, you are misdirected,
>   you have no faith,
> But when did you ever answer my question?
>
> As soon as I opened my eyes we were in war,
> In my father's hands was a gun instead of a pen.
>
> We could scarce make ends meet,
> And if we raised our voice we were told to shut up.
>
> For once let me tell what the story is,
> We both know what the pain is and what is its cause.
>
> For once let me believe I too am a human being,
> Imagine that I too live in a healthy society.
>
> Let me forget that for twenty years I have been slapped around,
> Stepped on like a piece of dirt – let me think for myself.
>
> Let me close my eyes to my sister's
> Nocturnal weeping and to the lump in my mother's throat.
>
> Let me close my eyes and imagine that I too am lucky.[9]

As evident in the music and lyrics of Shahin Najafi and much more in Iranian underground music, what the electoral crisis of June 2009 ushered in was no typical challenge to the legitimacy of the Islamic Republic. What we were witnessing in that fateful June was the commencement of a civil rights movement, the turn to a *societal* (as opposed to merely *political*) *modernity*, predicated on the rise of a post-ideological generation.[10] Iranian politics of the last three decades has always been on the brink; the Islamic Republic has been held together by the threat of a coup, the horrors of a war, and the immanence of an invasion – all fueled by a conspiratorially minded regime that refuses to let go of the memory of the 1953 coup, which serves its purposes well.[11] With the election of President Barack Obama, US/Israeli laser-targeting of the Islamic Republic's nuclear project did not relent, and indeed became keener. Hence under both the Bush presidency and, more so, under that of Obama, the Islamic Republic has faced its harshest international challenge since its very inception. Because of their enduring economic and strategic interests in Iran, Russia and China were among the few major powers that came to the aid of the Islamic Republic in its international woes. As the beleaguered Ahmadinejad government switched the playing field to the international domain, where it was strong, the Iranian electorate pulled it back to the domestic front, where the president – and the Islamic Republic – was the weakest.

The geopolitical *mise-en-scène* of the region, as a result, was thrown completely off-kilter with the rise of the Green Movement in the aftermath of the June 2009 presidential election and the global spectacle of its violent crackdown by the security apparatus of the Islamic Republic. This time the growing and expanding opposition pulled no punches and targeted the 'supreme leader' himself, as pictures and murals of Ali Khamenei were torn down and burned or defaced for the whole world to see, as chants of 'Death to the dictator!' reverberated throughout the country. Meanwhile, Ahmadinejad's lumpenism, exacerbated by the international embarrassment he kept creating by denying the Holocaust, was taxing the patience of an entire nation, taking sacrosanct ideas and principles to their rhetorical limits, *ad absurdum*.

The violent crackdown on the peaceful uprising put the brutal disposition of the security apparatus of the Islamic Republic on display. The internal bleeding of the clerical and political elite was also fully evident. Among them, Ali Akbar Hashemi Rafsanjani, Mohammad Khatami, Mir Hossein Mousavi, and Mehdi Karroubi essentially summed up almost the entire leadership history of the Islamic Republic from its inception. High-ranking officials of the Revolutionary Guards, meanwhile, became increasingly vocal in their threatening pronouncements against the uprising. To all intents and purposes, the Islamic Republic dropped all pretensions to republicanism and instantly transmuted itself into a porcupine, with its coat of armored spines sticking out in self-defense.

Among the serious charges of abuse that were now brought against the Islamic Republic were not just those of torture but of rape. The publication of a letter by Mehdi Karroubi, an oppositional presidential candidate, to Rafsanjani dared to speak openly about the most notorious public secret of the theocratic state – the rape of young men and women. Dated 29 July 2009, and released on 8 August 2009, Karroubi's letter provided a litany of wrongdoings that the heavily militarized security apparatus of the Islamic Republic had unleashed against peaceful demonstrators in the aftermath of the June 2009 presidential election, including kidnapping, beating, verbal abuse, illegal incarcerations, torture, rape, and outright murder.[12] The false halo of sanctity that the Islamic Republic had manufactured for itself in the Muslim world began to fade and the naked brutality of its rule of terror to expose itself.

The Green Movement had by now rained on the Islamic Republic's parade. As the world was watching a standstill showdown between the belligerent theocracy and the sole surviving global superpower, the Iranians reasserted themselves in the geopolitics of the region. The expectation of an imminent end to the Islamic

Republic was of course wrong and misguided. This was the commencement of a civil rights movement, and it was going to be a marathon. The clerical and security apparatus of the system had nowhere to go. Though more tyrannical in many respects than the Pahlavis, this regime had no figurehead like the Shah who would just pack his jewelry and secret bank account details and run away to the nearest Swiss chalet to wait for the CIA and MI6 to restore him to his throne. We were witness to the commencement of a new phase in Iranian political culture, in which the continuation or dismantling of the Islamic Republic was no longer relevant to the foundational institutions of civil liberties that any modern society had to establish to address its most basic concerns.[13]

While there were wild and exaggerated expectations of an imminent end to the Islamic Republic on one side, there were on the other sober wisecrackers who dismissed the whole Green Movement as ephemeral and moribund. 'What is being fought for today in Iran,' one such observer scoffed, 'is the preservation of a small space for political dissent and the prevention of the emergence of a militarized one-party system' – that's all.[14] Offering 'a lesson in humility,' the author of these words assured himself and others that 'the losers in the trade were the northern Tehranis who supplied the bulk of the street presence after the election.' He then concludes: 'Today [mid-December 2009] what is left of the green movement depends upon Ayatollahs Montazeri and Sane'i – both *personae non gratae* for years – for its religious legitimacy.' This pro-status quo reading was flawed, myopic, condescending, and patronizing; equally foolhardy and delusional were those among the expatriate oppositions who were packing to go back to Iran and secure a ministerial post in a restored Pahlavi monarchy. The thinking of both was short-term, one being rash revolutionary posturing; the other a condescending dismissal of the uprising. What escaped them both was not just history, but also demography, on which was predicated a seismic change in the political culture, which had been long in the making.[15]

The fate of the Islamic Republic was neither as threatened as its enemies wished, nor as rosy as its supporters believed. Both detractors and defenders thought and wrote in apocalyptic terms – blind to the fact that what we were witnessing in Iran was something entirely different from what they had hitherto dreamt of, dared to hope for, or feared, and something for which they had yet to find any formula in their old apothecary boxes.[16] In part, such defeatist options, insisting that the Islamic Republic would endure by the hook or crook of a coup, or else collapse under the popular pressure of a revolutionary uprising, were limited to the making of an enduringly colonized mind that in its most recent rendition can only see Iranian history as a 'short-term' society with no enduring historical memory, based on communal experiences, and leading to a public space and a collective wisdom. The person who has put forward this unfortunate notion of a 'short-term' society, or, as he colorfully puts it, *Jame'eh-ye Kolangi*, 'Disposable Society,' is the eminent Iranian historian and literatus Homa Katouzian, who evidently believes that, in contrast to Western Europe, his place of residence, his place of birth, Iran, has never had any enduring conception of history.

> Iran is ... a short-term society, a society which lacks continuity both at the individual and social level. I once wrote that up to a century ago, when an Iranian man left home in the morning he would not know whether, by the evening, he would be made a minister or be hung, drawn and quartered. I also wrote, on another occasion, that an Iranian may be a merchant this year, a minister next year, and a prisoner the year after. Obviously these are exaggerations, but they are close to the Iranian experience throughout its long history; a history which, though very long, consists of connected short terms. Ask an average Iranian what he would be doing in six months' time and you would

normally receive the reply 'In six months' time who is dead and who is alive.'[17]

Contrary to such theorizations of outlandish pessimism, there was perfectly evident rhyme and reason to what we were witnessing in the post-electoral crisis of June 2009. The Islamic Republic came to power by eliminating all its internal oppositions by activating and/or fabricating one external enemy after another. The constitution of the Islamic Republic was the violent distortion of Iranian polyvocal cosmopolitan culture. Thirty years later (1979–2009), when the Islamic Republic had finally exhausted all its enemy-making conjugations, at long last a young generation came to the fore that neither believed in nor could care less about these delusional 'enemies.' The Green Movement, in effect, returned and restored to Iranian political culture its cosmopolitan character and disposition. This time around, however, we had moved beyond the failed attempts at political modernity and opted for a qualitative breakthrough towards societal modernity (a fact to which Kolangi theories are blind). This was finally a post-ideological society – though both defenders and detractors of the Islamic Republic continued to defend or denounce it in outdated ideological terms, oblivious of the fact that this was a civil rights movement that had commenced with the simple question 'Where is my vote?'

'Where is my vote?'

In the annals of the Islamic Republic, 22 Khordad 1388/12 June 2009 is a day that will not be soon forgotten. Iranians are notoriously obsessive with dates, anniversaries, commemorations, ceremonies, and prone to reinvent their history in a manner that will define their present and change their future. This date will be no exception. On Iranian, Islamic and world (Christian) calendars, from the vernal equinox to the Arab conquest of Iran, to the martyrdom of the Third Shi'i Imam, to Labor Day (1 May), Iranians mark their multiple chronologies with colorful and robust memories. Of a total population of 72 million, some 80 percent of the 46 million eligible to vote participated in a fairly democratic election (a sign of their indomitable spirit rather than testimony to the democratic institutions of the Islamic Republic) within the severe confinements of a theocratic state. At every turn of the screw since the inception of the Islamic Republic both political practice and its evolving discourse have transmuted into varied kinds of civil disobedience by virtue of actors reaching for the particulars of a civil rights movement. On 23 Khordad 1388/13 June 2009 this civil rights movement entered a new, more forceful, phase.

It is quite a historical coincidence that the origin of the American Civil Rights Movement also dates back to a disputed presidential election. It was after the much-contested presidential election of 1876 that white supremacists resumed their political control of the South, put an end to Reconstruction and resumed their racist policies and practices. For almost two decades, between 1890 and 1908, racial discrimination against African Americans assumed systemic and widespread proportions – the so-called 'Jim Crow' system[18] – as the Democratic Party became a whites-only party and the Republican Party dwindled in significance. The fundamental flaws in the electoral process under the constitution of the Islamic Republic, the oddity of a so-called 'democratic theocracy,' is very much reminiscent of the discriminatory policies that Southern Democrats legislated in order to discourage African Americans from voting.[19] The unconscionable violence directed against demonstrators in Iran is reminiscent of the systematic police, corporate, and mass racial violence that targeted African Americans and other non-whites (Asians and Latinos in particular).

The non-violent modes of resistance deployed against institutionalized racism in the United States have a lot to teach the
Iranian civil rights movement. Such acts of nonviolent protest and
civil disobedience as the Montgomery Bus Boycott in Alabama
(1955–56); the Greensboro sit-in in North Carolina (1960); and
the Selma to Montgomery marches in Alabama (1965) stand as
exemplars. In the United States such protests reached critical mass,
producing a crisis that ultimately came to fruition in the Civil
Rights Act of 1964, the Voting Rights Act of 1965, the Immigra-
tion and Nationality Services Act of 1965, and the Civil Rights Act
of 1968. The American Civil Rights Movement is an exemplary
model in terms of both tactical perseverance and the significance
of protracted resistance.

The unfolding of events in the initial days of the 2009 Iranian
uprising will always be remembered for their spontaneity and
courage, challenging the monstrosities of a militant and violent
regime that did not hesitate in seizing its own citizens from the
streets, in holding them hostage in medieval dungeons, in beating,
torturing, raping, and even cold-bloodedly murdering them. The
day after the election, in the early hours of 13 June, the incumbent
president was officially and hurriedly declared the winner; and as
the principal contender, Mir Hossein Mousavi, called the official
results a 'dangerous charade,' thousands of protestors poured into
the streets chanting 'Where is my vote?' and charged widespread
fraud. There were violent clashes with the police.[20] The following
day, 14 June, as Mousavi, Karroubi, and Mohsen Reza'i – the
three leading oppositional candidates, insisted there had been
widespread fraud, pro-Ahmadinejad forces staged an officially
orchestrated rally on his behalf, which state-controlled national
television covered widely and magnified. This would be the first
of many staged demonstrations, engineered by the regime and
overcompensating for its fundamental absence of legitimacy.

Within a matter of days the fake formality of state legitimacy started to crumble and the naked brutality of the Islamic Republic began to reveal itself. 15 June saw a spontaneous and massive demonstration (estimates suggested up to 3 million people), with pro-Mousavi supporters marching in the streets of Tehran and gathering at Azadi Square. Other cities reported equally sizeable gatherings. Scores were arrested, beaten up, incarcerated. Two of the demonstrators, Neda Aqa Soltan and Sohrab A'rabi, were murdered; others were taken to the dungeons of Evin and Kahrizak prisons, tortured, raped, and murdered.[21] This was not the stuff of rumors generated by an 'opposition' outside Iran. These were charges brought by the most prominent former official of the Islamic Republic itself, Mehdi Karroubi, Speaker of the House 1989–92, 2000–2004, and corroborated by Mir Hossein Mousavi, the wartime prime minister (1981–89), and by Mohammad Khatami, two-term president of the Republic (1997–2005).

Over the following few days, sporadic demonstrations continued; foreign journalists were either expelled or forced to abide by extremely restrictive rules. Ahmadinejad defended his victory and pronounced it a major blow to 'the West.' In his much anticipated 19 June Friday public prayer sermon, Ali Khamenei corroborated and defended Ahmadinejad's 'victory,' stating that he considered the election perfectly legitimate, warned against foreign interventions, and held Mir Hossein Mousavi et al. responsible for the bloodshed that had ensued.[22] More demonstrations, more arrests, and more belligerence from the officials, matched by defiance from the dissidents, continued well into the second week of unrest in the latter part of June 2009. With every passing day, and in the face of a civil and nonviolent uprising, the regime was exposing more naked faces of its fundamentally flawed claim to legitimacy.

The Islamic Republic simply had no clue what had hit it and from where, and began reading from its tired, old, and cliché-ridden book, blaming a fictive 'enemy' – exactly as George W. Bush did after 9/11, and as Israel does striking an even more regular chord of monotony. Very early in the post-electoral crisis, the Islamic Republic opted to create a diplomatic crisis with a European country (on the model of a similar crisis involving the US early in the course of the revolution in 1979–80), in this case with the United Kingdom, accusing the British of plotting against it. At the same time, foreign journalists were similarly accused of plots against the Islamic Republic, as were the major human rights organizations like Amnesty International and Human Rights Watch. In his Friday sermon on 26 June, cleric Ahmad Khatami openly and angrily called for the execution of 'rioters,' accusing them of being agents of 'the West.' But by now major political groups like Majma' Rohaniyun-e Mobarez/The Organization of Militant Clerics, Sazeman-e Mojahedin Enqelab-e Islami/The Organization of the Fighters for Islamic Revolution – all, as their names indicate, among the leading organs of the Islamic Revolution – were actively siding with the pro-Mousavi demonstrators, as their leading members were arrested and jailed.

Central to the moral authority of the Green uprising at its earliest stages was the active and vocal support of Grand Ayatollah Montazeri and Ayatollah Sane'i, two high-ranking Shi'i clerics, for the dissidents and against Ayatollah Khamenei and Mahmoud Ahmadinejad. In his anticipated 17 July public prayer sermon, the former president Hashemi Rafsanjani also sided with the dissidents and suggested the Islamic Republic was in deep crisis. During the following week, on 20 July, former president Mohammad Khatami too called for a referendum on the legitimacy of the government. Meanwhile popular discontent was steadfast and unrelenting. On 30 July, clashes erupted after hundreds of Mousavi supporters gathered to mourn Neda Agha-Soltan at Tehran's Behesht-e Zahra cemetery, but police forced Mousavi, who had joined the gathering, to leave the scene. Hundreds of police fired teargas into the crowd to disperse protesters from nearby streets. The commencement of the Green Movement was thus entirely in tandem with the history of similar social uprisings in Iran – an older generation of activists leading a younger generation of impatient citizens. What was different was the societal disposition of the uprising, demanding civil liberties rather than a complete breakdown of the status quo – though there were sporadic signs of more radical demands as well.

In facing a mounting discontent, the Islamic Republic was now acting like a porcupine in danger and had all its spikes out. On 1 August, it put some of the leading members of the reform movement on public trial, and charged them with trying to overthrow the clerical establishment through a 'velvet coup'; as on 3 August the Supreme Leader Ali Khamenei formally approved the second-term presidency of Mahmoud Ahmadinejad. By 5 August, Ahmadinejad was sworn in by parliament in a ceremony boycotted by reformist leaders and marred by street protests.

What we were witnessing during the summer of 2009 in Iran was a historic sublimation of Iranian political discourse and disposition into the realm of a civil rights movement, via an active retrieving of its cosmopolitan culture, and in which *a public form of reason* was being cultivated at every instance of post-ideological confrontation. The ruling elite of the Islamic Republic was now deeply fractured. The population at large was at once divided and unrelenting. The propaganda machinery of the state apparatus was evidently at its wit's end, not knowing quite what to do with the momentum of the Green Movement. It went through the routine of expelling foreign journalists, creating a false diplomatic row, arresting leading political activists and charging them with treason, while systematically abusing the population at large – beating, incarcerating, torturing, raping, and murdering them in order to sustain its power.

Not just the demonstrators but the general momentum of the movement had now assumed an entirely different disposition. The most significant premiss of this movement was the active emergence of a public reason, which could no longer be assimilated into the dominant juridical discourse. This historic retrieval of Iranian cosmopolitan culture and the concomitant sublation of a failed *political modernity* into *societal modernity* was the defining moment of this movement. The movement was in obvious opposition to the ludicrous notion that 'Iran is a short-term society,' unfortunately betraying a deep-rooted colonized mind that has internalized grossly Orientalist assumptions about non-European societies, which are presumably long-term societies. All histories have long-term and short-term phases and durations. Do Iranians not learn from their experiences, do they not move forward, learn new strategies, abandon old clichés and sustain their historical progress towards the institutional achievement of their pride of place and sense of dignity? It is a racist nonsense to think Iranians just keep repeating themselves. Ours has been a consistent drive towards the formation of a public space, public reason, from political discourse to creative acts of civil disobedience, changing the moral map of our own political action, and thereby the dreadful colonial legacy called 'the Middle East.'

Identifying the June 2009 post-electoral crisis in Iran as a 'civil rights movement' is not to disregard the profound anger and sentiment mobilized against the very constitution of the Islamic Republic, which may indeed one day result in a complete collapse of the system and the establishment, in the near or distant future, of a democratic republic. But what is evident in this current uprising is a full-blown epistemic shift in Iranian political culture. The fact that the movement began with the slogan 'Where is my vote?' may indeed culminate in *Esteqlal, Azadi, Jomhuri-ye Irani*/'Independence, Freedom, Iranian Republic,' as some early slogans had it. That remains to be seen. But whether or not that eventuality comes to pass, the current crisis of the Islamic Republic is the commencement of a *societal modernity*, to use Habermas's apt term, that marks and transcends repeated failures in *political modernity*. And it is through this crucial paradigm shift that Iranian society has resumed its historic march towards democratic self-governance. In order to register this obvious fact, one must first break through the powerful mental barrier that colonialism seems to have installed in our mental perception, condemning us to a 'short-term history,' like a societal Tourette's Syndrome that cannot but stutter ad infinitum.

Contrary to persistent colonial assumptions, the public space in Iranian political culture and practice has been consistently expanding since at least the early nineteenth century and the transmutation of a medieval cosmopolitanism into an equally cosmopolitan anti-colonial modernity; meanwhile the Iranian political apparatus, via a negative dialectic between domestic tyranny and colonial domination and a state of permanent siege, has lagged pathologically behind.[23]

In an area infested with genocidal, homicidal, and suicidal violence, we are now witness to the rise of a non-violent civil rights movement that has caught the whole world by surprise. Unfolding before our eyes in Iran is the transmutation of the clichéd Iranian/Islamic question, 'Where is my gun?' into the far more powerful and enduring question, 'Where is my vote?' What has transpired has been in the making for a very long time, and yet no one ever dreamed that it would happen in our lifetime. The rise of the question 'Where is my vote?' marks the epistemic exhaustion of ideological metanarratives and the commencement of civil liberties, the categorical collapse of the useless notion of 'intellectuals,' and the birth of the far superior concept of 'citizens.' Inasmuch as absolutist ideological convictions were (and continue to be) coterminous with asking 'Where is my gun?,' the meticulous articulation of civil liberties and constitutional rights begins with the modest, but infinitely more powerful, question 'Where is my vote?'

FOUR

It's a Jungle Out There

CENTRAL TO THE INTERNAL STABILITY of the Islamic Republic and its ability to crush any form of dissent have always been the external pillars of its regional significance as the singular beneficiaries of the follies of the United States (our good old Lion) and its regional allies in that Ass of all prizes 'the Middle East.' As a quarterback with three wide receivers – Hamas, Hezbollah, and the Mahdi Army – the Islamic Republic is solidly placed to turn the favored football metaphor of American military strategists against itself. Since the events of 9/11, the Islamic Republic has strengthened its relations with three major national liberation movements in the region: Hezbollah in Lebanon (Shi'i), Hamas in Palestine (Sunni), and the Mahdi Army in Iraq (Shi'i). Despite the denominational differences among these three Islamist groups, they have in common a shared determination to oppose US/Israeli military domination in the region. The specific sinews of this commonality, and the reason for its power and durability, are the defining moments of an emerging asymmetric warfare that will define the next period of regional in/stability.

The general condition of the significance and power of the Islamic Republic in the region and in the Muslim world at large is the fact that a Christian empire (aided and abetted by a Jewish state) has invaded and conquered Muslim lands. It is not the fault of the Islamic Republic when American soldiers are caught by Al Jazeera organizing to convert Afghans to Christianity, with Pashto and Dari translation of the Good Word in good supply.[1] But the Islamic Republic becomes the beneficiary of the fact and the news. 'The special forces guys — they hunt men basically,' Lieutenant-Colonel Gary Hensley, chief of the US military chaplains in Afghanistan, is caught by Al Jazeera telling his congregated soldiers; 'we do the same things as Christians, we hunt people for Jesus. We do, we hunt them down. Get the hound of heaven after them, so we get them into the kingdom. That's what we do, that's our business.'[2] Forget about the Islamic Republic: who could blame al-Qaeda for calling Americans 'the Crusaders'? As an 'Islamic' Republic, Iran of course becomes the primary beneficiary of a condition in which Christian soldiers with the most deadly military machinery behind them are commanding the people they have conquered to convert to Christianity. 'From the United States' military's perspective,' Admiral Mike Mullen, chairman of the US Joint Chiefs of Staff, clarified, 'it is not our position to ever push any specific kind of religion, period.'[3]

Proselytizing might not indeed be a stated policy in the US military. But 'do we know what it means to proselytize?', as Captain Emmit Furner, a military chaplain, asked his flock? 'It is General Order Number One,' an unidentified soldier replies, according to Al Jazeera, which also reports similar missionary practices take place in Iraq. Sergeant Jon Watt, a soldier set to become a military chaplain, already has the answer: 'you can't proselytize, but you can give gifts. ... I bought a carpet and then I gave the guy a Bible after I conducted my business.'[4] It is in this

context that the central significance of an Islamic Republic ought
to be understood in Muslim lands.

It is thus not just Osama bin Laden, Mullah Omar, and the
custodians of the Islamic Republic who in varying degrees see
the US presence in the region and its unconditional support for
the Jewish state as the evident sign of a Judeo-Christian plot and
an attack on Muslims. Christian, Jewish, and Christian Zionist soldiers in the battlefields of Lebanon, Palestine, Iraq, and
Afghanistan see it that way too. Israelis believe that Palestine is
promised to them by God Almighty Himself, a view shared by
American Christian Zionists, who see the Jewish state as the fore-
runner of Armageddon. Hence also the language of civilizational
superiority and religious divination employed by George W. Bush,
Tony Blair, and Silvio Berlusconi. Even His Holiness Pope Benedict
XVI, in his Regensburg lecture in September 2006, went back all
the way to the fourteenth century – to the *Dialogue Held with a Certain
Persian, the Worthy Mouterizes, in Anakara of Galatia* – to find a passage
to insult 1.5 billion Muslims: 'Show me just what Muhammad
brought that was new and there you will find things only evil
and inhuman, such as his command to spread by the sword the
faith he preached.'[5]

Battle Formations

This is the age of asymmetric warfare. The superior military might
of the US and Israel (the Lion King of this jungle) fails the utility
test when compared to the lightweight resistance of combatants
defending their home turf – a fact that has surely been common
wisdom at least since the US involvement in Vietnam, but that
is now on full display in both the Afghan and Iraqi theaters of
operation, and even more so in the aftermath of the military
debacles of Israel in Lebanon in 2006 and Gaza in 2008–09. The

Revolutionary Guards (Pasdaran-e Enqelab) at the heart of the Islamic Republic know this only too well and are in full charge of its machinations. The links of the Guards far and wide into the region have been some thirty years in the making.

The political and military link between the Islamic Republic and Hamas is deep-rooted, organic, and enduring. The Palestinian cause is at the heart of the Islamic Revolution, and for obvious reasons the Islamist component of it is particularly dear to the Iranian leadership. Palestine has always been definitive for all progressive political forces in Iran – particularly among the Marxist left and militant Islamists. However, in the aftermath of the Islamic Revolution of 1977–79, militant Islamists appropriated the Palestinian cause (as they did many other things) exclusively for themselves. Nevertheless, for obvious reasons, among all the various factions in the Palestinian national liberation movement, Hamas and the Islamic Jihad Movement in Palestine are particularly close to the ruling Islamism in Iran.[6]

Soon after the Israeli military operation in Gaza in December 2008–January 2009, reports surfaced from Cyprus that an Iranian ship full of arms had been intercepted on its way to Gaza. 'Cyprus has searched a cargo ship,' the BBC reported, citing foreign ministry sources in Nicosia, 'suspected of smuggling weapons from Iran to the Gaza Strip.'[7] Suspicions surrounding this particular ship had been raised initially by the Americans. 'Some reports say,' the BBC specified, 'the US military boarded the Cyprus-flagged *Monchegorsk* cargo ship in the Red Sea last month, but could not legally detain it or seize its cargo. The ship then sailed to Egypt's Port Said, before arriving in Cyprus last week.' The link between the Islamic Republic and Hamas had long been evident, and the more Israeli atrocities in Gaza drew international condemnation, the more the Islamic Republic took advantage of that fact to extend its roots further into the Palestinian cause.

The link between the Islamic Republic and the Mahdi Army, the urban guerrilla organization led by Muqtada al-Sadr in Iraq, is even closer and more organic. Four years into the US-led invasion of Iraq, the link between the Mahdi Army and the Islamic Republic had become public knowledge and of grave concern to the Americans and their European allies. 'Senior commanders of the Mahdi army,' reported the *Guardian* in February 2007, 'have been spirited away to Iran to avoid being targeted in the new security push in Baghdad.'[8] This obviously was not the first time that the Shi'i militia's leadership was moving to Iran to regroup and rethink its strategies of fighting against the US occupation and to secure its share of power in the new Iraq. But this time around, according to an Iraqi official talking to the *Guardian*,

> the aim of the Iranians was to 'prevent the dismantling of the infrastructure of the Shia militias' in the Iraqi capital – one of the chief aims of the US-backed security drive.... The strategy is to lie low until the storm passes, and then let them return and fill the vacuum.... The Tehran authorities were 'playing a waiting game' until the commanders could return to Baghdad and resume their activities. All indications are that Muqtada is in Iran.[9]

Iran's support for the Shi'i community in Iraq in general and the Mahdi Army in particular has been a key strategic outcome of the post-US invasion. Repeated attempts by the US-led forces to compel the Shi'as into compliance with the new order have been futile. As internecine violence escalated under the US-led occupation, both the Iranian government and the Shi'i militia effectively used the US to do their work of clamping down on Sunni insurgents for them.

One should not think of the Mahdi Army as a disciplined and unified force. There is evident factionalism among its rank and file as well as its leadership. But Iran has managed to deploy its resources effectively to maintain a strong foothold in the militia. The presence of the Iranians among the Iraqi Shi'i forces had been sufficiently strong that President George Bush 'was convinced Iranian weapons were being used by insurgents in Iraq and promised to "do something about it."'[10] But the crucial point here is that, as the *Guardian* reports, 'Iraqi authorities, although regularly echoing the US charges against Syria, rarely repeat claims of interference from Iran, with which the Shia-led administration in Baghdad has close ties.'[11] So in effect Iran has leverage both with the US-backed Nuri al-Maliki government and with the anti-US Mahdi Army – as perhaps was best evident in President Ahmadinejad's visit to Iraq in March 2008, where he visibly flaunted his influence with both parties – in power and in opposition. As for the US accusation that Iran was interfering in Iraqi affairs, 'is it not funny,' Ahmadinejad asked reporters before leaving for Iraq, 'that those with 160,000 forces in Iraq accuse us of interference?'[12]

Like all grassroots guerrilla movements in the region, the Mahdi Army emerged as a community activism operation in the aftermath of the fall of Saddam Hussein and very soon assumed a militant demeanor. By June 2003, just a few months after the US-led invasion and occupation of Iraq, Muqtada al-Sadr had emerged as the leader of the Mahdi Army.[13] A militia estimated at 10,000, the Army is well placed to negotiate a powerful role based on its connections to the Islamic Republic and its tacit alliance with the US-backed prime minister Nuri al-Maliki. About a year after the US invasion, the Mahdi Army had emerged as a major force that the region had to acknowledge and accommodate. By spring 2004, it was the most effective guerrilla operation in Iraq resisting US occupation.

If the origin of the connection between the Islamic Republic and the Mahdi Army goes back to the US-led invasion of Iraq in March 2003, the Iranian link with the Lebanese Hezbollah is much older and deeper and goes back to the early 1980s, soon after the Isareli invasion of Lebanon in 1982.[14] More than two decades later, in the aftermath of the July 2006 Israeli invasion of Lebanon, the balance of power in the region went through seismic changes. After more than a month of relentless bombing of Lebanon, from air, land, and sea, the Israelis spent all they had only to put on public display the fact that they are a paper tiger – that their military power is entirely useless in the face of the new asymmetric warfare that has emerged in the region. The Israelis ran away from Lebanon leaving Hezbollah and its leader Hassan Nasrallah more powerful than ever. In collaboration with Syria, Iran was the clear winner in this emerging geopolitics of the region. The relationship between Hezbollah and Iran is of course not a mechanical one, but is predicated on an organic balance between two national polities, with Israel as the catalytic force bringing them ever closer together. The Islamic Republic uses Hezbollah as the first front of its strategic interests in the immediate vicinity of Israel. Hezbollah, as with all other factions in Lebanon, needs a strong foreign backer to enable it to operate effectively within the fractious world of Lebanese politics.

The origin of Hezbollah dates back to the Israeli invasion of Lebanon in 1982; its rise to prominence to the Israeli withdrawal in 2000, and to that of the Syrians in 2003. Hezbollah soon wedded its political agenda to the cause of the Palestine national liberation movement and effectively opened a second front against Israel. The fact is that some sixty years after the Palestinian dispossession no other military force, either of an Arab state or of a guerrilla organization, has so successfully challenged Israel as Hezbollah has since its inception in 1982. The alliance between Iran and Hezbollah remains firm on account of the plight of the Palestinians. The widely disseminated Washington view that Iran has a 'diabolic genius'[15] to create trouble in the region conceals the role of the US and Israel, whose purpose is served by the projection of the realpolitik of the region as the work of demonic forces. What is at issue is not any 'diabolic genius' on the part of the reigning mullarchy in Iran but a simple geopolitics of region underwritten by the end of conventional military operations and the rise of asymmetric warfare. In this geopolitics Russia, China, and even India are key (implicit) allies of Iran, and in the making of this asymmetric im/balance, Iran in fact need not obtain any nuclear arms. It is an entirely useless hardware and almost irrelevant in the configuration of realities on the ground – though it does flaunt some symbolic significance. It might be a matter of national pride for Iranians, but militarily it means nothing. Israel's belligerence against a nuclear Iran is just a pretext to hit it hard and challenge its military prowess, which in the age of asymmetric warfare means very little; in fact it would likely make Iran even stronger, with the consequence of revealing the Pasdaran Militia as the guerrilla operation that it is. What is lost on American and Israeli military strategists is the fact that the Islamic Republic remains at heart a guerrilla operation, successfully masking itself as a state apparatus, and waiting to hit the road at a moment's notice.

The al-Qaeda Factor

The relationship between the Islamic Republic, Hamas, Hezbollah, and the Mahdi Army casts the geopolitics of the region entirely in favor of the Islamic Republic, which at once creates and takes advantage of political crises to keep itself a strong and dominant force in the region.

What further complicates the situation (again in favor of the Islamic Republic) is the amorphous presence of the shadowy force that is called 'al-Qaeda,' which has successfully stretched its spectral reach from Afghanistan and Pakistan to Iraq and Yemen, and from there all over the Muslim (and even non-Muslim) lands. Osama bin Laden is no longer just a person but has been transmuted into a brand name – a fetishized commodity. From some fictive cave in Afghanistan he purportedly manufactures the illusion of an omnipotent and omnipresent threat that keeps the American military machinery abuzz. Like a dog chasing after its own tail, the US military races after al-Qaeda operatives around the globe and the exercise keeps what President Eisenhower termed the 'military–industrial complex' a profitably productive enterprise. The way it is projected by the US security analysts, al-Qaeda is not a reality in and of itself. Rather, it is the spectral shadow of US military might, its doppelgänger. Al-Qaeda metastasizes like a psychosomatic cancer through a global body-politic that is intent on devouring its own sense of sanity. The more the US army chases after this shadowy apparition, the more it exhausts its energy in a futile fantasy, and the more the Islamic Republic becomes the beneficiary of the deadly game.

As evident in the assessment of one (typical) US security analyst, Bruce Hoffman, in his article 'Al-Qaeda has a new strategy. Obama needs one, too,' the analytical screw on the logic of the matter is entirely loose.[16] The two crucial points that Hoffman raises are:

> First, al-Qaeda is increasingly focused on overwhelming, distracting and exhausting us. To this end, it seeks to flood our already information-overloaded national intelligence systems with myriad threats and background noise. Al-Qaeda hopes we will be so distracted and consumed by all this data that we will overlook key clues, such as those before Christmas that linked Abdulmutallab to an al-Qaeda airline-bombing plot. Second, in the wake of the global financial crisis, al-Qaeda has stepped up a strategy of economic warfare. 'We will bury you,' Soviet Premier Nikita Khrushchev promised Americans 50 years ago. Today, al-Qaeda threatens: 'We will bankrupt you.' Over the

past year, the group has issued statements, videos, audio messages and letters online trumpeting its actions against Western financial systems, even taking credit for the economic crisis. However divorced from reality these claims may be, propaganda doesn't have to be true to be believed, and the assertions resonate with al-Qaeda's target audiences.[17]

Whose fault is it if CIA gathers more (useless) data than it can decipher and analyze? Al-Qaeda's? If there is no purposeful manner of gathering intelligence, no intelligence behind the intelligence, who is to blame? Al-Qaeda? The American security and intelligence apparatus has gone on a whirlwind of wasteful and useless data collection that makes no sense and serves no purpose – and no one is to blame but the analysts who sit down poring over a mass of nonsensical facts. The second reasoning of Hoffman is even more bizarre. Decades of wanton disregard for human decency and of Milton Friedman-prescribed deregulation have wreaked havoc on the world's economy and created massive pockets of poverty – and al-Qaeda is to blame? If this assessment is 'divorced from reality,' as Hoffman suggests, then who is propagating it, al-Qaeda or Bruce Hoffman? Al-Qaeda is not responsible for the lack of intelligence behind intelligence – the CIA is. Al-Qaeda is not responsible for the financial crisis in the US and around the globe – Milton Friedman, Ronald Reagan, and Margaret Thatcher are. All of this is to say nothing about the fundamental structural deficiency in gathering real data – data about economic destitution and the politics of despair it engenders around the globe.

The Islamic Republic is not just the natural beneficiary of the delusion of al-Qaeda that US analysts have manufactured to keep them in business. The Islamic Republic is also the potential natural ally against that delusion – for its Shi'i disposition is inimical to whatever Salafi disposition informs the Wahabi-inspired gang of terrorists gathered around Osama bin Laden. This is not to reduce the Islamic Republic to its Shi'i denomination, for its strategic solidarity with Hamas (and, by extension, the Muslim Brotherhood), for example, defies such narrow sectarian interests. But the conceptual dissonance at the heart of the analytical manufacturing of 'al-Qaeda' works both to discredit the US and its security and intelligence analysts, and to empower the Islamic Republic. For if al-Qaeda is for real, and it is, by definition, a Salafi-based Wahabi movement that despises Shi'as more than it does 'the West,' then why not strike a deal with the Islamic Republic to combat that menace? The aging Lion does not seem to have all his wits about him. It has manufactured two Enemies that are mutually exclusive: one Sunni and the other Shi'i. It wants to keep them both as enemies, in two different terms, one transnational and the other national. In this transaction, the US (the Lion) loses credibility; the Islamic Republic (the Fox) gains the upper hand.

In this atmosphere of deceit and delusion, the Islamic Republic has its own nightmares, which keep feeding its hunger for power. Though the US is the chief operator in the situation that has inadvertently empowered the Islamic Republic, the role of the UK in keeping the Islamist theocracy in a position of regional advantage cannot be ignored. As a strategic sidekick to George W. Bush, Tony Blair both facilitated European consent to American military adventurism in Afghanistan and Iraq, and sought to secure a position of power for Britain far beyond its limited means.[18] But the hidden dimension of this belated British imperialism, or imperialism by US proxy, is that it invokes very dark memories in the Islamic Republic, which in turn wakes up in the morning and interprets as a sign of the old CIA/MI6 conspiracy to rob it of its national sovereignty and regional power. This, then, is a case where facts fuel fantasies. The fact of the US/UK alliance in warmongering in Afghanistan and Iraq fuels the fear of a reenactment of the CIA/MI6 coup of 1953 in Iran, which is at once real for the Islamic Republic and exploited to keep alive among Iranians the memory of that traumatic event. The fear of a coup aiming to topple it keeps the old Fox on his toes.

The Nuclear Nexus

Next to the amorphous disposition of al-Qaeda stands the prolonged nuclear issue that the Islamic Republic has effectively used to its own advantage. In one of his habitually insightful blogs on Al Jazeera, senior political analyst Marwan Bishara, contrary to the views of a myriad intelligence analysts in Washington DC, laid out the most fundamental dimension of the nuclear stalemate between the US/Israel and the Islamic Republic of Iran. Acknowledging the fact that 'Iran is not coming clean on its intentions over its nuclear programme,' and that in fact 'it is doing the absolute minimum under its International Atomic Energy Agency (IAEA) and Nuclear Non-Proliferation Treaty (NPT) obligations to underline how its nuclear programme is civilian in nature, when UN resolutions and mounting suspicion require more,' Bishara concludes that 'Tehran is managing a sensitive, even dangerous balancing act. It reveals the minimum required by its international obligations while making bombastic statements about its breakthroughs in nuclear enrichment.'[19] What additionally needs to be kept in mind is the fact that the US and its regional allies pick on one country at a time and set about preparing for military strikes against it. Between 9 September 2001 and 7 October of that year, when the US led the invasion of Afghanistan, there was 'mounting evidence' of al-Qaeda links not just to the events of 9/11 but to a whole host of other atrocities. And then, from about a year into the Afghan war up until 20 March 2003, when the US led its invasion of Iraq, there appeared additional 'mounting evidence' linking Saddam

Hussein to the same events of 9/11 and the equally compelling notion that he was amassing weapons of mass destruction. With no evident accompanying sense of irony, a couple of years into the Iraqi debacle the selfsame 'mounting evidence' against Iran began to be distilled from WINEP (Washington Institute for Near Eastern Policy) and its kindred souls among the neocon operatives extending from Washington DC to Stanford California. That the public sense of credulity had worn thin, even in the United States, the principal target of Washington-based spin-doctors, did not seem to bother them.

Bishara's principal insight is that as Iran 'tries to please the IAEA as an accountable member of the international community, it annoys, even embarrasses, the US and its European partners to please its nationalistic popular base.' In the aftermath of the June 2009 presidential election and the commencement of the Green Movement, that 'nationalistic popular base' had all but disappeared and was replaced by a sinister maneuver to use and abuse the nuclear issue to divert attention from the absence of any popular base. From mid-summer 2009, the nuclear game became perhaps the single most important ploy in the hands of Ahmadinejad's government and the regime at large to shift global attention away from the domestic Iranian scene towards the regional implications of a nuclear Iran.

As Marwan Bishara rightly points out, the only reason Iran would 'go through the trouble and risk of igniting stiffer sanctions and possible military attack' is that it believed 'that is the best way to safeguard its national sovereignty and strategic deterrence in a region dominated by a US and Western military presence'. But the scale of that risk is also worth considering. It is important to reiterate that, at its heart, the Islamic Republic remains a militant theocracy, and at the heart of that heart it remains a guerrilla operation with a very thin veneer of a state apparatus. It is Israel's worst nightmare, for it is the Islamic replica of the Jewish state. At this moment, as a result, the Islamic Republic will either have to emerge as a major regional power or else disappear – or be pushed back, as Israeli warlords love to say, 'half a century.' The Revolutionary Guards are thus fighting, or getting ready to fight, a life-or-death battle, and in that battle, and in those terms (and there's the rub), they need not 'instigate' any popular support or nationalist sentiment. They already have it. Iranians may despise the Islamic Republic, but there is a common nationalist trait in them that made even Ayatollah Khomeini invoke the memory of the Sassanid glory.

Marwan Bishara is also right that 'President Obama is well aware of Tehran's strategic anxiety and its search for strategic accommodation with Washington.' This is not just because the Islamic Republic cannot carve itself a share of regional power without the (however grudging) consent of the United States. It is also because such a bid for accommodation will also push the theater of operation away from the nuisance of domestic illegitimacy to where the Islamic Republic has learned how to play hardball. As Bishara points out, 'if Washington's agenda is nuclear, Tehran's agenda is national security and its future role in the region.' That future has now assumed an added urgency by virtue of the threat that the Revolutionary Guards feel not just from their regional foes without but from their own citizens within.

Bishara catches the US secretary of state red-handed:

It is disingenuous of the US secretary of state to claim that Iran refuses to sit down with Washington, and neglects to mention how Washington will not sit down with Iran to discuss the latter's regional concerns. With its neighbors to the north and south – Iraq and Afghanistan – occupied by the US and as it is threatened by Israel, Tehran demands explicit recognition of Iran's regional status and long-term US commitments and

assurances. Which begs the question: Is the Obama administration ready to discuss Iran's vision of the region or to recognize
Iran's regional power with all that it invokes in Tel Aviv, Riyadh
and Cairo?[20]

The answer to the last question is: of course not. Neither the
US nor Israel can imagine the region with another power outside
their sphere of influence. The two bumper zones that the Reagan
administration (1980–88) crafted around the Islamic Republic (the
Taliban and Saddam Hussein) to curtail its revolutionary zeal, the
Bush administration (2000–08) worked hard at dismantling one
at a time, leaving the Islamic Republic singularly positioned to
reap the benefit of American short-term memory and long-term
folly. Thus the Obama administration inherited a chaotic mess on
both sides of the Islamic Republic. Unless and until it is ready and
willing to engage in yet another military fiasco, it will have to
make an accommodation regarding its share of regional power.
Israel's choice in the matter is either to take a cold shower and
live with the 'existential threat' or else attack Iran and then really
face its existential threat. In either scenario, Israel and the US lose;
the Islamic Republic wins.

Bishara ultimately identifies the US attitude towards Iran in
three consecutive moves: 'charm/conciliation, coercion/sanctions
and regime change/war.' These three options pretty much exhaust
what is available to the Obama administration – and yet in any of
these three scenarios the Islamic Republic will win, and whichever
of them the US chooses it will end up facing the reality of a new
major power in the region, much to everyone's chagrin. Bishara
is not entirely oblivious to the Green Movement. If sanctions do
not work, Bishara suggests, 'Washington hopes Iran will implode
from within in light of the potent opposition to the regime, saving
America the trouble of waging another war in the Muslim world.'
But he leaves that assessment there rather than exploring it further

– despite the fact that the future of the Islamic Republic, and with it the region at large, is very much contingent precisely on that movement and how it will play out.

The Iraq Factor

In every conceivable respect, the Iraqi debacle has played to the great advantage of the Islamic Republic. The process began a year into the 1979 revolution when Saddam Hussein – encouraged, aided, and abetted by the Reagan administration and its European and regional allies – invaded Iran, and in the ensuing Iran–Iraq War (1980–1988) provided the Islamic Republic with the perfect opportunity to crack down and destroy internal opposition. The first US-led invasion of Iraq (1990–91), under President George H.W. Bush (the Father), dismantled the Iraqi military infrastructure but stopped short of destroying Saddam Hussein's government, fearing the advantage it would give to the Islamic Republic. His son was not so wise. President George W. Bush (the Son) and his neoconservative ideological gurus – ranging from Irving Kristol to Paul Wolfowitz, Richard Perle, William Kristol, Elliott Abrams and Douglas Feith, all institutionalized in the Project for a New American Century – thought they would make an example of Iraq, safe for Democracy and neoliberal economics. One million dead and 4 million refugee Iraqis and the infrastructure of a sovereign nation-state in ruins later, no one cares to remember these ignoble people, but the Islamic Republic does. It is the singular beneficiary of the follies of the American neoconservatives.

As George W. Bush & Co. ruined Iraq and laid the founda-tions of an Islamic Republic of Iraq, the Revolutionary Guards moved in to secure a solid sphere of influence in southern Iraq, as Turkey did the same in the north in Iraqi Kurdistan. The Iranians used Ahmad Chalabi (an Iraqi businessman-turned-politician who was instrumental in providing the US with false information in the lead-up to invasion of Iraq) – as Chalabi used, abused, and played like a violin his old neocon pals – to make sure that the make-up of the next generation of Iraqi leadership was entirely Iran-friendly, and the screening of Iraqis suitable for that purpose excluded not just the former Ba'athists, but all independent-minded Iraqi nationalists who loved their country and believed in its political integrity, and who as such were not just against American occupation but equally opposed to Iranian colonization.

In anticipation of the 7 March 2010 Iraqi election,

> a key Sunni Arab party [was] boycotting Iraq's ... elections because of what it says was Iranian influence that led to the banning of participants in the upcoming race, including the bloc's leader. The Iraqi Front for National Dialogue, headed by Saleh al-Mutlaq, said the move was prompted by remarks by a U.S. general and the American ambassador to Iraq about Iran's influence in Iraq's electoral process.[21]

Of course the Americans were not exactly in a position to point a finger. But what they pointed to was there.

Some seven years into the US-led invasion and occupation of Iraq, the Iraqi government was not in a position to reverse the trend and contain Iranian influence in the south. We were, in effect, back in the nineteenth-century Ottoman period, when the border between Iran and Iraq, due to both trade and Shi'ism, had once again become porous. As Robert Dreyfus rightly pointed out, 'Iran's influence in Iraq is semi-permanent. If anyone is going to force Iran to back down in Iraq, it will be the Iraqis themselves, not only at the ballot box but, it appears, in what may require a new outburst of violence, too.'[22] Ominous was Dreyfus's prediction, for it was at the behest of the Americans that Saddam Hussein invaded Iran in 1980, and it was now in the aftermath of the US-led invasion of Iraq that yet another bloody war might be in the offing. This is how Dreyfus summed up the situation in Iraq at the threshold of the 7 March elections:

> Here's the reality of Iraq in 2010: The damage is done. Seven years after the US invasion, Iran has the upper hand by virtue of its alliance with a network of Shiite religious politicians. ... Iran is multiply connected to the Kurds, as well. It has vast economic influence in Iraq. It's beyond absurd to suggest ... that Obama is to blame for that. When he took office, he inherited a disaster in Iraq. The plan to drawdown US forces was pretty much already written in stone by the US–Iraq accord negotiated in 2008 by President Bush – and Obama simply ratified it.[23]

As liberal and conservative Americans were blaming each other for the debacle in Iraq and the rise of Iranian influence, the Islamic Republic just sat there pretty, taking full advantage of a mess that President Bush had made and President Obama inherited and all but exacerbated.

The Watchful Fox

What we see in Iraq is equally evident in Afghanistan, and potentially in Yemen. President Obama has just committed the greatest folly of his administration by investing even more heavily in Afghanistan, and Yemen looks inviting to him too. These dual traps, one he inherited from President Bush and the other of his own device, are playing into the hands of the Islamic Republic. Again, here too, whatever President Obama does, the Islamic Republic will be the beneficiary.

In Afghanistan, the American military continues to do for the Islamic Republic what it cannot do for itself – waste American

time, energy, and resources, and destroy the infrastructure of
the Taliban. Meanwhile in Yemen, Iran has found a new reason
for Shi'i solidarity with the northern separatist movement of the
Houthis, as the Saudis and their US sponsors have come to the
aid of the central government. But that is not the whole story, for
after Somalia, Yemen is the new quagmire, into which the UK
and the US are drawn by al-Qaeda. As al-Qaeda had metastasized
from Afghanistan to Somalia to Yemen, the UK and the US were
getting more and more involved, first via covert operations and
then by the proxy armies of Saudi Arabia. But, again, before any
al-Qaeda 'cells' moved in, Yemen was already fractured along its
tribal, sectarian, regional, and ideological grounds, which means,
just like Afghanistan and Pakistan, it provided the best breeding
ground for the delusion of al-Qaeda to act out.

The central government in Yemen has had a problem sustaining its legitimacy against separatist movements in both the South
and the North anyway. What the idea of al-Qaeda does is to
confuse the political realities in a country like Yemen and drag
the US and its regional allies into a deep quaqmire. As with many
other disenfranchised populations, young Yemenis were initially
recruited by the CIA and sent to fight the Soviets in Afghanistan.
There they learned the few tricks of the trade, and now they were
looking for a job for which the CIA had trained them. President Ali
Abdullah Saleh has recruited the help of both the Americans and
the Saudis to quell the opposition to his reign from Yemeni Zaidi
Shi'is (the Houthis), since 2004, led by Abdel-Malik Badreddin
al-Houthi in the Saada district. By late February 2010, Yemen,
which was actively aided by the Saudis, seemed to be ready for
a truce with the rebels who had plagued the central authorities.[24]
Whatever this truce may have been worth, the southern separatist
moment was still very much in place, and in between them was
the specter of al-Qaeda.

All Fall Down

Meanwhile, preliminary investigations in Dubai in the United Arab Emirates indicated that Mahmoud al-Mabhouh, a Hamas official, was murdered by what the authorities termed 'a professional criminal gang' that had chased after him, cornered, and cold-bloodedly killed him in his hotel room.[25] The suspects had perpetrated their crime and then fled the United Arab Emirates. According to the BBC, 'doctors who had examined his body determined that he had died after receiving a massive electric shock to the head. They also found evidence that he had been strangled.' The BBC report added: 'Mr. Mabhouh's family also said he had survived two Israeli assassination attempts, including a poisoning six months ago in the Lebanese capital, Beirut, which left him unconscious for 30 hours.' Using (fake or real) European passports, the murderers were seemingly determined to make sure the investigators were aware of how proud they were of their act. 'The culprits,' UAE authorities said to reporters, 'left a trace behind which points to them and will help in chasing and arresting them.' The police chief declared: 'I cannot rule out the possibility of Mossad [Israeli secret service] involvement in the assassination of Mabhouh.'[26]

Confident of their mastery of the art of targeted assassination (or 'state-sponsored terrorism'), the Israelis of course said 'there was no evidence' that it had anything to do with the murder of Mabhouh. But the European countries whose passports were used or abused indicated (though not too strongly) that they were not best pleased with the Israelis. 'The European Union,' the *Financial Times* reported, 'signaled its displeasure with Israel by denouncing the use of forged European passports in the killing of a Hamas commander in Dubai.'[27] According to the report, 'The EU strongly condemns the fact that those involved

in this action used fraudulent EU member-states' passports and
credit cards acquired through the theft of EU citizens' identities.'
In other words, the Europeans (protesting too much) were far
more concerned with the fact that these passports were 'forged,'
than they were to denounce the actual murder. Others, however,
were shooting straight. According to the *Financial Times*, 'Dubai
authorities say they are all but certain that Mossad, Israel's intelligence service, was behind the operation, in which a squad of 11
individuals travelled on forged British, Irish, French and German
passports and Mabhouh was murdered in his hotel room.' The
EU authorities, for their part, worded their statement far more
carefully: 'Diplomats said the criticism of Israel was as strongly
worded as the EU could manage, given that Germany, Italy and
several other countries in the 27-nation bloc place great emphasis
on maintaining close relations with Israel.' In other words, the
degree to which European nation-states turn a blind eye to Israeli
terrorism is determined by and proportionate to their respective
atrocities during the World War II against European Jewry, for
which crimes the Palestinians, they have determined, have to
pay now. Israelis were, of course, entirely nonchalant about the
matter. According to the *Financial Times*, 'Danny Ayalon, Israel's
deputy foreign minister, said last weekend that he expected mini-
mal diplomatic fallout from Mabhouh's killing because France,
Germany and the UK – the EU's big three – all understood the
importance of combating terrorism.' Indeed. Ayalon has Germany
and Italy, with pictures of Hitler and Mussolini still hanging
somewhere in their collective subbasements, by their (as they
say in Brooklyn) vital organs.

It is a jungle out there, and the topsy-turvy world we frightened creatures inhabit defies augury. A decade into the twenty-
first century, Iran and Israel are gnarling at each other, with the
US as ringmaster, and no one knows who is going to jump the

gun first. It takes one to know one – and the Jewish state has finally found its match in the Islamic Republic: two fanatical furies staring at each other's mirror and not liking what they see. Their respective madness is reminiscent of two thugs who keep threatening each other by way of scaring the neighborhood into obedience of their mutual vulgarity. Israelis do whatever they please, and they do it so bluntly as if to flaunt their impunity. Who is going to stop them? President Obama? Just wind back the tape and listen to his AIPAC speech back in November 2009 soon after he was nominated by the Democratic Party. Chancellor Merkel or Prime Minister Silvio Berlusconi? Not likely. Speaking for an entire spectrum of Israeli banality, Zipi Livni in fact hailed the assassination of Mabhouh as a splendid act. 'The fact that a terrorist was killed,' said the foreign minister on whose watch the Gaza massacre of 2008–09 took place, 'and it doesn't matter if it was in Dubai or Gaza, is good news to those fighting terrorism.'[28] Livni is of course not the only Israeli, the only 'friend of Israel,' who flaunts so publically their utter disregard for human decency. Martin Kramer, a visiting fellow at Harvard's National Security Studies Program, went so far as to deliver a speech in which he urged a more drastic solution to the Palestinian problem by depopulating them through 'stopping pro-natal subsidies to Palestinians with refugee status.' In other words, as the *Huffington Post* reported, 'starve the Palestinians so they don't have babies and … starving the babies so they don't grow up.… That will help reduce the terrorist threat by preventing Palestinian babies from becoming "superfluous young men." It is, Kramer says, those "superfluous young men" who become radicals.'[29] Thus, with total impunity, Israelis have been systematically stealing Palestinians' lands, dispossessing them of their homeland, and, in one war after another, maiming and murdering them in full view of history – and nobody will risk being called an anti-Semite by telling them what it is they are doing. Well, Ahmadinejad does not have that fear, and his Islamic Republic can cover up its own atrocities by telling Israel what others dare not.

Zipi Livni's and Martin Kramer's counterparts in the Islamic Republic are no less part of this sad and sonorous spectacle. The principal reason that the Twelfth Imam (who is in hiding and whose appearance believing Shi'is expect) has not showed up yet is because Americans have not allowed him to come out and declare himself – this according to the colorful Ahmadinejad in a recent rally in Birjand in Iran, where he denounced the Israeli atrocity in Dubai in the next sentence.[30] Ahmadinejad, echoing like-minded Americans, reported to his audience that 9/11 too was an inside job. Zipi Livni and Mahmoud Ahmadinejad both live in a world shaped by their own dangerous delusions and, as such, care very little for reality, or else for the frightened and ailing body-politic each represents. In this mad game, though, the Israeli have finally met their match, and they, like the rest of the world, are clueless about how to deal with the Islamic Republic, just as the Islamic Republic is clueless about how to deal with the Green movement. Neither the Islamic Republic nor the Green Movement will go away. The fact that, almost a year into the Green Movement, a period in which the Islamic Republic has been processing ever richer uranium, Israelis have not hit Iran is not because they are scared of Ahmadinejad – but because they are scared of Neda Aqa-Sultan. I will return to Neda Aqa-Soltan, the icon of the Green Movement and the nightmare of AIPAC, in the next few chapters.

FIVE

Outfoxing the Wily Fox

THE UPSHOT OF MY ARGUMENT is that hard power has long since lost its effectiveness in the region, if not beyond, and will simply not work in the current sets of crisis the world faces in 'the Middle East.' This is the first and foremost lesson we must learn from the past before we know what the future holds. The ailing Lion has very little left in his arsenal, as the aging Fox has found new tricks in his bag. When it comes to dealing with Iran, in particular, President Barack Obama has inherited a paradox that will test his wits and wherewithal to unsurpassed levels. If he opts to attack Iran (with or without Israel) he will exponentially strengthen its power and turn the Iranian paramilitary forces (Basij, and Pasdaran) into a potent power of destruction in the region – with the Palestinian Hamas, the Lebanese Hezbollah, and the Mahdi Army in Iraq as its extended military wings; and if he opts to negotiate with Iran he will lend even more legitimacy to the beleaguered ayatollahs in a precarious position of power inside their own country – so that they can continue to suppress civil and human rights, women's rights, students and the labor movement in the country. If Israel, now under the apocalyptic leadership of Benjamin Netanyahu (himself at the mercy of the ultra-conservative power of Avigdor Lieberman, the leader of the ultra right-wing Yisrael Beiteinu party), opts for military action against Iran, with or without US approval, the effect on the region will be even more disastrous – not just for the civil rights movement in Iran, and peace in the region, but above all, and infinitely more so, for Israelis themselves, trapped as they are inside a theocentric soteriology that feeds on its own determined messianic fanaticism.

The use of hard power, first and foremost, we need to understand, will not work with Iran (as it did not with Hezbollah, Hamas, or the Mahdi Army), and will in fact exacerbate the volatile situation, make the ruling clergy even more belligerent, and further strengthen their hand in the region. This observation has nothing to do with the much exaggerated culturalist explanation of the 'Shi'i martyrdom complex' or any other such abstract delusion. It simply reflects the realpolitik of the emerging asymmetrical warfare. If there is any lesson to be learned from the past, it is the utter futility of surgical rashness on the part of a cowboy mentality. Has the nature of this paradox and the reality of this lose–lose situation dawned on President Obama? Under his administration, very little other than tone has changed between the US and the Islamic Republic. What we are dealing with in the region is the hardcore realpolitik of the balance of powers. The US continues to occupy Iraq and is even more deeply than before entangled in Afghanistan, and perhaps even more so in Pakistan. Israel grabs more Palestinian land in the West Bank, invades Gaza and kills Palestinians at whim, as Israelis elect the most warlike and belligerent government in their history. Iraqi resistance is more powerful and multifaceted than ever, with the Mahdi Army as the key militia with a staunch anti-American disposition. In Lebanon, Hezbollah dominates the political scene and still carries the clout of its 2006 victory over Israel. Obama's change of tone with Iran, as evidenced in his 21 March 2009 Noruz message, means very little if he does not comprehend that this most powerful set of alliances tips the balance away from the traditional pact between the US, the Jewish state, and the corrupt and/or medieval Arab potentates like Hosni Mubarak of Egypt and King Abdullah of Saudi Arabia.[1]

Prompted by the constitution that the US viceroy of Iraq Paul Bremer and his legal adviser Noah Feldman wrote for Iraq, and then by the book that that US military and strategic analyst Seyyed Vali Reza Nasr wrote expounding on that constitution, the Obama administration has inherited the delusion of an entrenched sectarianism in the region. In his *Shia Revival: How Conflicts within Islam Will Shape the Future* (2006), Nasr has sought to convince his military and foreign policy employers, and indeed the public at large, that an endemic sectarian violence is now coming back to divide the loyalty of Muslims in the region.[2] While at the tail end of George W. Bush's presidency, this thesis was quite treacherously instrumental in shifting the burden of responsibility for the Iraqi mayhem from its actual perpetrator to an amorphous sectarianism supposedly endemic to Iraq and the region, in the aftermath of that debacle it is now a positively delusional mirage that will detract from the overriding geopolitics that President Obama's administration faces.[3] In seeking to alleviate the burden of responsibility and dodge the legitimacy of charges of war crimes and crimes against humanity, the book flies in the face of historical facts and the challenge of peace among the warring factions in the region.

The sectarian violence in Iraq and the larger region is a red herring. It is there when US and Israeli regional politics and its Washington lobbyists and analysts gathered in the Washington

Institute for Near Eastern Policy so wish it and gone the instant trans-sectarian politics offers resistance to it. The assumption that the politics of the region is a rivalry between Shi'a-inspired Iranians and Saudi-led Sunnism is patently false. Sectarian and even racializing in its underlying assumptions, Nasr's thesis falls flat in the face of facts. Hamas is not a Shi'i force. Hamas is the Palestinian extension of the transregional Sunni Muslim Brother-hood – and no cause is more crucial for Iran or Hezbollah (and by extension the Mahdi Army – all Shi'as) than Palestine in general and Hamas in particular. It is only Paul Bremer, who had Feldman draft a constitution for Iraq along sectarian lines, and by extension US military strategists, who wish such sectarianism upon Iraq and then to extend it to the whole region (King Abdullah of Jordan likes Nasr's idea too). The assumption of a transregional Shi'i alliance (a so-called 'Shi'i crescent') is deeply flawed. Iranian and Iraqi Shi'as were slaughtering each other for eight long and bloody years – so what happened then to their transnational Shi'i solidarity? The assumption of an Iranian–Arab divide is equally deceptive, when not delusional and outright racialized in its prem-ises. Hamas, Hezbollah, and the Mahdi Army are Arab, and there are no stronger allies of the Islamic Republic of Iran than these movements, and vice versa. American strategic wishful thinking that the Sunni–Shi'a divide is underwritten by Iranian–Arab rivalry is illusory and self-deceptive; it is one of the oldest and tiredest colonial trickeries in the bag. The US is aggregating as its tactical allies Saudi Arabia, Egypt, Jordan, and the Persian Gulf states as the strategic extensions of Israel. This does not equate to an actual rivalry between Arabs and Iranians. US strategists like Nasr wish this were the case. It is not.

It is imperative to keep in mind that Iran has emerged as potentially more powerful than before the events of 9/11 not out of any creative commission of its own will, volition, and statesmanship, but by the fact of the delusional failings of the Bush legacy and his regional allies. Suspend this Orientalist notion of the so-called 'Arab Street'[4] and one will have a much clearer sense of what is happening in the region. From Morocco to Syria, influential public intellectuals, writers of newspaper editorials, academics, students, journalists, bureaucrats, businessmen, ordinary men and women are bitterly frustrated and angry when they see the pictures of defenseless Iraqi, Lebanese, or Palestinian women and children slaughtered by US or Israeli soldiers. This is not Iran's doing. It is the United States' and Israel's doing. Iran does not threaten Israel. Israel threatens Iran, as do illegitimate medieval potentates ruling in Arab capitals from the Persian Gulf sheikhdoms to Jordan to Egypt to Morocco. It is not the Iranian nuclear program that is the issue, but what is on every human being's mind when they see Palestinian civilians slaughtered by Israelis with total impunity: that if any country in the region was capable of dropping a single bomb over Tel Aviv, the Israelis would think twice before dropping hundreds of bombs on Gaza, in the blink of an eye and without the slightest hesitation and with not a care if images of hundreds of dead bodies of Palestinian women and children are paraded in the world's media. Iran has stolen the show over the Palestinian cause not because the belligerent custodians of the Islamic Republic are clever or committed to the Palestinians, but because, due to the Arab states' tacit or explicit implication in Palestine, Lebanon, Iraq, and Afghanistan, their complacency makes Iran look like God's gift to humanity. The Green Movement is here to tell the world it is not. That is the paradox that will unpack the politics of despair practised by the Jewish state and the Islamic Republic under the watchful eye of the Christian empire.[5]

The evident moral upper hand of the Islamic Republic has an immediate contextual relevance in the vicinity. Iran may not master the nuclear weapons technology any time soon, but if it does who is to point a finger? Israel? Pakistan? Russia – or the United States? Iran is surrounded by four nuclear powers, one of which, Israel, is so self-righteously belligerent and arrogant that it does not even sign the Nuclear Nonproliferation Treaty. So which of these powers has the legitimacy to tell Iran not to develop nuclear technology? How, why, and by what authority? Iran will develop its nuclear technology and soon nuclear weapons capability and there is not a thing that anyone can do about that fact – morally, politically, or militarily. In Israel, fanatical politicians like Avigdor Lieberman have their fingers on nuclear bombs. In Pakistan the equally fanatical Taliban are inches away from a deadly nuclear arsenal. The only means of preventing Iran acquiring the nuclear weapon is regional disarmament, first and foremost beginning with the military garrison that calls itself Israel.

The military fact on the ground, however, is that Iran does not need to develop nuclear weaponry. For it does not need it. How has it helped Israel protect its citizens, or Pakistan in providing its services to the US and Saudi Arabia in first creating and then seeking to combat the Taliban? Nothing. Today, after the futile (notwithstanding the hundreds of innocent lives lost) Israeli operations in Lebanon in July 2006 and in Gaza in December 2008–January 2009, more than ever it has become clear that we live in a time of asymmetric warfare – large-scale armies and military strategy drawn up on a big scale mean very little. Lightweight, strategic guerrilla operations are infinitely more effective – when creatively combined with urban uprising, civil unrest, and global activism of the sort that is now best represented by the International Solidarity Movement (ISM), of which Rachel Corrie (1979–2003) is a heroic symbol, or more recently by the British MP George Galloway, who mobilized a convoy to take humanitarian aid to Gaza in the aftermath of the Israeli invasion in December 2008–January 2009.[6]

Here the Palestinian intifada has taught the world at large and the people of the region a lasting lesson. Such a creative combination of operations, along with the global solidarity expressed in the Boycott, Divestment, Sanctions (BDS) movement, is infinitely more effective than the massive military machinery that Israel and the US combined have habitually mobilized. The wily foxes in Iran, and their allies in Iraq, Lebanon, and Palestine, know this – and to outfox the Fox you need not be smarter than him. You need to rob him of his *raison d'être*. You have to deny him the opportunity to prey on the gullible Ass. While the geopolitics of the region and the hypocrisy of the world community at large – having left the entire Palestinian people to the naked brutalities of Israel – could not but strengthen the Islamic Republic, its Achilles heel is totally exposed. The Green Movement, in turn, is now the very logic of the Palestinian intifada writ large, a shift from 7 to 70 million people. The Green Movement takes the very heart of this asymmetric warfare, eliminates all elements of violence from it, and runs home with it. The world does not know how to deal with the Islamic Republic precisely because of the logic of asymmetric warfare; and precisely with the same logic, the Islamic Republic does not know what to do with the Green Movement – whatever it does makes the movement stronger.

A Paradigm Shift

What is happening in Iran, and outfoxing the Fox, is a paradigm shift in its political culture – entirely unbeknownst to the world at large, busy as it is with its usual politics of despair. But what is the hinge of this paradigmatic turn in Iran?

In August 2009, a couple of months after the commencement of the Green Movement, Iranians around the world were commemorating the fifty-sixth anniversary of the CIA-sponsored coup of 1953, or, as Iranians call it indexically on the Persian calendar, *Kudeta-ye 28 Mordad*.[7] To that date Iranians usually don't even add the year 1332 on their calendar, for, just like 9/11, 28 Mordad has assumed such iconic significance that it is as if it happened in the Year Zero of their collective memory. But the phenomenon of 28-Mordadism as a political paradigm in modern Iranian political culture has now finally exhausted itself.

For generations of Iranians, the coup of 1953 is not a mere historical event; it is the defining moment of their lives. For it is the most haunting national trauma of their modern history – foreign intervention followed by domestic tyranny. Iranians cannot speak of 28 Mordad without a certain raw nerve suddenly being touched, an entirely involuntary process. The first thing Iranians do when they speak of 28 Mordad is to remember a personal story: where they were and what they were doing – very much like the assassination of John F. Kennedy (22 November 1963), Malcolm X (21 February 1965), or Martin Luther King Jr. (4 April 1968) for Americans. When the coup occurred, something certain died and something vague came to life. 28-Mordadism is the central traumatic trope of modern Iranian historiography.

The post-traumatic syndrome of the coup of 1953 was best summed up and captured in 'Zemestan'/'Winter' (1955), the now legendary poem of Mehdi Akhavan Sales (1928–1990). 'No one returns your greetings / Heads are dropped deeply into collars' became the talismanic opening of a poem that defined an entire generation of fear and loathing, self-imposed solitude and forsaken hopes. Akhavan Sales's other poems, such as 'Marsiyeh'/'Requiem,' 'Shahryar Shahr-e Sangestan'/'The Prince of Stoneville,' 'Chavoshi'/ 'Ballad,' were all written and read as lachrymal melodies for what might have been but was not. When, in 1978, Akhavan Sales's 'Marsiyeh'/'Requiem' gave Amir Naderi the inspiration for his dark foreboding of the revolution to come in his feature film

Marsiyeh/Requiem (1978), soon after his epic *Tangsir* (1974), the coup of 1953 was running quietly through the heart of the Pahlavi regime in two opposing directions – quiet desperation and euphoric hope.[8] Between Naderi's *Tangsir* and *Marsiyeh*, we might say, or between Ahmad Shamlou's defiant cry for freedom and Mehdi Akhavan Sales's painful dwellings on a lost future in a nostalgic past, or living in the middle of Forough Farrokhzad's poem 'Kasi keh Mesl-e Hich Kas Nist'/'Someone Who Is Like No One' and Sohrab Sepehri's 'Seda ye pa-ye Ab'/'Sounds of Footsteps,' an entire nation born and raised in the aftermath of the coup of 1953 learned how to oscillate between the depths of despair and ecstatic visions of hope. By now we had become bipolar in our remembrances of 28 Mordad. Thus 28-Mordadism, as if absorbing all our history in one fell swoop, felt like the birth pangs of delivery into an overwhelming awareness of our colonial modernity, of not being in charge of our own destiny, of everything that was best in us collapsing into mere phantom liberties, devoid of substance, of material basis, of formative force, of moral authority.

On the political stage, not just everything that occurred *after* 28 Mordad but even things that have happened *before* it suddenly came together to posit the phenomenon of 28-Mordadism: foreign intervention, colonial domination, imperial arrogance, domestic tyranny, an 'enemy' always lurking behind a corner to come and rob us of our liberties, of the mere possibility of democratic institutions. The result has been a categorical circumlocution – at once debilitating and enabling – that begins with the Tobacco Revolt of 1890–92, runs through the Constitutional Revolution of 1906–11, and concludes with the Islamic Revolution of 1979. Under the colonial condition that originally occasioned this mental state of siege and spun it around itself, we have lived through a persistent politics of *force majeure* in which we have experienced the forceful substitution of a revolutionary expediency in lieu of a public reason.

The June 2009 presidential election marks an epistemic exhaustion of 28-Mordadism, when the paradigm has finally conjugated ad nauseam. In the most recent phase, enacted by the custodians of the Islamic Republic, best represented in the Public Prosecutor's indictment against hundreds of reformists, the process has degenerated into a political Tourette's Syndrome. In this most recent version of the syndrome, an evidently psychotic political disorder has begun to express itself in involuntary tics, with vile and violent exclamations of coprolalia.[9] The Islamic Republic carrying 28-Mordadism ad nauseam is coterminous with an epistemic passage beyond it at the more commanding level of Iranian political culture, a discursive sublimation that is predicated on the crucial closure of a post-traumatic syndrome that commenced soon after the 1953 coup and concluded in the course of the Islamic Revolution of 1977–79.

The traumatic memory of the 1953 coup was very much rekindled and put to very effective political use in the most crucial episodes of the nascent Islamic Republic in order to consolidate its fragile foundations. When on 1 February 1979 Ayatollah Khomeini returned to Iran, soon after the Shah had left, the notion of an Islamic Republic was far from certain and there was an array of opposing political positions and forces, ranging from nationalists to socialists to Islamists. On 30–31 March Khomeini ordered a national referendum, and on 1 April he declared that the Islamic Republic had been overwhelmingly endorsed and established. But by no stretch of imagination was this referendum convincing to major segments of the political and intellectual elite, or indeed to the population at large, for which reason as early as early June Khomeini was lashing out against what he termed 'Westoxicated intellectuals.' By mid-June, the official draft of the constitution of the Islamic Republic was published. But there was no mention in it of any *Velayat-e Faqih*, namely the overriding political authority of a senior Shi'i cleric. Khomeini endorsed this draft, as he continued his attacks against the 'Westoxicated intellectuals,' meaning those who at this point were actively demanding the formation of a Majles-e Moassessan, a Constitutional Assembly to examine the terms of the constitution (I was present at one such meeting in Tehran University in July 1979). Khomeini openly opposed this idea, announcing that there would be 'no Westernized jurists' writing a constitution for the Islamic Republic – 'only the noble clergy.' Meanwhile Khomeini's doctrine of *Velayat-e Faqih* was being actively disseminated in the country. By early August, the newspaper *Ayandegan*, which was actively questioning the notion of *Velayat-e Faqih*, was savagely attacked by the Islamist vigilantes and then officially banned. At the same time a major National Democratic Front rally at Tehran University soccer field was viciously attacked (I was present at this rally). By mid-August, the Assembly of Experts had gathered to write the constitution of the Islamic Republic, and by mid-October they had completed their deliberations and drafted the constitution, with the office of *Vali Faqih* in it.[10]

The constitution of the Islamic Republic was written under conditions that included both intellectual and militant opposition to it, and Khomeini's circle showed an aggressive dermination to consolidate and institutionalize it at all costs. A perfect opportunity was given to them when on 22 October the deposed Shah travelled to the US for cancer treatment, which Khomeini instantly called a plot, invoking the memory of 1953 to lend the charge credibility. When on 1 November the liberal Mehdi Bazargan was pictured shaking hands with then US National Security Adviser to President Jimmy Carter, Zbigniew Brzezinski, in Algeria, not just the Islamists but even the left thought the Americans were up to something again.[11] Iranians were bitten by a snake in 1953, as the saying goes in Persian; now they were afraid of any black or white rope.

The American Hostage Crisis began on 4 November 1979, and lasted 444 days; by the time it had ended, on 20 January 1981, it had used and abused the memory of the 1953 coup to consolidate the fragile foundations of an Islamic theocracy.[12] Two days after the hostages were taken, the weak and wobbly Bazargan was pushed aside and forced to resign. By now the Lion King was showing signs of his weakness and the wily Fox was showing more cunning. The militant Islamists assumed a warring posture. They were now fighting the Great Satan, and the left and the liberals, the fainthearted and the soft-spoken, had better stay clear of the fight. In this atmosphere, on 2 December, Khomeini ordered the newly minted constitution of the Islamic Republic to be put to the vote, following which he reported that it had been massively approved, and he duly became the Supreme Leader. Soon after that, on 25 January 1980, the first presidential election of the Islamic Republic was conducted and Abolhassan Bani Sadr was declared the winner. Soon after that, on 15 March, the first parliamentary election was held, with Hezbollah vigilantes attacking the headquarters of all surviving opposition parties, especially the Mujahideen-e Khalq Organization, dismantling and discrediting them so they couldn't participate in the parliament. That was not enough. On 21 March, the eve of the Persian New Year, Khomeini ordered a 'cultural revolution,' and thus commenced the militant Islamization of the universities by the intellectual echelon among his devotees (some of them are now the leading oppositional intellectuals). All of these crucial steps towards the radical Islamization of the Iranian Revolution (and with it political culture) were done under the *force majeure* of a repetition of 1953 – 28-Mordadism at its height.

As if Khomeini needed further excuse to prove that a US plot against the revolution was in the offing, on 25 April Operation Eagle Claw to rescue the American hostages met with a catastrophic and (for President Jimmy Carter) embarrassing and costly end in the Iranian desert, providing further fuel and momentum to Khomeini's revolutionary zeal, so that during May, June, and July further Islamization of the state bureaucracy took place, purging anyone suspected of not being committed to the revolution.[13] This in effect amounted to the mass expulsion from the state apparatus of all Iranians suspected of ideological impurity. The story was the same after the 11 July Nojeh coup attempt, which fuelled Khomeini's fury even more, resulting in the persecution of alternative voices and movements and the radical Islamization of the revolution – during which time the shadow of 1953 was kept consciously, deliberately, successfully on the horizon.

Finally, on 27 July, the Shah died in Egypt and the American hostages began to lose their usefulness to Khomeini. When, on 22 September, Saddam Hussein invaded Iran and the grueling eight-year Iran–Iraq war started, the hostage crisis had successfully performed its strategic function as a smokescreen for Khomeini's radical Islamization of the revolution and the brutal elimination of all alternative forces and voices. By 26 October, Iraqi forces had entered Iran and occupied Khorram-Shahr and Iran was fully engaged in a deadly war with Iraq.[14] On 20 January 1981, Khomeini allowed the American hostages to be released, and shifted his attention to the Iran–Iraq War, during which took place more domestic suppression, along with further radical Islamization of political culture, society and, above all, historiography.

With the birth of the Reform movement in the late 1990s, 28-Mordadism began to lose its grip on Iranian political culture, after decades of abusing it to sustain an otherwise illegitimate state apparatus. Though the custodians of the Islamic Republic continue to abuse it *ad absurdum*, the paradigm has to all intents and purposes exhausted itself. The end of 28-Mordadism does not of course mean the end of imperial interventions in the historical destiny of nations. It simply means that now there is a renewed and level playing field on which to think and act in postcolonial terms.

The White Moderates

This is of course the case only in Iran, and to the degree that foreigners care to know and understand its history and political culture. But who can expect powermongers of one sort or another to try to understand anything. As Iranians were getting ready emotively to put the traumatic memory of the coup of 1953 behind them, an equally treacherous intervention of another sort began to come their way from the selfsame Americans, and, as it happens, from the selfsame CIA vintage. 'I must confess,' wrote Martin Luther King Jr in his famous 'Letter from a Birmingham Jail' (16 April 1963),

> that over the past few years I have been gravely disappointed with the white moderate. I have almost reached the regrettable conclusion that the Negro's great stumbling block in his stride toward freedom is not the White Citizen's Councilor or the Ku Klux Klanner, but the white moderate, who is more devoted to 'order' than to justice; who prefers a negative peace which is the absence of tension to a positive peace which is the presence of justice.[15]

Precisely in the same terms, the Green Movement in Iran now faces the problem of these 'white moderates.'

The only reason why the world at large should take the slightest notice of what American pundits think of the Green Movement in Iran is that their self-indulgent punditry reveals much about the troubled world in which we all live, and they think they must lead. One of the most magnificent aspects of the unfolding civil rights movement in Iran is that it serves to expose the bizarre banality of American foreign policy punditry and its habitual

limitations regarding how to deal with the rest of the world. Those in American foreign policy circles who are of the 'Bomb Bomb Iran' persuasion are a lost cause and, just like the Ku Klux Klan among white supremacists, scarce need further consideration. It is the functional equivalents of what in a different, though similar, context the late Martin Luther King Jr. called 'the white moderates' who need to be paid more urgent attention.

Perhaps the single most important problem with American politics, policymakers, and pundits – left or right, liberal or conservative, Democrat or Republican – is their belief that anything that happens anywhere in the world is about them, or at least is their business. It is not. The imperial hubris that seems to be constitutive of the DNA of this political culture wants either to invade and occupy other people's homelands and tell them what to do, or else to disregard people's preoccupation with their own domestic issues and impose – demand and exact – what they call an 'engagement' on them, whether they want it or not.

Take a recent piece of nonsense published on the civil rights movement in Iran by Flynt and Hillary Leverett, 'Another Iranian Revolution? Not Likely,'[16] which has absolutely nothing to do with or serious to say about the Green Movement, and yet reveals everything about the pathology of American politics as determined in the self-delusional cocoon inside the Beltway (the proverbial highway around Washington DC). As early as mid-June 2009, the Leveretts were up and about defending the fraudulent election of Mahmoud Ahmadinejad: 'Without any evidence,' they charged in an article, 'many U.S. politicians and "Iran experts" have dismissed Iranian President Mahmoud Ahmadinejad's re-election Friday, with 62.6 percent of the vote, as fraud.'[17] That millions of Iranians had also poured onto their streets and put their lives on the line with the same charge did not seem to bother the Leveretts. Among the 'experts' who had corroborated these charges and supported those demonstrators, and whom the Leveretts placed in quotation marks by way of denigrating and dismissing them, were the leading Iranian scholars within and outside their homeland – from Iran to Europe to the US to Japan to Australia – and the Leveretts would do well to exercise a degree of humility in the face of their superior competence and knowledge of their own homeland. If the Leveretts have issues with kindred souls among US experts 'on the other side of the isle,' as they say inside the Beltway, that is their problem, not the Iranians'.

The Leveretts made a name for themselves during the Dark Ages of Bushism by standing up to neoconservative plots to impose more 'crippling sanctions' on Iran as a prelude to a military strike. Those of us who recall the nightmare of those years remember the Leveretts with an abiding affection and admiration.[18] But this time around, by categorically and condescendingly dismissing a massive civil rights movement altogether, they are falling off the roof from the other side of Bushism – and in doing so they reveal something deeply troubling in American political punditry.

In addition to adopting a dismissive tone regarding the civil rights movement, about whose origin and disposition they know relatively little, the chief characteristic of the Leveretts' critique is the positing of non-existent targets and then shooting them down. The result is that everything they say reflects the besieged and bunkered mentality inside the Beltway and has nothing to do with the Green Movement. For example, 'The Islamic Republic of Iran,' they believe, 'is not about to implode. Nevertheless, the misguided idea that it may do so is becoming enshrined as conventional wisdom in Washington.'[19] But whoever said it was? No scholar or otherwise serious and informed observer of Iran writing in Persian or any other language and retaining a sense of balance and proportion can predict whether the Islamic Republic will or will not fall. And even if it did fall, that would have nothing to do with what 'the conventional wisdom in Washington' (whatever this contradiction in terms may mean) opts to enshrine or not to enshrine. If there are some inside the Beltway who think that the Islamic Republic will fall any day now, that Abbas Milani will become the American ambassador to Iran, or the Iranian ambassador to the US, depending on the season of his migrations to the left or right, and that *Lolita* will soon become required reading in Iranian high schools, they are entitled to their view, but it would represent a dangerously delusional politics. Such hallucinations have nothing to do with the Green Movement.

These Washingtonians live in a world of their own, with little or no connection to reality. A massive civil rights movement has commenced in a rich and diverse political culture, and it embraces a wide range of positions and possibilities, about which people trapped inside the Beltway (physically or mentally) have no clue. Thus what American pundits, of one persuasion or another, make of it is entirely irrelevant to its course or consequences. This is a civil rights movement some two hundred years in the making, whose very political alphabet is Greek to these commentators, and whose course and contours will be determined inside Iran and by Iranians, and not in the corridors of power in the United States by American politicians, their pundits, and their contingents of native informers.

No Iranian cares what people in the corridors of power in the United States think of their uprising, unless and until they start harming it. There are two sorts of obstacle that they can put in the way of the Green Movement: (1) economic sanctions, covert operations, and a military strike, as advocated by one kind of imperial hubris in the United States (aided and abetted by Abbas Milani);[20] or (2) engaging with the illegitimate and fraudulent government of Mahmoud Ahmadinejad.

Back to the Geopolitics of the Region

To be sure, it is not just those Martin Luther King Jr called 'the white moderates' who are encouraging dialogue between President Obama and Mr Ahmadinejad. Marwan Bishara, senior political analyst for Al Jazeera, effectively concurs with the Leveretts in that recommendation, and he cannot be accused of either shortsightedness (though he runs his 'Empire' show from Washington DC) or being trapped in the bunker mentality of the Beltway. Be that as it may, Marwan Bishara too believes that 'the US needs to drop the false dichotomy of sanctions or war and embrace direct talks' with the Islamic Republic.[21]

Bishara's frame of reference, it must be said, is far more comprehensive and based on a solid reading of the geopolitics of the region and the globe at large. It starts by noting the early March 2010 meeting between Ahmadinejad, his Syrian counterpart Bashar al-Assad, and the leaders of the Lebanese Hezbollah and Palestinian Hamas, which, as Bishara rightly says, 'have ruffled many feathers in the US, Europe and Israel.'

Bishara discounts the bellicose language of the meeting and believes 'the anti-Israeli gathering has sent a primarily strategic not polemical message: We stand united – an attack on one of us is an attack on all.' This gesture Bishara reads, again correctly, as 'A deterrent message to both Israel and the US, [which] comes against the backdrop of increased war speculation in Israel and mounting pressures to pass a new round of tougher sanctions against Iran.'[22]

Bishara shows how the US attempt at rapprochement with Syria in order to cause a rift between it and Iran has failed. In other words, the strategy of isolating Iran in the region has patently not worked. Secretary of State Hillary Clinton, General Petraeus, Admiral Mike Mullen have, in various ways, tried to convince

Arab states of the danger of the Iranian nuclear program, but to no political effect, for the obvious reason that

> the Gulf states are the first to be affected by long-term tensions or military escalation between the US and Iran. Recent US naval deployments in the Gulf and its sales of sophisticated weapons to Gulf countries have not calmed their fears that an escalation of those tensions could bring down their economies and affect their security. The same could apply to other parts of the 'Greater Middle East' such as Afghanistan, Iraq, Lebanon and Palestine which could be affected by an escalation between the US and Iran.[23]

Meanwhile, neither Russia nor, a fortiori, China (both veto-carrying members of the UN Security Council) will succumb to pressure to isolate Iran, for political and economic reasons. Additionally, the two countries are reluctant to go down this road for fear of domestic fallout. Bishara shrewdly observes: 'They worry that the political and security overspill from widening the landscape of confrontation in the Muslim world could end up affecting their substantial Muslim minorities and eventually their internal stability.' The upshot of Bishara's argument is this:

> All of which should send the Obama administration back to the drawing board. Has President Obama truly exhausted the diplomatic track before the US attends to sanctions or war? In other words, has the Obama administration truly extended a hand or unclenched its fist for the sake of a peaceful resolution to the Iranian Middle East impasse? The answer is an unequivocal NO. It is time to remind Barack Obama of his willingness as a candidate to meet with his Iranian counterpart as president if that can protect US interests. ... Well Mr. Presidents, it is time.[24]

What, then, is the difference between the white moderates' position and that of Marwan Bishara? Isn't Bishara's recommendation for 'rapprochement' what the white moderates also suggest? Aren't both saying the same thing: hurry up and negotiate with Iran?

Yes indeed – but what separates them is the Green Movement. The key aspect of Bishara's analysis, and the sign of his superior geopolitical intelligence, is that he just *ignores* the Green Movement – he does not *dismiss* it. Bishara waited for more than eight months, before he opted to *disregard* it in his analysis of the geopolitics of the region. The Leveretts, on the contrary, have been gung-ho supporters of Ahmadinejad and dismissive of the Green Movement from the word go, and immediately came out full blast to endorse their favorite candidate, as early as 15 June 2009, when they published their 'Ahmadinejad won, get over it' in *Politico*.[25] That is, on the very day that the biggest anti-government demonstration in the history of the Islamic Republic marked a new beginning in modern Iranian history, the Leveretts were out and about in the streets and alleys of the Internet chanting for Ahmadinejad. Ever since, the former CIA analysts have consistently dismissed the civil rights movement in Iran as non-existent – and they have continued to consult their fortune-teller native informer and persisted in denigrating and dismissing, even ridiculing, the Green Movement.

The superior strategic intelligence of Bishara is precisely in not needing to consult Mr. Marandi or any other native informer to tell him what to think of the Green Movement. When it was clear to him that the Movement could not topple or seriously weaken the Islamic Republic, he turned back to analysis of the geopolitics of the region and stayed the course. The result is that his pitch-perfect analysis does not discredit the Green Movement but, rather, lends it more legitimacy. Bishara's cogent reading of the situation returns us to the same paradox: the US/Israel may impose sanctions or invade Iran, or they may opt to sit down and negotiate, but either way they will strengthen the Islamic Republic and further alienate and antagonize their regional allies. Bishara's understanding of the region leads him to recognize the strategic power of the Islamic Republic and the fact that it has cornered US/Israel into coming to terms with its regional interests. So he opts for one of the two scenarios that will make the Islamic Republic even stronger than it is – the scenario of engagement. But because Bishara does not play down the significance of the Green Movement, we remain within the logic of the same solid double jeopardy. Whatever the US/Israel does (because these two entities are just one), it will strengthen the Islamic Republic, just as whatever the Islamic Republic does will strengthen the Green Movement. Nobody can defeat the Islamic Republic; it has defeated itself by generating its own antithesis in the Green Movement. Likewise, no one could militarily defeat Zionism, until Zionist military might turned against and defeated itself.[26]

Bearing Witness

Before events unfolded in Iran over the second half of 2009, national politics had become all but irrelevant. The geopolitics of the region were locked, from Pakistan and Afghanistan to Israel/ Palestine, from Central Asia to Yemen, into a terrorizing balance of power, a stifling politics of despair, in which the term 'peace process' had contracted into a four-letter word that everyone knew by heart but no one dared or cared to utter.

In the Islamic Republic itself, over the last thirty years there have probably been more presidential, parliamentary, and city council elections than in the entire Arab and Muslim world put together. But these elections were not the insignia of a healthy democracy. They were the desperate signs of an Islamic Republic that was seeking to legitimize a deeply troubled theocracy with the simulacra of democratic institutions. That public secret was finally blasted into thin air in a simple statement in the fall of 2009 by the late Grand

Ayatollah Montazeri (1922–2009), the revered Jurist posthumously dubbed the moral voice of the Green Movement, who observed that the Islamic Republic was neither Islamic nor a republic.

Beyond Iranian borders, national elections in the region are either a sad excuse for a joke (from Morocco and Tunisia through Libya and Algeria to Egypt and Sudan, to Jordan and Syria) or else regionally inconsequential (from Israel to Turkey). But this is not so in the case of Iran – at least not since June 2009, when the Islamic Republic emerged as the ground zero of a civil rights movement that will leave no stone unturned in the moral fabric of the modern Middle East.

Six months into the Iranian presidential election, the civil rights movement that it had unleashed in ever more creative terms was writing a new page in modern history of the country and its troubled environs. The children of the Islamic Revolution, systematically brainwashed into militant zombies by one obscene cultural revolution after another, were now turning against parental banalities like there was no tomorrow. Turning the rhetoric of the Islamic Republic on its head, this generation of Iranians has now used every occasion since the June 2009 election to challenge the mendacity on which they have been raised. The end of the Islamic Republic, which may or may not come tomorrow, will not be the end of the Green Movement. Similarly, the unfolding ends of the Green Movement will not be confined by the limited imagination of the Islamic Republic or of its expatriate nemesis, or indeed of ex-CIA supporters.

The Changing Cosmopolis

The Green Movement is a cosmopolitan uprising, variably centered in major Iranian cities, gathering storm in the capital Tehran, before becoming, with a form and ferocity unprecedented in history, a cyberspace rebellion the full scale of which we are yet to fathom. In a New York cab on my way to the CNN studio for an interview I receive on my iPhone an email from a former student on the streets of Tehran, which I use in the analysis I offer ten minutes later to a global audience. The student writes back to say that he liked my analysis – 'and the cool color of my tie' too! This circularity of information and the speed with which history is a witness to itself are strange and exhilarating.

This is a self-propelling machinery made of Baroque architecture and postmodern engineering, the Haiku-like poetry of Tweeters echoing through the arcades and colonnades of the bizarre bazaar of Facebook – all as banal as they are beautiful, bordering the supercilious with the sublime!

But how do we recognize, acknowledge, and honor a generation that is smarter, gentler, more forgiving than their parents could ever dream of being? Iranian political culture is cleansing itself. The spectacle is no longer solely Islamic. It is Manichaean, cosmic, good and evil mixed and matched to overcome themselves. 'Bearing witness' is all, but at once the most noble thing, that anyone can do. And it will do.

Because it has stolen the regional show and drawn it into a dramatic national scene, the Green Movement is very much at the mercy of one major power that can break its back by yielding to Ahmadinejad's preference for distracting global attention from his domestic troubles. Paradoxically, the only man who can help Ahmadinejad in his desperate determination to turn everyone's attention away from the Green Movement and towards regional politics is President Obama. One picture of President Obama with Ahmadinejad would be a dagger to the heart of the Green Movement, an event to be remembered longer than the CIA-engineered coup of 1953 has been – and to traumatize US–Iran relations for another half of a century. It would not kill the Green Movement

– nothing will – but it would serve to mark Obama's presidency with ignominy.

President Obama's reaction to the violent crackdown during the initial stages of the Green Movement was balanced and measured. While he condemned 'the iron fist of brutality,' he continued to insist, and rightly so, that 'what's taking place in Iran is not about the United States or any other country. It's about the Iranian people,' while at the same time insisting that 'we will continue to bear witness to the extraordinary events that are taking place' in Iran.[27] That 'bearing witness' means and matters more than the president's critics can dream of in their philosophy.

The pressure on President Obama 'to do more for Iran,' especially when it sports a 'Bomb Bomb Iran!' pedigree, deserves a term stronger than 'hypocrisy.' The Iranian people have every right to peaceful nuclear technology within NPT regulations, and the international community has every right to doubt the trustworthiness of Ahmadinejad's government. The worst thing that President Obama could do, not just in terms of the best interests of Iranians as a nation, but also with regard to his own stated ideal of regional and global nuclear disarmament, would be to sit down and negotiate with Ahmadinejad. For such would, *ipso facto*, legitimize an illegitimate government while failing to produce a binding or reliable agreement with this Iranian president. While, for his part, Obama would not be a credible partner in negotiation if he failed to address the issue of regional disarmament. The alternative to shunning direct diplomacy with Ahmadinejad is neither more severe economic sanctions nor, *horribile dictu*, a military strike, which would backfire and hurt the wrong people.

The only option for President Obama has always been to believe in what he has said – 'bearing witness.' But that presidential rhetorical device should be taken to its logical civil society conclusion: Americans could, for example, send delegations of civil rights icons, film and sports personalities, Muslim leaders, human rights organizations, women's rights activists, labor union representatives, student assemblies, and so on, to Iran. They could connect with their counterparts in Iran, exposing the banality of the illegitimate government that has suffocated the democratic aspirations of a nation for too long.

If the international media have watched or have turned away, the Green Movement has been gaining ground consistently and apace. The Islamist regime is giving it all it has, and it does not stint – kidnapping people off the street, murder, torture, rape, kangaroo courts, obscene official websites and news agencies making fools of themselves by failing to report the truth, and instead distorting, ridiculing or else attributing it to phantom foreigners. But it has all failed. The Islamic Republic is cornered; its fake halo of self-ascribed sanctity exposed, the public space is appropriated. Iranians within and outside their country, young and old, men and women, rich and poor, pious or otherwise, right wing and reactionary or left wing and progressive, are all coming together. 'Bearing witness' is an investment in the future of democracy in a country that is destined to change the moral map of a troubled but consistently vital part of a very fragile planet.

A decade into the twenty-first century the internal politics of Iran is changing, and changing fast, while at the same time regionally the usual politics of despair reigns supreme – a violent politics of fear and desperation. From monarchy Iran turned fast into a brutal mullarchy – but now the Green Movement is challenging and fundamentally altering the very political discourse of contemporary Iranian history and our reading of it. The rest of the world is yet to catch up with what is happening in Iran. Thus the world – meaning those in a place to read and interpret it from a position of power and publicity – denigrates and dismisses the Green Movement, disregards it, or else wants to abuse it for ulterior motives. But, and here is the rub, the world at large is incapable of handling the Islamic Republic and will strengthen it whatever it does; just as the Islamic Republic is incapable of stopping the Green Movement and by its actions will only further its ends. Following the white moderates' advice, the US/Israel might opt to negotiate with the Islamic Republic and thus disregard the Green Movement, thereby legitimizing a vicious and brutal theocracy; or else it might listen to Senators McCain and Lieberman (or other, even more menacing, voices) and impose 'crippling sanctions' or attack the country. Either option would strengthen the Islamic Republic. The same goes for the Islamic Republic and the Green Movement. The regime will either go all the way and trigger a military coup, further exposing its naked violence, and thereby strengthen the moral standing of the Green Movement, or else it will moderate its position, tolerate the Movement and allow its moral authority and magic to work on the theocracy. Just as the Jewish state has found its match in the Islamic Republic, so the Islamic Republic has bred its own antithesis. The dialectic that has ensued will act itself out – one way or another.

SIX

Paradox Redux

THE STORY of the ailing Lion King, the wily Fox, and the unfortunate Ass from the *Kalilah and Dimnah* is in fact told by a monkey – a Monkey King to be exact, Kardanah his name, a monkey who narrates this story by way of an example, an admonition, in order to point out to a Turtle who had falsely befriended him that he, the Monkey King, was not a fool like that proverbial Ass in the story. The story of the Monkey King and his false friend the Turtle is itself curious and instructive too.[1]

Kardanah the Monkey King used to rule over a vast kingdom of monkeys on an island with evident majesty, glory, and magnanimity. But gradually his royal charisma and political power left his person as old age and frailty finally caught up with him, and a young and more robust monkey, a relation, managed to win over his army and arrange for a *coup d'état* and depose the Monkey King. Robbed of his kingdom and majesty in his old age, Kardanah was forced into exile in a remote corner of the island where there were enough fruit trees for him to go on with a decent existence.

One day Kardanah was sitting on top of a fig tree and enjoying himself when he accidentally dropped a fig into a pond that was under the tree. He loved the sound that it made and dropped another one. This too pleased him immensely, and so he kept dropping figs down into the pond and enjoying their music. There was a Turtle in that pond, casually wandering under that fig tree when he saw the Monkey dropping figs down towards him. The Turtle thought the Monkey was doing this by way of friendly magnanimity to share with him some of the delicious fruit he was enjoying. 'If he is so generous to people he does not even know,' the Turtle thought to himself, 'one can only imagine how generous he would be with his friends.' So the Turtle called on to Kardanah the Monkey King, who was indeed quite bored with his sad state of solitude, expressed his friendly enthusiasm and they gradually became very close, even intimate, friends.

Meanwhile the Turtle's wife was at home worried sick as to what had happened to her husband. She finally confided to a close and enterprising friend, who in turn informed her, with much hesitation and trepidation, that the reason her husband had not come home to her (for by now the news had reached the Turtle's homeland) was that he had befriended a monkey in a faraway island and that he evidently preferred his company to hers. The Turtle's wife got quite upset and asked her friend for advice. The two women, so the story goes, conspired and came to the conclusion that the only way out of this predicament was to kill the Monkey. The Turtle's wife, following her friend's advice, pretend she was terminally sick and sent a message to her husband to that effect and asked him to hurry home.

Upon receiving the terrible news, the Turtle asked Kardanah for his kind and friendly permission to leave to pay his wife a visit. The Monkey King readily agreed, and the Turtle headed back home to his wife and family. Upon reaching home, however, his wife (following her conniving friend's advice) refused to talk or have anything to do with him. The Turtle turned to her friend and asked her what was the matter with her. 'Well,' she promptly responded, 'how do you expect a woman who so ill that she is about to die to talk to you?' The Turtle was heartbroken. 'What sort of illness does she have,' he mumbled sorrowfully, 'and what is the cure?' The friend paused for a moment and said, 'She has a gynecological illness and her cure is the heart of a monkey!' The heart of a monkey – the poor Turtle mumbled to himself. He was instantly faced with a conundrum: what was he to do, let his wife die or kill his friend Kardanah, the Monkey King, and bring his heart for her cure? It was a tragic dilemma and it kept the wretched Turtle awake for nights on end. Finally his love for his wife triumphed over his friendship for Kardanah and he decided to go and kill the monkey and bring her his heart.

The Turtle traveled back to the exiled Monkey King with a heavy heart. Upon their being reunited, he soon found out that he had really missed him; nevertheless he thought he had no choice but to lure him to his house, kill him and feed his heart to his wife to save her life. 'Would your gracious majesty condescend to come to your humble friend's abode so my family can meet you and all my friends and neighbors can see you are indeed my friend – for they have heard so much about you.' Kardanah listened attentively. 'Yes,' he said kindly, 'I will happily come to your house; the only problem is I don't know how to swim and your home is on the other side of this sea.' Without the slightest hesitation the Turtle said, 'Not to worry. I will be happy to carry you on my back.'

So, carrying Kardanah on his back, the Turtle started swimming towards his home. Halfway through the journey, pangs of guilt attacked the Turtle's conscience and he became hesitant about so treacherously luring his friend to his death. As he was questioning his conscience, the deposed Monkey King noticed the change in his friend's demeanor and asked what the matter was. 'I am afraid,' the Turtle said, 'that when we arrive my wife will be too ill to prepare for a proper welcome and a feast for you.' The Monkey King told him not to be concerned. 'Among friends,' he added, 'such considerations are not necessary.' The Turtle resumed swimming. Yet after a while guilt again overcame him, and once more the Monkey asked him what was the matter. 'I am preoccupied with my wife's illness,' he finally spitted it out. 'I understand,' Kardanah said, 'but what exactly is her illness and what can cure it?' 'It is a gynecological issue,' the Turtle said almost involuntarily, and then added, 'and its cure is a Monkey's heart.'

The world suddenly darkened for Kardanah and he regretted the moment he had been fooled by this traitorous Turtle. He had no choice but find a way out of his predicament, sitting as he was on the back of a turtle on his way to be killed so that his heart would be fed to his wife. Not a happy scene. 'But,' he offered with a measured tone to his voice, 'I have absolutely no problem with you giving my heart to your wife. This is a common illness among woman of our island and we monkeys regularly dispense with our hearts and offer them to our womenfolk. I just wish you had told me before we left the island so I could have brought my heart along with me.' 'You have left your heart back on the island, but why?' the Turtle responded. 'Well,' Kardanah said, 'we monkeys have a habit that when we go to a friend's house we leave our heart behind so we won't worry about any mistreatment we might receive. We wish to enjoy ourselves and indulge in our friend's kindness and hospitality, without worrying too much about one thing or another we might hear or see. But now that I know the full measure of your predicament and am aware of how much you love your wife, it would not be good of me to come without bringing my heart along to offer it in friendship and solidarity. Do please take me back so I can come along with my heart.'

The Turtle duly turned around and they swam back to the island. As soon as they reached the shore, the Monkey King Kardanah instantly jumped off and climbed the fig tree, while the Turtle waited for him to return. After a while the Turtle called out to Kardanah and asked him to hurry so they could leave. At which point the Monkey called back to the Turtle, addressing him from the safety of the top of the fig tree, telling him that he is not a fool; he has experienced much in the world and is not like that Ass who was fooled twice and lured to his death for his heart and ears. And it is this wisdom that the wise Brahman wants to impart to his young King, to whom all these animal fables are told by way of advising him how not to lose the reign he has earned so easily and freely by ignorance and stupidity – just as the Turtle did the Monkey after having initially deceived and won him over so readily.

Brahmanic Wisdom

President Obama left Columbia University, where he completed his undergraduate education, just before I started teaching there, and so I never had the opportunity to teach him anything – even if I'd had any Brahmanic wisdom I could impart. Right now he is far beyond my reach, guarded by variations on the conventional wisdoms of might and empires that have landed us in the mess we see before us. But if I could I would ask him to read this splendid book of *Kalilah and Dimnah* and wonder in what particular ways he is capable of doing what no one before him ever dared to do: changing once and for all the DNA makeup of the American global menace, and creating a nation among nations, sharing its fears and contracting its hopes, for this is what the horrid events of 9/11 should have accomplished – enabling Americans to feel, not just 'to understand,' what it means for buildings to crumble and innocent lives perish. With weak or conniving turtles, agile but gullible monkeys, and tired and abused asses, the jungle that young or aging lions wish to rule is far more unruly than anything that fits the wobbly wisdom of the think-tanks that have long plagued Washington DC.

What passes for realpolitik in Washington DC, and by extension wherever else the US thinks it must tell people what to do, is actually a politics of despair that keeps abusing the weak and enabling unprincipled opportunists. What the wise Kardanah managed to do and what the gullible Ass failed to do both fit the received rules of the jungle that the wise Brahman wishes to teach the young prince to ensure the enduring majesty of his reign. We have long since passed the age and the ailing of such royal endurance, but, alas, not the wisdom they entail. What passes for politics, policy, and punditry in the US/EU theaters of operation has categorically failed to alter the course of a fragile planet in a more sustainable direction. Between the world 'as it is' and the world 'as it ought to be' there is a wide range of possibilities that can recast the vision of, and the perspective that informs, our global predicament.

What we basically have in full view are tired old lions (there used to be two, the US and the Soviet Union; there is now only one) who still have a foggy but overwhelming memory of their power to rule the jungle the way they wish and a fundamental mental inability to come to terms with the fact that they no longer do, and who are in fact manipulated by weak turtles or wily foxes in one way or another. The United States now looks like

that tired old Lion, Israel like that self-righteous and conniving
Turtle, the Islamic Republic like that wily and treacherous Fox,
and 'the Middle East' oscillating between that gullible Ass and
that saved-by-the-skin-of-his-teeth Monkey, alternately abused
and disabused. Now, if we take Barack Obama as the most recent
personification of that Lion King, the sublime Brahmanic wisdom
that is to guide him has slipped in the direction of ridiculous
Washington think-tanks that vie for his attention and pull and
push him in one direction or another. The net result is business
as usual, with very little leverage that the US (or even the UN)
can apply to belligerent forces on the ground.[2]

In that frame of reference, the usual and habitual bifurcation
between Republicans and Democrats, Conservatives and Liberals,
or even Liberals and the Left has simply collapsed into the modus
operandi of a politics of despair that is unable to see beyond its
proverbial nose. In that politics of despair, all successive US administrations do is crisis-mis/management of one sort or another,
and when they do have a philosophy, a vision, or a theory it is of
the sort that the neoconservative cabal manufactured, imposed,
and practiced as the modus operandi of world domination during
the eight dark years of the George W. Bush presidency.[3]

In the makeup of that crisis-mis/management code-named
'realpolitik,' there is a structural functionalism that is epistemically
dominant in both right-wing aggression and left-wing opposition
that has never sought to alter the terms of engagement with the
politics of despair that is dominant in this entity we have inherited
from the old colonial map of the region and call 'the Middle East.'
Even the most progressive analysts of the region are trapped in
a jigsaw puzzle they see (and rightly so) laid out in 'the Middle
East' and can do nothing but rearrange the players ever so gently
to see what the alternatives are. We are in the mess we are in
precisely because the view from the ground up (the so-called

'realist' school of politics) is the view most trapped inside the rules of the jungle.

The history of all nations, however, is marked by moments of elation when politics-as-usual gets momentarily suspended, like when Mohammad Khatami was elected president of the Islamic Republic in 1997, or when Barack Obama became the US president. Like Mohammad Khatami in Iran, Barack Obama ran for the presidency with much hope and anticipation that he would be a different man in the White House. He achieved widespread adulation in his own country and beyond with ease and grace. When he won the Nobel Peace Prize many scoffed and wondered what he had done to deserve it. I was among those who celebrated his prize, arguing that he had in fact awoken a euphoric hope in his country, particularly among the idealistic youth, that deserved recognition.[4] His speeches in Ankara and Cairo and his Noruz message in March 2009 were all indices, at least at the rhetorical level (which is precisely the discourse-shifting level I have in mind), that this optimism was legitimate. But before long the air people breathe in Washington DC began to identify and exacerbate a 'pragmatism' in President Obama that tilted instantly to politics-as-usual – from climate control to healthcare.[5]

The almost instant retrieval of a debilitating pragmatism (structural functionalism is a better term for it, though political scientists in the Washington state of mind call it 'realism' too) in President Obama coincided with the commencement of the civil rights movement in the aftermath of the June 2009 presidential election in Iran, which in and of itself is an unprecedented development that will either pull the region out of its present politics of despair or else be pulled under by the overriding goblin of cynicism and desolation. This movement has handed President Obama an unparalleled gift to push precisely in a direction that might save not just the region but with it the infested cynicism it has historically inherited and cultivated – and which the US and its regional allies have in fact sustained and exacerbated.

The answer to the paradox the wily Fox has concocted for itself is very simple. Eliminate the temptation of the Monkey or the Ass's heart and the wretched Fox and the conniving Turtle are undone. Is President Obama ready to be part of the solution, and not constitutive of the problem, and willing to outmaneuver the Islamic Republic (and its Jewish mirror image in Israel) and rob it of its one abiding excuse over which it has hung its self-perpetuating paradox? The answer seems to be no, though everyone had hoped it would be yes. What the future holds for the region is entirely contingent on the cancerous growth of the politics of despair that from Morocco to Pakistan – with Palestine, Lebanon, Iraq, and Afghanistan now as its epicenter – has metastasized into the body-politics of the region.

The geopolitics of the region cannot, of course, be reduced to the Palestinian predicament; however, nor can it ever be divorced from it. The fundamental historical fact of the last half a century is that there is no bleeding wound on Arab and Muslim consciousness deeper and more hurtful than the plight of the Palestinians and the barefaced theft of their homeland. No American administration has ever mustered the bold and creative imagination to rescue American foreign policy from its Israeli Achilles heel, to listen to what ex-president Jimmy Carter and John Mearsheimer and Stephen Walt, the wisest Brahmans this political culture could produce, have argued and demonstrated for close to a decade now. Of course some 7 million human beings trapped inside a militant figment of their own imagination they call 'Israel' are entitled to safety and security, as is everyone else in the region and in the world; and the selfsame 'of course' applies to the fact that these 7 million are not entitled to a racist colonial settlement that, akin to South African apartheid, continues to steal another nation's homeland on an almost daily basis. Disengage American foreign policy from the blindfolded interests of a self-defeating apartheid state and allow the Israeli Peace Now movement and the combined forces of the Palestinian national liberation movement (which includes but is not limited to Hamas) to come together on a fair and level playing field. Allow for an obvious and natural alliance between Israeli progressive forces (small but multifaceted as they are) and their counterparts in the region, particularly the Palestinians.[6] Only by seeing the similarities between a Jewish state, a Christian empire, and Hindu fundamentalism can President Obama deprive the Islamic Republic of its three trump cards in Palestine, Lebanon, and Iraq.

Were the Islamic Republic deprived of these cards, the shallow nature of the mullarchy ruling with an iron fist and a medieval jurisprudence over 70 million Iranians trapped inside their own country would be exposed, the reformist movement of the 1990s given a new lease of life, and the charismatic American president with 'Hussein' for a middle name and a book full of references to Malcolm X might be able to do wonders for human, civil, and women's rights in Iran, and indeed for the rest of the Arab and Muslim word, as he saves his own country from an old, fatigued, and self-defeating political culture of hubris and complacency. Will he rise to the occasion, or will he slide further and faster into the usual politics of crisis-mis/management?

The Case of Thrasymachus

There are two complementary moments in the story of the deposed Monkey King and his false Turtle friend that illustrate perfectly the point I wish to make in this chapter. The first is when Kardanah sits happily atop a fig tree, enjoying himself, eating figs and taking in a splendid view of the jungle, from above the fray, as it were, before he accidentally drops a fig and the traitorous Turtle picks it up and the sad saga of the Monkey begins. The second is the moment of closure at the end of the story when Kardanah is saved by the skin of his teeth, returns to his abode and the first thing he does is climb to the top of the selfsame fig tree, there not just to be a safe distance from the treacherous Turtle who wanted to kill him and feed his heart to his wife but also to regain that liberating panoramic view of the jungle unknown to those trapped within it. Those two moments of descent and ascent, which frame the story of Kardanah, are what I have in mind as figures of entrapment within a narrative modus operandi and, alternatively, of its transcendence.

The rules of the jungle are what ordinarily inform the politics of despair and thus demand and exact the politics of survival in that jungle. One might suggest that from Socrates down to Machiavelli there is a structural functionalism about the theory and practice of politics that accepts the 'facts on the ground' and tries to regulate them morally or pragmatically. The usual division of political stances between the left and the right is in fact both defined and practiced 'within' the box of this structural functionalism. This is precisely the reason that the distinguished German sociologist Ralf Dahrendorf (1929–2009) turned his attention to the principal nemesis of Socrates in Plato's *Republic*, Thrasymachus, to take the history of that structural functionalism to task. He suggested that

> Tradition has been rather less than fair to Thrasymachus of Chalcedon, who ... deserves to be remembered for the remarkable achievement of holding his own in an encounter with that champion dialectician, Socrates. Despite the impressions of some of the bystanders and perhaps of Socrates himself, Thrasymachus emerged unconvinced by Socrates' arguments, and with his heavy irony intact, from the vicious debate about justice.[7]

Why would a German sociologist of the post-World War II era turn to the philosophical subconscious of Socrates, and beyond him turn towards the repressed trauma of 'Western' political philosophy?

Why this retrieval of Thrasymachus, up against the cherished (almost sacred) memory of Socrates? The timing of Dahrendorf's essay 'In Praise of Thrasymachus' (1968) is of extraordinary significance. Most of the material collected in *Essays in the Theory of Society* (1968), where this essay first appeared, was in fact published in the 1950s – in the aftermath of the German Nazi disaster of the 1930s and early 1940s – when leading German thinkers were reflecting on the terror their homeland had perpetrated against itself and upon others. In the aftermath of World War II, as the horrors of Nazi Germany were haunting Europe, and as at the same time the atrocities of the Soviet Union were discrediting Stalinism, the space that was created between the structural functionalism of the status quo and the failure of Soviet Marxism to offer a viable alternative gave rise to a moment of renewed importance for the sociological imagination, of which Ralf Dahrendorf was a leading exponent.

Dahrendorf believes that this dual conception of the republic – Socratic structural functionalism and Thrasymachus's defiance in the face of such stabilizing presumptions – to be 'the single most persistent conflict in the ranks of those who seek to understand the working of human society.'[8] He goes so far as suggesting that the result of this reorientation of political theory would posit what he considers 'the pattern of the good society in our time.'[9] He believes that the debate between Socrates and Thrasymachus about 'justice' has remained central to social and political thought, down to the moment when Georg Simmel asks his almost existential question, 'How is society possible?'[10] Dahrendorf traces Socratic structural functionalism directly to that of Talcott Parsons and Neil Smelser, 'and many others whose analysis rests on an equilibrium model of social life.'[11] This is an entirely post-Holocaust recognition, for the horrors that Europeans had perpetrated upon themselves had suddenly jolted their memory to go back all the way to Plato and his Socrates and pinpoint a moment when the Greek sage had been taken constitutionally to task. Under normal circumstances – normal meaning when Europeans were doing to others what they did to themselves during World War II – the structural functionalism of Socrates was the epitome of 'Western civilization.' But now, in the 1950s, a decade into the horrors of the Holocaust, a leading German sociologist goes back to the time of Plato for a bit of revisionist philosophical history.

This is not conjectural, for Dahrendorf narrows in exactly on National Socialism in Germany and asks, pointedly, 'Why what happened had to happen.'[12] His position is that the 'equilibrium theory is ill-adapted to identifying the rate, depth, and direction of social change in pre-Nazi and Nazi Germany.'[13] His conclusion is that, 'In a Thrasymachean theory, power is a central notion. It is seen as unequally divided, and therefore as a lasting source of friction; legitimacy amounts at best to a precarious preponderance of power over the resistance it engenders.'[14] This is an absolutely remarkable moment in the history of European political philosophy, when a European finally recognizes that 'resistance to power' is as crucial as 'power' to an understanding of political philosophy. In other words, just a taste of the medicine that European colonialism had been *administrating* (Adorno's term) to the world at large was sufficient to send the German sociologist back in history to retrieve a singular soul who had taken Socratic structural functionalism to task and recognize that in the face of structural violence codenamed 'state' or 'republic' there is resistance, defiance, rebellion, uprising – equally if not more important than the structural violence of the state itself in understanding the central trope of political philosophy.

Ralf Dahrendorf's conclusion in this seminal essay is that

> Socrates became the first functionalist when he described justice
> as the state in which everybody does what he is supposed to
> do. This is clearly a miserable state, a world without rebels or
> retreatists, without change, without liberty. If this is justice,
> one can understand Thrasymachus's ill-tempered preference for
> injustice.[15]

Dahrendorf is pleased that neither Socrates nor his followers
have succeeded in establishing this definition of justice; instead, he
believes, the world has taught us a different conception of justice.
'Justice, then,' he says, 'would appear to be not an unchanging
state of affairs, whether real or imagined, but a permanently
changing outcome of the dialectic of power and resistance.'[16] The
world at large, the world beyond Europe, and the world before
and after Holocaust, has known this entirely independent of a
philosophical retrieval of the Socratic subconscious. But the fact
that Dahrendorf discovers this *after* the Holocaust in and of itself
is a crucial truth that has much to teach us about the moment
of revelation when a political culture, under the influence of a
traumatic crisis, transcends itself.

The sense of frustration with structural functionalism felt and
theorized by Europeans responsible for engulfing their own in a
Holocaust is in fact constitutive of a colonial condition that the rest
of the world has inherited from the European (and now American)
legacy of global domination. If *power* is defining of Platonic political
philosophy, *resistance to power* is defining of its manufactured civilizational others. European thinkers like Ralf Dahrendorf discover
Thrasymachus in the dire circumstance of post-Holocaust angst,
of Europe in general and of Germany in particular, but the rest
of the word is in fact in a permanent state of Thrasymachus, as
it were; so ours is not so much *a will to power* as *a will to resist power*.

The key conceptual hangover of the post/colonial moment for the world is when the idea of 'the West' both creates and imposes itself as the modus operandi of the world – having always already worlded the world, we seem not to have any option but to inhabit it. European philosophical imagining imposes itself (in spirit and theory, manner and matter) on the world without the slightest awareness of its consequences. A recent expression of such would be the way that during the Oscar Academy Awards the world watched with incredulity as Kathryn Bigelow, director of the award-winning film *The Hurt Locker* (2009), praised the US army as 'real heroes,' and uttered not a word about 26 million Iraqis who have suffered the murderous consequences of that 'heroism.'

To come to grips with the defiant disposition of the Green Movement in Iran, a longstanding promise just about to be delivered, we need to ensure our angle of vision is confidently on the colonial side of modernity, on the site of the abuse of labor by globalized capital writ large, for there and then is the defiant moment of postcoloniality. It is long since overdue to strike back not with the self-defeating nativism of 'Islam versus the West' but with an alternative cosmopolitanism, to which Islam is of course integral but not definitive, which means nothing more than re-worlding the world with the world we have known and lived and experienced, *before* it was de-worlded by the false binary of 'the West and the Rest.' *Resistance to power* is defining of the postcolonial moment that will forever remember its birth pangs of colonial modernity. Without coming to terms with this postcolonial moment, the Green Movement makes no sense in the current context of a realpolitik that always banks on a deep-seated and shortsighted contemporaneity. In the Green Movement that has just unfolded – and it may take a very long time before it produces tangible democratic results – Iranians are retrieving their historically repressed cosmopolitan political culture, and by denouncing violence for the first time in their modern history they are getting ready to institutionalize, rather than fantasize, their civil liberties.

Brownshirts, Blackshirts, and Plainclothes

Atop the fig tree, Kardanah has shifted his angle of vision to his habitual distance (at once critical and intimate) and sees the jungle very differently from the rest of the creatures down below. In the aftermath of the Nazi atrocities, Ralf Dahrendorf also adjusts his vision and opts for a rediscovery of Thrasymachus as the ancient philosophical moment of resistance to power, and thus rediscovers the balance of power/resistance as the site of justice. There is a wisdom that one learns in the aftermath of traumatic experiences, whether caused by a conniving Turtle or by a dictatorial psychopath like Hitler. To understand the rise of the Green Movement in Iran as a sustained struggle for civil liberties, we too need to rise above the habitual politics of despair embedded in the geopolitics of the region, and recognize the site of a renewed resistance to the banality of the status quo. To do so, we also need to know how new social formations (webs of group affiliations, in Georg Simmel's language) have been at work to enable that productive shifting of vision.

Let's start with where all totalitarian regimes thrive, namely the atomization of individuals, their severance from social networks, their insularity within the totalitarian state apparatus, and with the process whereby such policies generate their own antithesis. In the case of the Islamic Republic this has assumed a particularly poignant turn. Majid Mohammadi, a distinguished Iranian sociologist, has offered the term *Obash-salari*/'thugocracy' as the apt manner of referring to the way the Islamic Republic now operates its security apparatus and sustains its military control over its own citizens. What Mohammadi believes to have happened over the last thirty years of the Islamic Republic is its transmutation from a theocracy to a 'thugocracy,' as its social basis has also shifted from widely popular to rampant lumpenism.[17] Majid Mohammadi's assessment is that the Islamic Republic initially began with solid support among

> the middle class and the poor, merchant class and the clergy, and to some extent the technocrats and the university-affiliated groups, but eventually, as the state became more absolutist and totalitarian, a significant proportion of this political capital was lost. The clergy and their merchant class supporters became the beneficiaries of the system, but they could not protect themselves and their accumulated wealth, and they did not trust ordinary people to protect their power either. They needed a rootless and obedient class for that task. Ayatollah Khamenei clearly recognized that fact about twenty years ago [in the late 1980s] and began to organize the neighborhood thugs and hoodlums [obash va lat-ha-ye mahallat] in the Basij and plainclothes security apparatus throughout the country, and then systematically purged these organizations of disobedient elements.[18]

Mohammadi's argument is that as the popular basis of the state shifted (over the last thirty years) from ordinary people of various classes and groups, the structure of power also moved from the clerical authority of the theocracy towards what he terms 'thugocracy.' When government officials talk about 'the people,' Mohammadi suggests, they are really talking about these pressure groups that have prevented borj-e larzan-e hokumat/'the shaky tower of government' from falling. The religious establishment, the Rohaniyat, Mohammadi believes, always prefers the obedience of these rootless and classless lumpen elements to that of even the most compliant among the educated ranks. The neighborhood Hey'ats/Religious Community Centers, Mohammadi suggests, are the main locus of the gathering of these lumpen individuals, and

under Ahmadinejad's government massive resources have been al-
located to expand and strengthen them. Ahmadinejad is in fact the
best-known representative of this group, which has now become
fundamental to the operation of the Islamic Republic.

Mohammadi also offers a discourse analysis of this lumpen
stratum, identifying their speech patterns and use of language,
again as best represented by Ahmadinejad's own interviews,
speeches, and idiom. Historically, the link between the clerical
establishment/Rohaniyat and the lumpen population has been
vital to their popular support, not least their utilizing of the
latter's propensity towards pseudo-mystical absolutism in their
devotions to a supreme religious figure like Khamenei, whom they
refer to simply and honorifically as *Agha*/'Sire'! Mohammadi refers
to the rape and torture of young men and women in Kahrizak,
as widely reported in the aftermath of the post-electoral crisis in
the summer of 2009, as the best example of how the religious
establishment gives free rein to these lumpen elements. These
are mercenary forces who serve the powers that be, including
moving against the late Ayatollah Khomeini's own family when
they defied the command of the reigning Supreme Leader, Ali
Khamenei.

One may disagree with Mohammadi's conclusion that Islamism
as a political project began and is now ending with this organic
link between the clerical class and lumpenism, for, as he himself
indicates at the very beginning of his essay, the 1979 revolution
began with massive popular support among all classes, and yet
the Islamic Republic eventually lost that broad legitimacy and
began clumsily to manufacture a simulacrum of artificial and
forced consent. Mohammadi also glosses over the poor and
disenfranchised classes and communities whose very livelihood
is contingent on the security apparatus of the Islamic Republic
but who are not in any shape or form part of what he rightly

identifies as lumpenism. Lumpenism is indeed a factual and troubling phenomenon in Iranian politics, as it has been throughout modern Iranian history. But the Shah's famous *lat*/thug, Sha'ban bi-Mokh/Sha'ban the Brainless, was squarely in the service of the monarchy and instrumental in the CIA-sponsored coup of 1953. So this lumpen class is seemingly attracted to power per se, not just to clerical power. They would turn to Reza Pahlavi, the late Shah's son, overnight if that is what served their thuggish demeanor and parasitical existence. Equally untenable is Mohammadi's categorical linkage between the clerical class, *in toto*, and the phenomenon of lumpenism, for this totally disregards the extraordinarily positive role that certain progressive segments of the clergy in Iran, and indeed Iraq, have played in the course of the Constitutional Revolution of 1906–11.

Be that as it may, the importance of Mohammadi's essay is in pointing out the systematic atomization of individuals, alienated from their republican citizenship and placed squarely within the security apparatus of the theocracy as the functional equivalent of the Italian *Camicie Nere*/Blackshirts, the Fascist paramilitary groups in Italy between the two world wars, and the the *Sturmabteilung*/Stormtroopers (SA), the Brownshirts, who functioned as a paramilitary organization of the Nazi Party and were instrumental in Adolf Hitler's rise to power in the 1920s and after. Like their Italian and German counterparts, the Iranian lumpen stratum, or *lats* ('thugs' or 'hoodlums') as they are called in Persian, are drawn from the lowest, and socially parasitic, strata of society. (A cultural expression of this phenomenon is the genre of Iranian cinema knows as *Jaheli*, from *Jahel*, meaning 'ignorant' – another way of referring to this underclass. It is, however, very important to distinguish between this disenfranchised, rootless underclass and the working class, who because of their position in an organically weak oil-based national economy have historically had a very limited (though nevertheless crucial) presence and influence in social uprisings.

The security force known as 'the Plainclothes' (*Lebas Shakhsi-ha* in Persian), the Stormtroopers of the Islamic Republic, is now the ground zero of the state apparatus, where it stands all but erect.[19] This is where the oil money goes; it is where the anxiety of an Islamist regime that has completely lost its popular base is most evident. The Plainclothes are no recognizable entity – vacant, vacuous, non-citizens, non-soldiers, non-police, non-workers, asexual, androgynous, non-existent. They can do whatever they wish and are responsible to no one, for they do not exist; they have no mark, no uniform, no address, no identity, no home, no habitat. They are the *tabula rasa* of a monotheist theocracy, and will always be that way – the plain page of an unwritten, illiterate, unlawfulness that has eradicated its own citizenry and stands erect on nothing but an illusion of citizenry. Yet the Plainclothes are the building blocks of the Islamic Republic – plain, simple, amorphous, omnipresent, vacuous. The Plainclothes are shells of human beings, simulacra of citizens – the soulless, murderous expression of a theocratic nightmare.

Social Networking and the Making of a Civil Rights Movement

Kardanah shifts his viewpoint, his perspective on the customary rules of the jungle, almost immediately after his traumatic experience with that false friend of a Turtle, in a manner similar to that of Ralf Dahrendorf reaching for Thrasymachus to offer an alternative vision of the structural functionalism that had defined realpolitik (the rule of jungle) since Socrates. Both returned to the ground zero of their respective cultures in order to resume a political narrative that had been abandoned. Iranians, too, are now back to that ground zero in the aftermath of the prolonged trauma of an Islamic Republic, built on the broken back of a cosmopolitan revolution. On this site, founded on retributive justice, the belligerent custodians of the theocracy base their rule on a vacated citizenship, one in which the intermediary institutions of civic life have been all but suffocated. Here, citizens have been stripped down to their 'naked lives' (Agamben's phrase) by being deprived of the means of civil sociability, used as a faceless security cadre, an underclass of atomized individuals shorn of identity and any meaningful social setting. It is against this background, the ground zero of the rootless, utterly alienated individual, that the significance of cyberspace social networking can be assayed.

An intriguing reference to a prominent nineteenth-century philosopher makes a letter sent by Mir Hossein Mousavi to the late Ayatollah Montazeri in September 2009 of some urgent interest. More than three months into the post-electoral crisis of June 2009, the chief oppositional candidate, who had cried foul following the officially declared victory of Mahmoud Ahmadinejad, had written the letter to the aging Ayatollah soliciting his support for his decision to lead what was now dubbed the Green Movement in a purposeful direction. Mousavi reminded the ayatollah that the prominent seventeenth-century Shi'i philosopher

> The late Molla Mohsen Faiz Kashani [1598–1680], in his *Olfat-nameh/Book of Affinities*, considers the ultimate purpose of religious duties to be the attainment of *mohabbat va olfat-e ijtema'i* [social empathy and affinity]. The result of this social empathy and affinity is what in modern social sciences is called *shabakeh-ha-ye ijtema'i* [social networking].[20]

Mousavi then proceeds to indicate that he intends this constellation of social networking to be used to 'resist the government, prevent it from repeating its past mistakes.' These networks will also 'result in social rejuvenation, contain the emerging energies

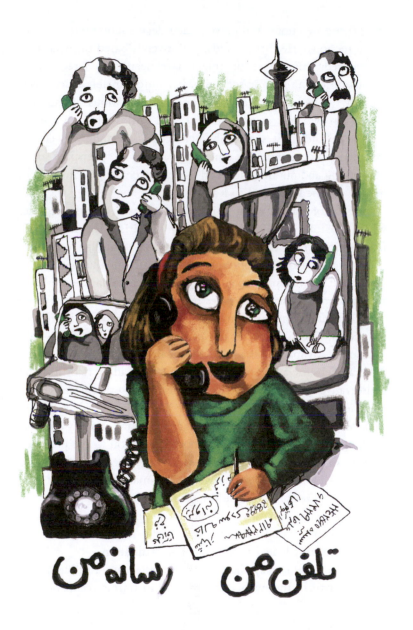

رسانه من   تلفن من

and excited affections, and prevent their degeneration into destruc-
tive directions.' He further adds, plaintively: 'based on what Faiz
has offered, this suggestion might have been considered a new
adaptation of the Islamic scripture, but unfortunately it has been
unfairly dubbed an idea copied from the CIA.' Mousavi's shrewd
invocation of a text of a prominent Shi'i philosopher, in a letter
written to the most senior Shi'i cleric in the land, was clearly
intended to domesticate the emerging patterns of cyberspace social
networking and put them to good use in the civil rights movement
he now seemed destined to lead.

The tug of war between Mir Hossein Mousavi and the regime,
which he took implicitly to task by soliciting the fatwa (official opinion) of the leading oppositional ayatollah over and
above the head of the Supreme Leader Ayatollah Khamenei, was
predicated on the prominence of cyberspace social networking,
which over the last two decades had redefined the terms of mass
communication in Iran, almost simultaneously with the rest of
the world. The widespread use of mobile phones, SMS, Twitter,
Facebook, MySpace, LinkedIn, personal weblogs, political and
cultural websites, and the Internet editions of leading reformist and
conservative newspapers, had skyrocketed among significant sectors
of society in the decade leading to the June 2009 presidential election. Mousavi was not initiating any cyberspace strategy. He was
banking on it. In precisely the opposite direction to the practiced
policies of the Islamic Republic, which was in effect striving to
eradicate all forms of social networking to manufacture devotional
obedience to *Velayat*, the pseudo-mystical authority of the Supreme
Leader, Mousavi was now depending on the further cultivation
of the subterranean (Internet-based) social networking that was
creating unprecedented modes of group affiliation.

In a remarkable way the rise of computer use and literacy in
the early part of the twenty-first century in Iran is comparable to

the growth of newspapers and magazines early in the nineteenth century, when one of the first groups of Iranian students sent to Europe returned with the first printing machine and with it founded the country's first periodicals, thereby expanding the spectrum of the public domain and civil society, and engaging the collective consciousness of a society on the verge of monumental changes. Almost a century later, the press had undergone such growth that it played an instrumental role in a massive social uprising in the country, whereby an absolutist monarchy was forced to accept a constitution. By the time of this Constitutional Revolution, 1906–11, the press had helped expand, define, and circumscribe the boundaries of the public domain beyond anything hitherto achieved. The post-electoral crisis of June 2009 echoed and built on those momentous developments in the early nineteenth and early twentieth centuries. The constitutive feature linking these epochal expansions of the public domain has been the organic development of social networking on the site of *resistance to power* – Thrasymachus, as it were, overseeing the modernity of a political culture.

What we have witnessed over the last decade, however, reaching a dramatic crescendo in the course of the presidential election crisis of 2009, is the steady and exponential expansion of the public domain into cyberspace, to the point that it has had a catalytic, and arguably overwhelming, effect on physical space. In this respect the issue of access to a personal computer or degree of computer literacy is entirely irrelevant, just as basic literacy was irrelevant earlier in the earlier periods, for all that is required is just one person per family, or a few per neighborhood, to account for the entire public domain. We have descriptions from the early twentieth century of newspapers being read on street corners to a gathering crowd; and I have vivid memories from my own childhood in the late 1950s and early 1960s in southern Iran of one television set serving an entire neighborhood. Basic literacy early in the nineteenth century and computer literacy early in the twenty-first century may indeed be directly comparable in terms of numbers – for common to both is the catalytic effect on society at large, which is now globally wired.[21] It is crucial to note here that the rise of literacy and the new mode of public participation have both been coterminous with the emergence of oppositional politics.

The effective use of social networking in the course of the 2009 presidential campaign was predicated on the preceding three decades of the Islamic Republic, where an overwhelmingly young population was increasingly drawn into the electronically savvy age. When Mir Hossein Mousavi declared to his followers that har Irani yek setad, 'every Iranian [is] a campaign headquarters,' he was paying tribute to the resourcefulness of his young admirers. By then SMS instant messaging had become central to campaign organizations: so, alongside the routine messages of friends and family members, a sudden rush of political messages began to redefine the medium, as it expanded the modus operandi of social mobilization and political campaigning. By now mobile phones had become an integral part of the urban scene, and millions of young Iranians used Facebook and Twitter. The skeletal structure of cyberspace, well-oiled and operative due to mundane use, was now instantly turned into an effective mechanism of social mobilization, political opposition, and generation of dissent.

The same mobile phones that were used to take photographs of friends and family to share with others within and outside the country were now being used to take pictures and shoot videos of massive demonstrations around the country and then made available to millions of others who were not there. The primary purpose of these snapshots or short (between thirty seconds and two minutes) video clips was entirely domestic, for disseminating information, enabling mobilization, and regrouping and organization, but before long this visual evidence found its way into the studios of BBC, CNN, Al Jazeera, and other global networks. Soon after the 12 June election, all major foreign correspondents were either severely restricted in their movements or else their visas were cancelled and they had to leave the country. By then, though, the very architecture of journalism was in the process of being redefined. CNN's senior correspondent Christiane Amanpour sat in London looking at the snapshots and videos trying to piece together the story. The notion of 'citizen journalist' had by now assumed a particular poignancy in the nascent civil rights movement.[22]

Though it was in the offing long before the June 2009 presidential election, the Iranian *hozeh-ye omumi*, or public domain, rapidly extended into cyberspace, with political protest as a modus operandi of civil society and its discontent. Events following the election transformed Facebook into an active site of social networking beyond the cyberspace coffeehouse where people vicariously met each other. Did Facebook produce the Iranian civil rights movement or did the Iranian civil rights movement save Facebook? This question became an adage that came down on the side of the frequenters of the coffeehouse.

The effective and creative use of cyberspace social networking by the demonstrators obviously caused the security apparatus of the Islamic Republic to extend its surveillance procedures to that domain. High-ranking Revolutionary Guards made it quite clear, and publically announced, that the demonstrators should not think that the Internet was immune to their surveillance. Suddenly, almost overnight, many Iranian users of Facebook changed their name and profile, assuming 'Neda' (in reference to Neda Aqa Soltan, who had assumed iconic significance following her murder by the security apparatus) as their first name and 'Irani' or 'Iranian' as their last name. Nokia in particular was singled out for attack and boycott because it had evidently sold the security forces surveillance software. By no stretch of the imagination, however, did this extended form of surveillance prevent people from continuing to use Facebook and other forms of social networking – though the instant use of pseudonyms and the fear of reprisal became palpably evident on the Internet.

Almost a century before Facebook gave a new cyberspace meaning to the term 'social networking,' Georg Simmel (1958–1918), in his *Web of Group Affiliations* (1922), suggested that while social groups are composed of individuals, it is through group affiliations that we become and are defined as social personae. Without seeing something in different contexts, it is difficult to define it as what it is. Simmel suggested that each new group that we join or with which we become affiliated defines us in terms of what was potential but unrealized in us. Our individuality, or social persona, to be more exact, is born at the center of the different confluences that socially situate and publicly affect us. In the Iranian context, social networking has made people more social than insular; while the fear in North America and Western Europe is that the same social networking is providing a false and fictive sociability in lieu of the real thing. Iranians have used cyberspace to turn their politics of despair into a dramaturgy of hope. Instead of their reality being subsumed into the irreality of cyberspace, the amorphous possibilities of cyberspace have expanded the political efficacy of their public domain – and that is precisely what frightens the custodians of the medieval theocracy most, deeply troubled as they are by this particular 'fifth column' that is not the work of any external Enemy, but just the frivolous doing of a band of playful geeks out to commandeer their country from its illegitimate usurpers. The significance of Mir Hossein Mousavi urgently invoking the distant memory of Kashani in his letter to

Montazeri is precisely in providing a modus operandi for that reappropriation of the social space; a Shi'i twist to an otherwise amorphous reimagination of the public persona. If Kashani's ancient predecessor, Socrates, was the philosopher preoccupied with an analytic of power and status quo, Thrasymachus' younger and distant followers were busy navigating the contours of a revolt that was yet to be adequately named or mapped out.

SEVEN

The Fox in the Box

WHO CAN SPEAK FOR IRAN – or for the Green Movement? Not Iranians obviously. When one reads the work of some US commentators it seems that interpreting the Green Movement, as something serious and to contend with or else as something irrelevant and whimsical, is a matter to be decided between them, on the one side, and their counterparts of other political shades in Washington DC, on the other. It seems that it was not for Iranians themselves to think through this movement and inform the world (Washington included) what was happening in their homeland. It was for US journalists to tell their fellow analysts (ex- or current CIA agents in particular) what was happening in Iran. No one, they contended, should take 'the so-called Green Movement,' as they termed it disparagingly, seriously or read anything into millions of Iranians marching, or indeed pay attention to what Iranians themselves had to say about the matter – for their 'Iranian contacts' (they like to stick with their old-fashioned CIA terminology) had told them otherwise.

How could that be? Were the Iranian people not in a better position to speak for themselves? That millions of Iranians inside and away from their homeland were marching in support of the Green Movement, and that their most prominent scholars, public intellectuals, civil servants, artists, journalist, bloggers, musicians, and others were actively behind this movement, going to jail or being exiled for it, did not seem to concern these 'white liberals' (to use Martin Luther King's label) who had taken it upon themselves to denounce a massive and unprecedented civil rights movement of whose origin and destination they were blissfully ignorant. How is this possible? That four prominent former officials of the Islamic Republic itself – two former presidents (Ali Akbar Hashemi Rafsanjani and Mohammad Khatami) who between them had run the country for sixteen years; a former prime minister (Mir Hossein Mousavi) who was in post for eight years; and a former Speaker of the House and a founding member of the Islamic Republic (Mehdi Karroubi) – were the leaders (of one sort or another) of this movement did not seem to concern these pundits, who don't even speak the language of these people. Isn't it strange that millions of Iranians had poured onto their streets, risking arrest, incarceration, torture, rape, and murder, but they seemed to arouse no interest in the critics of the movement. Nor did the fact that thousands of university professors had written letters of protest to officials, or that leading intellectuals and artists had been arbitrarily arrested, or that hundreds of journalist were forced into the indignity of exile, or that mothers were mourning the torture, rape, and murder of their children. Instead we were informed that 'The so-called green Movement ... was not what many Iran analysts and other foreign policy and political pundits have cracked it up to be.'[1] Where do people get the authority to say such things – to represent another people they scarcely know, whose language they cannot speak, of whose history, fears, and aspirations they know nothing? 'By what authority doest thou these things?' asks the Bible 'and who gave thee this authority'? (Mark 11:28).

Whence the Green Movement

The Green Movement has appeared within the geopolitics of the region as if out of the blue, *ex nihilo*. But of course it has not. Like everything else, it has a history, a geography, a demography, and a deep-rooted place in modern Iranian political culture – and thus it will not disappear. The belligerent custodians of the Islamic Republic cannot wish it away, or club it to death. It will triumph.

What we witness unfolding in Iran today is a civil rights movement whose moment is long overdue. Central to its history is a cosmopolitan political culture that has been conversant and communicative with the world at large, an integral part of the world, with a worldliness written in its character, not least through the crucial intermediary of expatriate Iranians leaving their homeland as political exiles, students, diplomats, merchants, dissident intellectuals – all of them traveling troubadours of liberty. The nature and disposition of that cosmopolitan culture shaped the most significant event of modern Iranian history, the Constitutional Revolution of 1906, and influenced all subsequent social movements, including the 1977–79 revolution, before it was viciously hijacked and brutally Islamicized, and are now reasserting themselves in the form of the Green Movement.

Crucial in concealing that cosmopolitan worldliness is the false binary opposition stubbornly upheld between *Islamism* and *Secularism*, or between *Tradition* and *Modernity*, or between *Islam* and *the West*, all now best represented in the clash between *religious intellectuals* and *secular intellectuals*. This false binary, the origin of which goes back to the mid-nineteenth century and Iranians' encounter with colonial modernity, is today the single most traumatizing consequence of the last thirty years of militant Islamism that has ruled Iran. What the Green Movement has done, effectively, is to leave behind the false binary and run faster than imagined possible ahead of this lost and losing game. This movement is generating its own thinkers, its own theorists, its own activists, and above all its own abiding sense of citizenship. Perhaps finally, now, in the course of this movement, the presiding idea of citizenship may come to supplant the debilitating and self-indulgent notion of 'the intellectual.'

Historically, the immediate origin of the Green Movement can be traced back to the student-led uprising of the summer of 1999, and the Reform Movement of the 1990s, marked by the presidency of Mohammad Khatami (1997–2005); before that was the militant resistance to the Islamic theocracy that resulted in the mass execution of prisoners in the 1980s; and before that was the original enthusiasm of the 1979 revolution. One could, of course, go further back: to the Marxist guerrilla uprising of the 1970s; the Islamist revolt led by Khomeini in the 1960s; the nationalization of the Iranian oil industry in the 1950s; the persistent resistance to the autocratic rule of Reza Shah in the 1930s and 1940s; resentment against the colonial occupation of Iran during both World Wars; and even to the mother of all modern social upheavals, the Constitutional Revolution of 1906–11, and, before that, to the reformist projects and revolutionary uprisings of the nineteenth century.

Yet the important difference between the Green Movement and its historical antecedents is that, for the first time, the focus of the democratic project has shifted away from the dismantling of the political status quo and the ruling regime, and towards the securing of civil liberties. The position that some observers believe to be a sign of Mousavi's limitation or weakness, that he is committed to the Islamic Republic, is in fact his strongest and most enduring political virtue, for he insists on civil liberties rather than on blind political destabilization. That he is both a key founder and an important product of the Islamic Republic, which qualifies him to talk about its 'original' aims, also makes him (in an exhilarating paradox) more deeply implicated (however inadvertently) as a catalyst in facilitating a retrieval of the cosmopolitan political culture he was once instrumental in suppressing.

Geographically, the Green Movement is also geared, in its demeanor and disposition, towards a retrieval of Iranian cosmopolitan (not 'secular,' not 'Islamic,' but *cosmopolitan*, which includes both and is reducible to neither) culture, the harmonious synthesis of its various strands into a confident location in the world. Iran has experienced the crosscurrents of world historical events, all the way from the ancient Persian empires to medieval Islamic dynasties to modern European colonialism. Nothing is either alien to that cosmopolitan culture or nativist in it disposition. The false binary of 'Islam versus the West,' or 'Tradition versus Modernity,' or 'Religious versus Secular' (which to this day plagues the very language of Muslim and Third World intellectuals) has long distorted the fact of that cosmopolitan phenomenon. Not just beyond its borders, but also within it, this polyvocal worldliness defines the effective history of Iranians of all regions and ethnicities. The ethnicized diversy among Iranians – from the Azaris and Gilakis in the North to the Baluchis and Khuzestanis in the south to the Kurds in the West and the Turkmens in the East – is integral to this cosmopolitan culture.

The geographical spread of this cosmopolitanism extends into the Indian subcontinent, Central Asian territories, and the former Ottoman domains of Turkish, Arab, and Muslim disposition. The Green Movement, in its character and culture, and after thirty years of forced and violent over-Islamization of Iranian polyvocal culture by the Islamic Republic, predicated on half a century of forced, extravagant, and presumptuous 'Westernization' (so-called) by the Pahlavis, is now reaching out and retrieving that cosmopolitanism. Jalal Al-e Ahmad's unfortunate and misguided term *Gharbzadegi*/'Westoxication' epitomizes this calamitous historical distortion, which paved the way for Islamization, in reaction against a presumed 'Westernization.'[2] The currency of the false binary has been a plague, ravaging the palpable fact of Iranian (which is similar to any other) cosmopolitan worldliness. Jalal Al-e Ahmad and such among his critics as Dariush Ashuri (a prominent Iranian intellectual who wrote a famous critique of 'Westoxication') are two sides of the same false coin – one insisting that all ills come from 'the West' and the other believing that the selfsame 'West' is the cure of all ills – both, *ipso facto*, corroborating, consolidating, cross-referencing and authenticating a delusional fantasy they kept calling 'the West.' 'Europe is the invention of the Third World,' Fanon once famously said, and we must re-signify it, in more sense than one.

Demographically, all these factors and forces are carried forward into a new generation of Iranians – 80 per cent of them under the age of forty, 50 per cent under the age of twenty-five – that has scarcely any memory of the Islamized revolution, and that in the age of globalized mass communication is widely wired and integrated within a renewed worldliness. The combination of a very young population trapped inside an oil-based economy that cannot generate enough jobs, and a social movement that is deeply seated within the modernity of its political culture, has given the current combustible condition in Iran an entirely restless and volatile disposition. The political boundary of Iran as a nation-state no longer means much to this generation of Iranians, millions of whom now live 'outside' their homeland – by virtue of manual, professional, and intellectual labor migration – and yet are deeply invested in and committed to its future. The whole binary of inside/outside the country now increasingly means very little, at a time when a significant proportion of the population get their daily dose of news from BBC Persian, Voice of America Persian, or else from a myriad websites based in Western Europe and North America. Young Iranian bloggers inside and outside their homeland are adept participants in the rapid circulation of news, and millions are 'friends' of each other on the Facebook and Twitter social networking sites, which renders the fictive frontiers guarded by border police fairly meaningless. The medieval and modern border-crossing of Iranian/Islamic cosmopolitanism has now effectively entered the postmodern age of globalization.

Those among the European and American 'left' (or right or center for that matter...) who either dismiss or else celebrate the Green Movement as just another colorful revolution inspired by George Soros and neoliberalism are all, categorically, wide of the mark, for they pay no attention to, or else have no knowledge of, the deep historical and social underpinnings of the Green Movement. With the explosion of this civil rights movement in Iran, Tehran could well emerge as the ground zero for similar movements that will leave no Middle Eastern country untouched, including Israel. 'The unrest in Iran,' the prominent Israeli columnist Gideon Levy wrote in *Haaretz* soon after the Green Movement started, 'makes me green with envy.'[3] Whether the lame-duck Ahmadinejad is forced to step down or serves out his full term, his weakened position will produce a domino effect in the region. This will not be limited only to the allies of the Islamic Republic – Hamas and Hezbollah in particular – but will extend well into the domains of its nemesis (from the US and Israel to Saudi Arabia and Egypt), for the options available to the United States and its regional allies regarding Iran's nuclear ambitions have become much compromised in the aftermath of the Green Movement. The idea of economic sanctions, a blockade, or a military strike has become much harder to sell to the international community now that the fate of millions of young Iranian protestors is a global concern. How could anyone starve Neda Aqa Soltan's soulmates – or, even worse, bomb them?

A severe crackdown by the security apparatus of the Islamic Republic may seem to dampen the spirits of the civil rights movement one moment, and yet it bounces back on the next festive or mournful day on the calendar. Scores of demonstrators were killed or injured during the 2009 demonstrations; there have been disturbing reports of political prisoners being raped, tortured, or murdered; hundreds of civic leaders and public intellectuals have been arrested; major opposition figures have been accused of treason and threatened with execution; human rights organizations are routed; and even worse developments might yet to come. But morning has broken, the parable is undone, and the Fox is outfoxed.

Two facts thus confront each other – that of a massive civil rights movement that the whole world can see, and that of its powerful mis/representation by US analysts who have made it their business to insist that what the rest of the world is witnessing does not in fact exist. History, and whatever lesson it may have to offer, will be the judge – not only of the events occurring now, but also of what has happened to create, condition, and sustain them.

Home and Exile

In terms of its scale and varied dimensions, the Green Movement that emerged in 2009 is rightly compared to the Constitutional Revolution of 1906–11 – and indeed it is instructive to go back to the preparatory stages of that critical moment in Iran's encounter with colonial modernity in order to understand more fully what is happening in Iran today.[4] One might consider the Islamic Revolution of 1977–79 to have been the concluding chapter of the book to which the Constitutional Revolution of 1906–11 was the introduction. However, although modern Iranian history is conventionally

constructed as a succession of revolutionary uprisings, the record
in fact shows a more sustained pattern of reformist thought and
institution-building between the two defining moments of violent
upheaval and change. Underpinning the historical narrative of
reformist movements and revolutionary uprisings are a few key
and momentous figures who have cast a long and lasting shadow
over the making of modern Iran.

Arguably a crucial factor in the making of the Green Movement
has been the active involvement of Iranians around the world
– a tangential and supplementary point of view that complicates
the idea we tend to have of 'Iran.' It is not accidental that the
enthusiasm of Iranians living outside the political boundaries
(or, as Firoozeh Kashani-Sabet marvelously puts it, the 'frontier
fictions') of their homeland is no less and perhaps even more
passionate than that of their compatriots inside.[5] One might go so
far as to argue that the very idea of 'Iran' as a modern nation-state
was fostered in a pivotal way by Iranians outside Iran – by travel-
ers, merchants, students, diplomats, expatriate political activists,
intellectuals, and scholars in exile – during which time, the Qajar
dynasty, it was in reality being ruled by a medieval potentate.
One can scarcely name any significant nineteenth-century thinker
instrumental in the shaping of the Constitutional Revolution who
did not, in one way or another, leave his homeland first in order
to return to it, either physically or in his convictions and writing,
to define it as a homeland.

'Iran' has been imagined from the outside ever since the
formative nineteenth century, sometimes involving dramatic and
bloody events. The story of the brutal beheading of three rebellious intellectuals under a wild rose tree, following their arrest in
Istanbul and extradition, is perhaps one of the more disturbing
narratives of modern Iranian history.[6] The date of this execution
was 15 July 1896, the location the city of Tabriz in north-western

Iran, whence the three revolutionary activists had been dispatched from the cosmopolitan center of the Ottoman Empire. Who were they and why were they arrested in Istanbul, dispatched to Tabriz, and cold-bloodedly murdered? Their story, especially their brutal ending, has remained in the collective unconscious of an entire nation ever since – like an adolescent trauma that refuses to loosen its grip on the grown-up man it has long preoccupied.

It is impossible to exaggerate the significance of these three pioneering intellectuals – Mirza Aqa Khan Kermani, Sheykh Ahmad Ruhi, and Khabir al-Molk – in the history of the Iranian encounter with colonial modernity in the mid-nineteenth century, or to overstate the degree to which their exilic life has shaped the meaning of homeland in modern Iranian history. The most prominent among the three was Mirza Aqa Khan Kermani (1853–1896), a leading intellectual of uncommon learning who abandoned his homeland for the more hospitable and cosmopolitan environment of Istanbul. Mirza Aqa Khan was born and educated in Kerman. By the time he was 25 years old, he had already mastered all the major classical fields of Islamic learning, published his first book, *Ridwan*, and learned English well enough to translate a book on astronomy into Persian. Moved by his precocious mind and impatient disposition, Mirza Aqa Khan Kermani soon got into trouble with the political authorities in his native Kerman, wherafter he moved to Isfahan for a short while, and soon after that to Tehran, and from there he was finally forced into exile in Istanbul, where he lived his most fruitful and significant years, and from which he helped shape the meaning of 'homeland' in his country.

From the vantage point of expatriate intellectuals like Mirza Aqa Khan Kermani, the Istanbul of the late nineteenth century was the capital city of a cosmopolitan worldliness whose significance went beyond the Ottoman Empire proper and reached widely and deeply into Central Asia, Iran, all the way to South Asia and North

Africa. One might in fact think in terms of a *cosmopolitan crescent* that began from the farthest reaches of Central Asia, came west towards the Ottoman territories, turned south and extended all the way to Egypt and beyond, with Istanbul as the hub of this vast, multi-cultural, and worldly terrain. While for late-nineteenth-century Turkish intellectuals like Namik Kemal (1840–1888), London or Paris was the center of the universe, for Iranian intellectuals of the same period Istanbul was a far more exciting, hospitable, consequential, and effervescent cosmopolis. It was a home from home – at once close and yet distant from the notion of 'home-land.' This is not to say that colonizing capitals like London or Paris did not cast their magic spell over Iranian intellectuals as well. It is rather to identify Istanbul as the cosmopolitan center of an entirely distinct normative and moral imaginary, far closer to home and far healthier in its worldly offering of a hospitable space for critical and creative thinking and action. Istanbul, then, was both home and not home. Living and writing there did not mean a state of permanent exile from home. Quite the contrary: it meant you could dream of and design home ever more creatively. You could both live and work in Istanbul and feel connected to home – that is, the home you were busy imagining. A generation or two later, if an Iranian intellectual moved to Berlin, London, or Paris (or, years later, to New York or Chicago), there was a sense of almost permanent removal from one's homeland if this crafted idea of it was not carried along too – a feeling with which the debilitating experience of *exile*, of *exilic conditions*, or, worse, of *diaspora* was identified. Istanbul for Iranian intellectuals of the late nineteenth century was a creatively liminal space: they were close enough to home to feel implicated in its destiny, and yet far enough away to allow them the freedom to navigate their normative and moral imaginations, with which they were now busily creating their *vatan*/homeland. Without coming to terms with that liminal space, where the centrifugal and centripetal forces of a culture meet and productively grow, social uprisings (including this very Green Movement) will not yield their full political force.[7] It is no accident that Mirza Aqa Khan Kermani and his comrades chose Istanbul as the center of their intellectual life and political activities. While in Istanbul he collaborated with the leading intellectual organ of his time, *Akhtar*, and earned a living as a teacher at an Iranian school. A particularly important event in Mirza Aqa Khan's life while residing in Istanbul was his acquaintance with Seyyed Jamal al-Din al-Afghani (1831–1897), by far the most globally celebrated Muslim reformist of his time. The two intellectuals struck up an immediate friendship in their shared struggles against tyranny in Muslim lands.

A young revolutionary activist by the name of Mirza Reza Kermani fled the tyrannies of Qajar Iran, met Jamal al-Din al-Afghani in Istanbul, and encouraged by him went back to Iran and assassinated the reigning monarch, Nasser al-Din Shah Qajar (1831–1896), and thus triggered a chain of events that ultimately resulted in the Constitutional Revolution of 1906–11.

The presence of expatriate intellectuals like Mirza Aqa Khan Kermani outside their homeland generates and sustains a dialectic of reciprocity between them and activists inside the country, without which both sides of the mobilizing dynamic would lose momentum and synergy. That momentum, operational at least since early in the nineteenth century, is still very much alive and instrumental within the Green Movement. A principal concern of the security apparatus of the Islamic Republic is to dismantle oppositional websites such as *Jaras* or *Gooya* (among a myriad others) in which leading Iranian intellectuals regularly post their analysis of current events. The television networks BBC Persian and Voice of America Persian are equally troublesome to clerical power in Iran.

The case of Mirza Aqa Khan Kermani is not the exception
but rather the rule in the shaping of Iranian (moral, normative,
and intellectual) anticolonial modernity and the struggle against
domestic tyranny into such a potent political force. Another
equally compelling example is the case of yet another friend and
comrade of Mirza Aqa Khan, a leading literary figure named Mirza
Habib Isfahani (d. 1893). The extraordinary achievement of Mirza
Habib Isfahani, who was one of the most distinguished literary
figures of the late nineteenth century, is equally representative of
this expatriate group of intellectuals who crafted Iranian literary
modernity while living in Istanbul. Mirza Habib was born in
Chahar Mahal, educated in Isfahan and Tehran, and spent a few
years in Baghdad. Upon his return to Tehran he was accused of
having composed a satirical poem against Mirza Hasan Khan
Sepahsalar, a Qajar court official − a charge that forced him to
flee the tyrannical reign of the Qajars altogether and seek refuge
in Istanbul, where he worked as a teacher, translator, manuscript
copyist, and also as a bureaucratic functionary. In Istanbul, Mirza
Habib earned a meager living to support himself and his family,
and commenced a reading and writing career that before his death
in 1897 had revolutionized Persian literary modernity. A principal
achievement was the writing of a number of Persian grammar
books based on an entirely new and systematic model. This he
did while living outside Iran. Literary historians suggest that the
very grammatical foundation of modernist Persian prose-writing is
almost entirely indebted to Mirza Habib's groundbreaking work on
Persian grammar in the 1870s. The literary output of Mirza Habib
between his arrival in Istanbul in 1866 and his death in 1893 laid
the foundation of modernist Persian literature for decades, and
perhaps centuries, to come.[8]

A crucial aspect of living and working in Istanbul for Iranian
intellectuals was their ready access to the most progressive and

revolutionary ideas from European and Russian struggles against their own medieval tyrannies – sources that were otherwise difficult to access given the severe Qajar censorship. A similar situation obtains today in the Islamic Republic – where leading Iranian scholars and intellectuals cannot live or visit without landing in jail, whilst sympathetic foreign analysts are regularly welcomed and given the red-carpet treatment. Exilic conditions proved exceedingly productive for Iranian intellectuals. Mirza Habib had a solid command over the French language, and among his major achievements while in Istanbul was the translation of Alain-René Lesage's (1668–1747) *Gil Blas* (written 1700–1730), the novel that was instrumental in making the picaresque form a major European literary sensation, and that would have an enduring effect on Persian literary modernity.

By far the most important achievement of Mirza Habib Isfahani while living in Istanbul was his Persian rendition of James Morier's novel *The Adventures of Hajji Baba of Ispahan* (1824). Ever since the publication of the English edition in 1824 and the Persian translation by Mirza Habib Isfahani in 1892, the work has generated much discussion and controversy. At the beginning of *The Adventures*, Morier states that he has translated the text from the Persian. Is that merely a literary device or did he mean it literally? Morier was a bureaucratic functionary and colonial officer with a modest and clumsy command of Persian. The English diction includes a great deal of verbatim and entirely ludicrous English renderings of Persian phrases. This enigma has baffled literary historians for decades. Some believe that Morier's text is actually a translation and not an original work. Others wonder how a text of such astounding colonial racism in its English original could become so seminal a text in its Persian translation during the course of the Constitutional Revolution. The controversy turns on a single, and singularly baffling, fact:

whereas James Morier's original is a horrid piece of Orientalist and racist farce, Mirza Habib's Persian text is a literary gem of unsurpassed beauty and elegance, a work both foundational of Persian literary modernity and a shaping factor in the Constitutional Revolution of 1906–11. How could a bad Orientalist English novel become a definitive text of the moral imagination at the core of the Constitutional Revolution? Some historians of Qajar rule who view Morier's text as 'an Orientalist project par excellence' have identified the reception of Mirza Habib's Persian work as 'an early example of the masochistic Persian modernists who were fascinated with everything Western, even to the extent of deprecating their own culture. This internalization of Orientalist stereotypes found resonance especially among the intelligentsia of the Constitutional Revolution and thereafter.'[9] This ludicrous explanation stems from a factual confusion rooted in a failure to understand how a literary work of art is written and received.

Mirza Habib, Mirza Aqa Khan, and Sheykh Ahmad collaborated with each other, reading and editing each other's writings, while they lived in Istanbul. The first manuscript of Mirza Habib's translation of The Adventures of Hajji Baba of Ispahan that reached Iran was in fact in Sheykh Ahmad Ruhi's handwriting. Thus it was thought to be his book and consequently the first published edition was misattributed to him. Sheykh Ahmad Ruhi was no run-of-the-mill activist. He was a major force in the course of the Constitutional Revolution. A year after the publication of The Adventures in Persian, he and his comrades were cold-bloodedly murdered by Qajar executioners. It was thus the presumed authorship of that novel, and the radical condition of its revolutionary reception, that turned its publication into a defining moment both in the rise of literary modernity in Iran and in the Constitutional Revolution, regardless of nonsensical notions about 'masochistic Persian modernists.'

Had it not been for Mirza Habib Isfahani's masterful Persian translation, Iranians inside Iran would never have known about James Morier's English text; a racist tract would not have been transformed into one of the literary cornerstones of the Constitutional Revolution. This observation is one that holds more broadly for the émigré community at this time. All Iranian expatriate intellectuals in the Ottoman territories enjoyed direct access to European literary, philosophical, scientific, and political developments, and acted as a bridge enabling their introduction to their homeland. It is hard to imagine the Constitutional Revolution without the groundwork that literary and revolutionary figures like Mirza Habib Isfahani or Mirza Aqa Khan Kermani had prepared in this crucial period. Their work, and that of others, gave the Constitutional Revolution – a defining moment in modern Iranian history – a profoundly cosmopolitan character, a disposition that has remained a vital feature of Iranian culture to this day, all the violent attempts of the Islamic Republic to dismantle it notwithstanding.

Mirza Aqa Khan Kermani's arrest and execution by the Ottoman authorities marks a particularly poignant moment in modern Iranian intellectual history. One might argue that nineteenth-century Istanbul was the birthplace of Iranian (and also Egyptian, Indian, Central Asian, etc.) cultural modernity. In thinking through the history of Istanbul as a cosmopolis, it is crucial to locate it in its own imaginative geography, as the home to generations of public intellectuals from all over the world – from Mirza Aqa Khan Kermani and his circle in the late nineteenth century to the German literary theorist Erich Auerbach (1892–1957) in the early twentieth. This perspective will radically remap the world that hitherto has been so awkwardly and jarringly divided between a metaphysical East and an everlasting West – a division valid only in the colonial imagination of a white supremacist thinking unable to perceive the world in alternative, more democratically liberating, ways.

Imagining a Liberated Homeland

The Green Movement is the retrieval of an Iranian cosmopolitan
political culture that has been consistently in the making from
early in the nineteenth century, and that the Islamic Republic has
spent thirty cruel years misrepresenting and suppressing in the
name of an Islamized absolutism. As the ancestral faith of Iranians,
Islam is of course integral to that cosmopolitan culture, but it is
not constitutive of it. The cosmopolitan worldliness embedded
in the intellectual life of the nineteenth century ushered in the
political culture of subsequent decades and defined the disposition of the social movements to come. Imagining a liberated
homeland from a position outside became the formative impulse
in the founding of twentieth-century cosmopolitan culture in
Iran. Mirza Saleh Shirazi, whose *Safarnameh/Travelogue* (composed
1815–19) is considered a pioneering text in the history of the
Iranian encounter with European modernity, was among the very
first Iranians to become aware of his civil rights as the potential
citizen of a republic. *Safarnameh* is perhaps the single most important gift to his homeland that Mirza Saleh brought from his visit
to England. Throughout his journey from Iran to Russia to England
and back, he recorded perceptive observations regarding the
absence or presence of civil liberties in Europe – always with an
eye towards his readership back in Iran.[10] Due to his knowledge of
both English and French, Mirza Saleh became deeply immersed in
European traditions of liberalism and the Enlightenment, and was
thoroughly familiar with the writings of such thinkers as Voltaire
and Rousseau. On his way back from England, Mirza Saleh brought
a printing machine, on which he subsequently published the first
widely circulated newspaper in Iran. In this way he introduced
the notion of civil society, and showed how its constitution was
contingent upon civil liberties.

In addition to the Ottoman territories and Western Europe, Central Asia and Russia proved to be equally fertile resources in the making of this cosmopolitan culture. From his native Azerbaijan, Mirza Fath Ali Akhondzadeh (1813–1878), a leading literary intellectual of his time, was deeply attracted to Russian culture and literature, and through that familiarity pioneered modern drama and became widely popular. A consequence of this influx of new ideas from outside was the active rise of a defiant and critical discourse that enabled Iranians to think about the modernity of their condition. Another prominent thinker, Mirza Yusuf Khan Mostashar al-Dawlah (d. 1895), was the author of a singularly significant treatise he titled *Resaleh Yek Kalameh/A Treatise on One Word*. That one word, which he thought his homeland desperately needed to learn, was the rule of 'law.' In this very period, Seyyed Jamal al-Din Asadabadi (aka al-Afghani, 1838–1897) became the epitome of such traveling troubadours of liberty. He journeyed from one end of the Muslim world to the other and then to Europe and back. He had an important influence on political developments in both Iran and Egypt, and inaugurated a wide range of reformist and revolutionary ideas and movements. He was a Shi'a who pretended he was a Sunni, an Iranian who posed as an Afghan, or a Turk, or an Arab, or an Indian, depending on his immediate purposes for instigating defiance against the status quo. The politics of identity or the homeland meant very little to him. His revolutionary authenticity was predicated on cultural inauthenticity. The world was his home. He was vital to the making of a political culture that would navigate all the major and minor social revolutions of the twentieth century and after in Iran.

The education of another leading thinker and statesman, Mirza Ali Khan Amin al-Dawlah (1844–1904), was fairly typical of a learned Qajar aristocrat. He was aware of the historic changes that were happening around him and sought to bring them about in his homeland. He became immersed in French Enlightenment ideals, for which he developed an abiding respect and admiration. When Nasser al-Din Shah (ruled 1848–96), the reigning Qajar monarch, asked al-Dawlah to write a treatise for him on what he had learned from the French, Montesquieu's *The Spirit of Laws* (1748) was the paramount text. For a short period during the reign of Mozaffar al-Din Shah (ruled 1896–1907) Amin al-Dawlah served as prime minister, in which brief interval he was instrumental in bringing a sense of order and responsibility to the central administration. He was particular in guaranteeing freedom of the press, and had a passion for establishing modern schools, which made him an enemy of backward elements within the Shi'i clergy. Amin al-Dawlah's *Khaterat-e Siasi/Political Memoir* is suffused with anger against Qajar tyranny and replete with admiration for European societies and politics, which he praised for their rule of law and their civil liberties.[11] Al-Dawlah was a nationalist who was deeply troubled by the rule of clerical fanaticism and monarchic tyranny, believing the alternative to this dual calamity was to learn about the ways and manner in which Europe had achieved its civil liberties. This was all happening as a prelude to the defining moment in Iranian political culture, the Constitutional Revolution.

In the making of this cosmopolitan culture, intellectuals from religious minorities were as instrumental as those with a Muslim background. Mirza Malkom Khan Nazem al-Dawlah (1833–1908) was an Armenian, originally from Jolfa in Isfahan, who studied in Paris and became imbued with French Enlightenment ideas. As a translator, he was instrumental in helping European teachers employed at Dar al-Fonun, the European-style college that the reformist prime minister Amir Kabir had founded in 1851. Malkom Khan visited Istanbul and Europe on many diplomatic missions, but he is chiefly known for having published the exceptionally important oppositional newspaper *Qanun/Law* from London, the writings in which became integral to the revolutionary aspirations that resulted in the drafting of the Iranian Constitution early in the twentieth century. The central significance of Malkom Khan among the leading intellectuals of his time is symbolic of the non-denominational, cross-religious, and multi-ethnic disposition of an Iranian cosmopolitan political culture that refuses reduction a false secular–religious divide.

Returning Home

If we are to consider the Constitutional Revolution of 1906–11 a major threshold in the passage of Iran into political modernity, which it was, then we need to consider the fact that the weak and wobbly Iranian bourgeoisie at the time exacerbated the overwhelming rural disposition of the country at large. The unpropitious alliance struck between fanatical and backward components of the Shi'i clerical establishment and the corrupt and decadent Qajar aristocracy makes it impossible to understand the cataclysmic event as a social revolution engineered by a robust bourgeoisie against an entrenched feudal aristocracy. The role of liberal ideas, the demand for the rule of law, and an appetite for civil liberties were infinitely more powerful in the making of this social uprising. No document is better testimony to this fact than a novel published just a year before the assassination of reigning Qajar monarch Nasser al-Din Shah in 1896, a publishing event that bears comparison with the publication of Harriet Beecher Stowe's *Uncle Tom's Cabin* (1852) just before the Civil War in the United States. Amin al-Dawlah's *Political Memoir* refers to a book he identifies as *Siyahatnameh Ibrahim Beik/Ibrahim Beik's Travelogue*, which, he says, 'needs no introduction.' What is this book and why was its reputation such that it needed no introduction? Haj Zayn al-Abedin

Maraghe'i (1839–1910) wrote his *Siyahatnameh Ibrahim Beik* (composed 1894–1918) as a fictional narrative in which an Iranian returns to his homeland to find it in utter desolation. This gave Maraghe'i occasion to reflect creatively on the real social malaise gripping his homeland, which he ascribes to political circumstance and to tyranny. The publication of the novel was a momentous occasion in the avalanche of new and path-breaking ideas that were flooding the Qajar realm at the time, incrementally pushing it towards a massive social uprising consequent upon the strong desire for the rule of law and civil liberties.

The first volume of the book was published in 1894, the second volume ten years later in 1905, and the third volume four years after that in 1909.[12] The first tells the story of the protagonist's journey through Iran and gives a detailed account of his social and political observations. The second narrates his return to Egypt, his love affair with Mahbubeh, and ultimately their untimely and tragic deaths. The third relates a dream of Ibrahim Beik's traveling companion/servant Yusuf Amu, in which he travels through Heaven and Hell, a story that seems to have been influenced by Dante's *Divine Comedy* (1308–21) and in other respects anticipates Kafka's short story 'In the Penal Colony.' Yet even in this third volume, all the inhabitants of Heaven and Hell are Iranians and still afflicted by the selfsame maladies as in this life. Noting the date of the publication of the third volume (1909), Mohammad Reza Fashahi, a leading historian of the period, reads this last part of *Siyahatnameh* as a premonitory account of the Constitutional Revolution of 1906–11, which was just about to take place.[13] These texts not only conditioned the rise of the Revolution and gave it its narrative disposition; they defined the literary cosmopolitanism of subsequent generations.

The printing and publication of *Siyahatnameh Ibrahim Beik* in Cairo by an expatriate merchant/intellectual is the best example of how both the very notion of 'Iran' (its ills and its aspirations) as a homeland and the most radical ideas to transform it into a modern nation-state came in fact from outside the physical entity of the country, and were fashioned by a peculiar class of merchants, diplomats, and expatriate intellectuals, who paradoxically discovered their homeland when they were no longer resident there. If today we are witness to an especially passionate commitment on the part of the Iranian expatriate bourgeoisie in particular, one must trace its origin back to this time, when a very formative period for the Iranian national bourgeoisie among the class of merchant capitalists was interwoven with an abiding love of homeland nurtured from a distance.

Born to a Sunni Kurdish family in Azerbaijan, Haj Zayn al-Abedin had a perfunctory education and soon began his early life as a young merchant. His business ventures eventually took him to Russia where he soon became a citizen of that vast and tumultuous empire. But fifteen years into his new citizenship suddenly a fierce sense of nationalism overcame Haj Zayn al-Abedin, whereupon he spent four years fighting the Russian bureaucracy to give back his citizenship. He was so utterly elated when, in February 1904, he finally succeeded in relinquishing his Russian citizenship that he began singing and dancing in joy, perceiving himself as a born-again Iranian. Nevertheless, Haj Zayn al-Abedin spent the remainder of his life in the Ottoman territories and never physically moved into Qajar, in part due to the relative freedom he enjoyed in Istanbul, in part on account of his business interests, and in part because Istanbul offered him an infinitely superior social and intellectual milieu than Tehran would. Like most other expatriate or itinerant Iranian intellectuals, Haj Zayn al-Abedin spent the rest of his life imagining a homeland for himself that was far superior and more advanced than that in which his fellow countrymen were actually living. His commitment to and preoccupation with that imaginary Iran is amply evident in his fictional masterpiece.

One crucial fact regarding this seminal novel is that Haj Zayn al-Abedin published the first of the three volumes anonymously for fear of persecution, even though he was in exile. This was perhaps because, as he put it himself, he felt embarrassed that in the book he waxes poetic about his love for his homeland but was not in fact living in Iran, which he thought might be taken as a sign of duplicity. There was wild speculation as to the identity of the author of *Safarnameh Ibrahim Beik*. When Haj Zayn al-Abedin published the second and third volumes of his novel he finally introduced himself, but now people did not believe him and thought there were thematic and narrative discrepancies between the first and the subsequent two volumes. Moreover, some wondered how a simple-minded merchant could have such a deep knowledge of his homeland. Be that as it may, all major historians of the Constitutional Revolution – from E.G. Brown to Ahmad Kasravi – concur that the author of all three volumes of *Siyahatnameh Ibrahim Beik* was indeed Haj Zayn al-Abedin Maraghe'i and that his novel had an instrumental role in exciting public sentiment against the Qajar tyranny.

Perhaps the most crucial aspect of the novel is the directness of its style, which resonates with Mirza Saleh Shirazi's concern with the simplification of Persian prose at the expense of ornamental casuistry, in order that the narrative's democratic message might reach a wide readership. This democratization of Persian prose, developed outside Iran by members of the expatriate Iranian intelligentsia, is perhaps the single most important literary corollary of the formation of the public space in Iranian modernity. Persian prose and poetry were historically the exclusive domain of the aristocratic court – from their *bazms*/banquets to their *razms*/battles. Thus, from Mirza Saleh Shirazi early in the nineteenth century to

the later work of Haj Zayn al-Abedin Maraghe'i, all social reformers and revolutionaries were very particular in their determination
to bring Persian prose and poetry out of the court and into the
public domain, and their solution was to craft a much leaner
and more agile narrative. That Haj Zayn al-Abedin had opted for
a work of fiction, and specifically for travelogue as a narrative
device, is testimony to his deliberate design to reach a wider
audience. *Safarnameh Ibrahim Beik* soon became a banned book and
Amin al-Sultan, the notorious prime minister of Nasser al-Din
Shah, had anyone caught with a copy arrested and jailed.

The plot of the novel is very simple. Ibrahim Beik is the son
of a prominent Iranian merchant who lives in Egypt but deeply
loves his homeland, and he invests that love in his son. Just before
his death, the Iranian merchant asks his son to travel to Iran,
which the dutiful son does soon after his father's death. Ibrahim
Beik and his companion/servant Yusuf Amu spend some eight
months traveling from one end of the country to another record-
ing in some detail its material poverty and moral decay. People's
destitution, the charlatanism of the clerical class, the tyranny of
the Qajar aristocracy, and the domination of European colonialism are paramount among his concerns. Ibrahim Beik's travels
through Iranian cities are also a ruse behind the cover of which
he encourages his fellow Iranians to revolt against the tyranny that
has ruined their homeland.

Haj Zayn al-Abedin Maraghe'i was a man of the world rather
than of learning (like Mirza Aqa Khan Kermani); nevertheless
his extensive travels, and particularly his knowledge of Russian,
had exposed him to many progressive ideas, instilled in him
an abiding (though phantom) nationalism, and led him to care
deeply for his homeland. Chief among his concerns were the
need for constitutional precepts, political reform, and the rule of
law, as well as the dangers of colonialism. Intellectual freedom

and freedom of expression, both deeply influenced by European liberalism and French Enlightenment thinkers like Rousseau, Voltaire, and Montesquieu, were the driving force of Maraghe'i's passionate nationalism. In Maraghe'i we also witness the birth of the idea of a merchant/intellectual. Deeply influenced by the French Revolution and the Declaration of the Rights of Man and the Citizen of 1789, and the Russian Revolution of 1905, Maraghe'i is as much beholden to Europe as he is to Japan. He never uses the word *Gharb*/West in his prognosis of regional and global conditions, for the term had no meaning at the time, but the word *Farang*/Franks designates both colonialism and progress. In his novel, Maraghe'i declares and practices not just a new democratic prose but also a worldly literary space, liberated from classical Persian pleasantries. He is a deeply nationalistic man, and as such thoroughly influenced by European nationalism, which he turns against European colonialism by crafting an anti-colonial nationalism, which in his case is equally influenced by Russian revolutionaries. He radically opposes the role of the clerics in social and political matters, although in instigating revolt he does appeal to them to come and speak on behalf of the wretched of the earth. Parliamentary democracy, however, is his paramount ideal. Though in many moments of anger and frustration he revolts against tyranny and calls for revolution, his ideals and aspirations for this revolution are thoroughly liberal in disposition and character, to be led by an autonomous and prosperous national bourgeoisie.

Amin al-Dawlah, in the same passage in his political memoir in which he discusses Maraghe'i's *Siyahatnameh Ibrahim Beik*, also mentions that while in Dagestan he stayed with a friend, Abd al-Rahim Talebof (1834–1911), 'the author of *Ketab Ahmad/The Book of Ahmad*,' another key text in the movement of nineteenth-century literary and intellectual cosmopolitanism. This finds an intertextual echo in the narrative of Maraghe'i's novel, wherein Ibrahim Beik and his companion/servant Yusuf Amu enter Istanbul on their way to Iran and stay for a few days in the narrator's home. Iranians read these and many companion texts as highlights within a seamless historical narrative that weaves the current struggles of Iranians for liberty together with those of their past generations. In these literary and historical narratives, home and exile very soon fused, forming a powerful binary in the Iranian political imagination. The expatriate community of literati and intelligentsia in effect built the idea and ideal of a homeland when they were in fact far away from it. It is that creative and critical imagination that has now, as it has repeatedly over the last two centuries, returned to inhabit and inform another massive social uprising that is set to redefine a people's fate.

Can Iranians Speak?

The key question facing Iranians who care about the future of their homeland is whether Iranians – as a people, a nation, a country – are able to speak for themselves, and in a language that the world at large can understand, or must be spoken for by self-appointed foreign analysts who distort their voices and misrepresent their country and its cultures. That is, can Iranians speak?

Many prominent Arab, Muslim, African, Latin American, and even Western European and North American public figures and leading intellectuals are, to various degrees, suspicious of the Green Movement and wary of its implications for the geopolitics of the region. Progressive Arab and Muslim intellectuals in particular are concerned that even though this movement is genuine and indeed involves the grassroots, the US and its regional allies might nevertheless still abuse it according to their own agenda. Consequently Iranians actively involved in the movement, whether writing in Persian or in other languages, have been hard at work trying to understand the internal dynamics and progressive dimensions of the Green Movement and to determine to what degree, if any, it is being manipulated by outside forces, for their own purposes.[14]

What, then, is the standing of the Green Movement today? Some leading Arab and Muslim intellectuals distrust it, while at the same time American neocons are trying to abuse it. The pro-Israel US Senator Joe Lieberman staunchly defends it, while his friend Senator John McCain enthusiastically endorses it. American neoliberals are infatuated with the Green Movement, while the American and European lefts categorically dismiss it. So, is it possible for Iranians – the subalterns of this power-play game of representation – to speak in a manner whereby these players and others will allow them to represent themselves, or must they continue to be represented?

Quite obviously, Iranians do not all speak with one voice. To begin with, there are millions who oppose the Green Movement, many believing it to be the evil design of foreigners. As Mir Hossein Mousavi has repeatedly stated, the primary task is to win over this significant portion of society, and enable them to see the movement not as hostile but rather as directly conducive to their interests. For the custodians of the Islamic Republic cynically abuse the trust and beliefs, as well as threatening the livelihoods, of the mass of people, in order to maintain the illusion that it has a popular base. On the other hand, there coexist a range of perspectives among those who wholeheartedly support, and even those who are active in, the Green Movement. After all, supporters come from a variety of social backgrounds and represent a range of political outlooks, so by no stretch of the imagination could their differing class, gender, and ethnicized interests be articulated in a straightforward way.

The most immediate consequence of this observation regarding the dissonant voices in Iranian society and, in particular, the multiform nature of the Green Movement's support base is, as Gayatri Spivak has made amply clear in her important essay 'Can the Subaltern Speak' (1988),[15] the fact that the subaltern, or the nation in a condition of agitated and potentially revolutionary subalternity (in terms of its ability to speak for itself), has no claim to a quintessence that can or cannot be represented. Iranians, like the population of any other nation, come in a multiplicity of identities, with numerous persectives on their country and the world, thereby representing a complex class, gender, and ethnic diversity. The same is true of the Green Movement. Hence no one – and this includes those in the think-tanks of the US and Europe – can speak for the collectivity with any degree of overarching authority or incontrovertible legitimacy. The 'epistemic violence' of which Spivak rightly speaks, and against which she warns, pre-empts any essentialist or totalizing claim to representation. But what exactly would that mean – that any act of representation is as flawed, and even as mischievous, as any other? That is, since no one is entitled to speak for the Green Movement, does it follow that no one should speak for it?

Perhaps the most immediate issue we need to resolve, in order to answer that question, is that first and foremost social movements are not predicated on statistical analysis of those who support or oppose them, but on the inner dynamics of the movement itself. Social movements have a 'social' logic of their own, whether they succeed or fail in terms of that dynamic. Did the American Civil Rights Movement, concerned at most with the fate of 10 percent of a nation, represent a significant statistical factor within American society? How many people did it take to lead the Cuban Revolution, or the Russian and Chinese revolutions for that matter? Since I insist that what we are witnessing in Iran is a civil

rights movement, it is arguably best compared with the American
movement; and that includes registering the fact that support for
the Green Movement is certainly proportionately greater than the
entirety of the African-American community that was behind
American Civil Rights.

The problems with Spivak's disabling rhetorical question regarding who can speak for this movement are manifold – but first
and foremost in the fact that it is an arresting inhibition posing as
an innocent question. The answer that the question solicits, indeed
requires, is obviously 'No, the subaltern cannot speak, forgive
us for presuming that it does or that we do on the subaltern's
behalf!' This answer, then, is embedded in the question. The
question, which begs itself (in the classical form of the Aristotelian
petitio principii in his *Prior Analytics*), is actually a rhetorical answer
in the negative; this negative answer pre-empting the affirmative
masquerades as a question that is open to either.

Thus it is the question itself, not the obvious and implicit
answer it carries within, that needs to be questioned; for a question that resolves itself obviously needs no answer but, *ipso facto*,
calls itself into question, thereby exposing the anxieties of its
origin. That is, the question Spivak has asked should thus not be
answered – it should be questioned.

The main problem with the question 'Can the subaltern speak?'
is that it posits a fictive, but all too potent, white supremacist,
'Western' interlocutor as the principal arbiter of truth, judge
of history, target of any issue that the subaltern might raise or
query. The question Spivak asks reinscribes the colonial constitution of this fictive white man as the Scribe-in-Chief of History,
the Prophet of Truth, the Lord of the Mansion. In other words,
Spivak's own question confers misplaced concreteness on the
fictive manufacturing of the notion of 'the West,' reinscribing all
utterances as addressing 'the West.' All his life, indeed, Edward

Said had such a white interlocutor dwelling authoritatively up in a prominent mansion in his own mind; and he tried to convince that white interlocutor that Palestinians have been wronged. Said, by far the most eloquent spokesperson of the Palestinian cause, spent a lifetime addressing this fictive white man, trying to convince him that Palestinians had been dispossessed, and yet he died uncertain that he had succeeded – and he had not. The same is true about Atom Egoyan's film *Ararat* (2002), in which unless and until a white Canadian custom officer is convinced that the Armenian genocide happened, it is as if it did not happen.[16] The simplest and most immediate response to this supposition is (paraphrasing Travis Bickle's/Robert De Niro's menacing question, but with the same attitude, in Martin Scorsese's *Taxi Driver* of 1976): 'You talkin' to me? You talkin' to me? – well, I'm not talkin' to you!' Whether or not the subaltern can speak is not for 'the West' to know – or, better still, it is for the subaltern to know and for the fictive white interlocutor to guess. This imperial assumption that anything that happens anywhere in the world is the business of 'the West' is at the heart of Spivak's question.

Another problem with the question is its presumed mimetic absolutism regarding any act of representation – that the act of representing the subaltern is total, final, and definitive. That seems a particularly strange position for a prominent deconstructionist to hold. No act of representation – in good or in bad faith – is ever complete or total, and the mimetic gap that remains between the fact of the phenomenon and the act of representing it always (already) dismantles and discredits any legislative contract between the represented and the representative. In political acts of defiance, in particular, which is the subject of the subaltern's revolt, acts of representation chase after the event, the act of the revolt, rather than the other way around. This particular problem with the question that Spivak raises points to a specific issue regarding academic attempts at representing/theorizing political acts of revolt, where the academic intellectual thinks s/he is causing or representing what s/he is barely trying to understand. In the case of the question 'Can the subaltern speak?' the intellectual places the horse behind the carriage and wonders if the carriage can pull the horse.

Related to this latter problem is the fallacy of taking the representation of something for the thing itself. The subaltern acts in collective ways (strikes, revolts, uprisings), or else speaks through critical and creative works of its own making (art, literature, cinema, photography, poetry, etc.). All of these actions and works exist *before* they (e.g. deeds, words, images) are represented, packaged, reported, theorized, or dismissed by the academic theorist. The armchair intellectual, identifying with the subaltern or questioning this identification, has nothing to do with those acts, words and pictures of actual and figurative revolt. At best s/he will report or fail to report them, understand or fail to understand what they mean or anticipate.

Even more fundamentally, the question 'Can the subaltern speak?' categorically glosses over the central political parallax of class antagonisms that don't just pre-date but foreground any act of representation. Writing or speaking about revolt is an *ex post facto* narrative option: it does not pre-date the political act, it follows it; it does not cause it, and it may succeed or fail to explain its cause(s). The question 'Can the subaltern speak?' confuses the condition and the act of revolt with the epiphenomenon of its historiography. Subalternity is not a literary proposition; it is a political condition. Suppose the subaltern cannot speak; can it not act? Speaking is not the *conditio sine qua non* of subalternity; action is.

The most obvious response that the rhetorical and self-indulgent question 'Can the subaltern speak?' hides is: yes, of course the subaltern – notwithstanding the sum total of the misery that the abusive world economic system and the tyrannies that sustain it have generated and sustained – speaks, sings, dances, paints, makes movies, writes and directs plays, and so on; but the subaltern does all those things in front of and for the other subalterns who sit there and watch, reading, listen and, above all, rise up in revolt. Whether or not the intellectual can hear the subaltern speak, sing, dance, play, or revolt is not the subaltern's problem. Perhaps the academic intellectual needs a hearing aid.

No critique of logocentricism, with which the Derridian position dismantles all acts of representation, or the constitution of the knowing subject, leads to the conclusion that the subaltern, as subaltern, cannot speak. This is particularly the case in literary and artistic traditions such as those in Iran or prevalent among Muslims in general, where this logocentricism of philosophical discourses (in the plural) is constitutionally compromised by the nomocentricity of law and the homocentricity of mysticism. These multiple narrative devices and strategies do not posit a speech impediment for the subaltern; they enable them to act and speak more eloquently. It is particularly crucial to keep in mind, in this respect, the fact that social uprisings (in which the subalterns revolt) are not primarily *speech acts*; they are *social acts*, and as such operate through the open-ended working of what some sociologists used to call 'symbolic interactionism,' a mode of sociological analysis that was particularly pertinent in its application to urban sociology and social movements.[17] Extrapolated from the work of George Herbert Mead (1863–1931) and Charles Horton Cooley (1864–1929), symbolic interactionism considered social actors as developing their attitudes towards their social actions based on the meaning they derived from specific social conditions. Sociability and social action are the conditions in which social actors attribute meaning to their deeds. At times, these deconstructionist strategies are predicated on very positivist notions of text, textuality, and meaning. Symbolically mediated social interactions and the open-ended interpretations they entail are the primary modus operandi of the meaning people attribute to their social actions. The subaltern is no exception, and in fact more so in moments of social uprisings – long before anyone speaks for them.

Can Iranians speak? Of course they can. Of course the subaltern can speak. The right question is, is the theorist able to listen and learn? Nobody speaks for the subaltern. The subaltern acts and speaks for the subaltern, and when subalterns act collectively they speak through the social, symbolic, and collective language of their uprising. Iranians are out and about and mobilized in a civil rights movement that speaks its own language to those who care to decipher and understand it. Those who dismiss, denigrate, or question its domestic rootedness will face the (not so gentle) judgment of history. The cosmopolitan character of that history that has given birth to and is now defining the character and disposition of the movement will unfold in terms distinct to that culture and worldly in disposition. In the making of that cosmopolitan culture, the two opposing categories of home and exile, through the intermediary role of expatriate intellectuals – building the ideal of a homeland when far away from it – have given birth to a far more worldly attitude towards their otherwise estranged, or else nativized, culture. It is precisely that cosmopolitan imagination that has now returned to inhabit and inform the Green Movement in Iran.

EIGHT

Retrieval of a Cosmopolitan Culture

IN ORDER TO MAKE MY CASE for the Green Movement as the return of Iranian cosmopolitan culture, beyond any measure of sustained control by the Islamic Republic, I have so far provided both a deep history and a wide range of contemporaneous indices of its theory and practice, its thinking and modes of aesthetic manifestation. In this final chapter, I wish to present a final body of evidence: the body itself – the return of the repressed in the body of the *corpus eroticus*.

Love Letters

Dwelling in the hidden subconscious of the story of the Monkey King Kardanah is the misogyny implicit in the message that the treacherous Turtle's wife and her female friend conspire to send to her husband informing him that she is terminally ill and that he needs to rush home, whereupon they plan to kill the Monkey King. Medieval Persian wisdom narratives are peppered with such misogynist leitmotifs, and it is precisely against those enduring narrative themes that the feminist dimensions of a defiant subject are today to be assayed. It is thus to the reversal of that repressed misogyny, and the agential assertion of women as social actors, that we need to return in this conclusion, and revisit the 'message' (in the form of a letter) of an entirely different sort that Iranian women were sending to their jailed husbands in the course of the Green Movement's mobilization in the aftermath of the contested June 2009 presidential election. In these letters we are witness to a living body of evidence.

During the rise and subsequent unfolding of the Green Movement in Iran in the aftermath of the June 2009 election, BBC Persian Television and its website emerged as a major force and principal source of daily information about the uprising, with the Voice of America (VOA) Persian program as its major contender. Benefitting from a superior cadre of professional journalists, BBC Persian soon became a key factor in the unfolding drama, a fact reflected in the aggressive hostility that the custodians of the Islamic Republic and its security apparatus displayed both to the BBC and to its perceived sponsor, the British government. To be sure, the mushrooming of Persian weblogs and websites had by then seriously challenged the primacy of news organizations per se, BBC Persian or otherwise, as the source of news. Weblogs and websites, along with mobile phone images and short videos taken by Iranian demonstrators themselves, achieved an almost exclusive currency within their own civil rights movement. Nevertheless, BBC Persian had established a certain canonicity for itself, if for no other reason than that the name 'BBC' had carried an authority ever since World War II in Iran and in the rest of the region formerly under the colonial gaze of the British Empire.

In a memorable piece aired late in February 2010, BBC Persian concentrated on the spouses of some of the leading Iranian reformers who were jailed soon after the June 2009 election, and specifically on the public love letters that these women were writing to their incarcerated husbands.[1] To be sure, the program segment revealed nothing new to those following the unfolding events closely through the myriad Persian weblogs and websites. The departure was in the fact that the women were expressing their affections for their husbands as well as using the occasion to expand the public domain of the political discourse, merging and fusing it with the private and thereby articulating the democratic cause for which their husbands were being intimidated, harassed, jailed, and in some cases kept for months in solitary confinement. Thee letters were beautifully composed, endearing in their diction and expressions of affection, revealing the personal and private aspects of the lives of some very public figures. The love letters had a palpable erotic intonation.

Referring to the infamous prison in Tehran, 'Asheqaneh-ha-ye Evin'/'Evin Love Letters' was BBC Persian's way of catching up with what bloggers and website news addicts had known and been following closely for some time. Fatemeh Shams and Fakhr al-Sadadt Mohtashami-pour were the respective spouses of two prominent political prisoners – Mohammad Reza Jalaipour and Mostafa Tajzadeh, respectively – that the BBC report was featuring as prime examples of the writers of these love letters. Fatemeh Shams was filmed writing, left-handed, in her notebook one of her famous letters to her husband Mohammad Reza, and then saying how much she missed him. Fakhr al-Sadat Mohtashami-pour, for her part, had been reached by telephone in Tehran and her voice recorded reading a short passage from one of her widely publicized letters to her husband. The piece so far was quite effective, interjected with a melodic love song, matched by a sympathetic reporter's voice-over. We were witness to something new and exciting, certainly unprecedented: Iranian women expressing love publicly for their husbands.

Covering the Evidence

The BBC Persian piece was progressing well when suddenly a professor of nineteenth-century Iranian history from Santa Barbara in California was introduced by way of providing an expert analytical commentary on these women and their love letters. With the introduction of the professor's voice and image, against the backdrop of a row of colorful books on a bookshelf, and her professorial demeanor, with its condescending attitude and discourse, the two authors of love letters to their husbands were turned into 'traditional' specimens, with their identities frozen as 'Muslim.' They were thus instantly transformed into objects of the professor's ethnographic curiosity, *ipso facto* casting her as the distant and distancing authority who analyzes and makes sense of such letters, which otherwise would evidently have been mis-understood. Here was an authority on love letters; those love let-ters needed an expert's opinion and professorial exposition. Thus the piece became a strange case of flawed journalism, whereby the introduction of a small measure of one wrong ingredient suddenly reduced the force of the narrative and irretrievably destroyed the significance of the program.

By the time the BBC piece had run its course, the two thus ethnicized and denominated 'Muslim women' (one marked by her scarf, the other present only by her voice) were made – entirely unbeknownst to themselves – to provide ethnographic samples and testimonials for the professorial mind and voice to analyze and explain. With the introduction of a single factor, suddenly the professor, the BBC reporter, the BBC Persian program, their presumed audience, and the entire verbal and visual idiomaticity of the piece were all cast on one side as *spectator* and Fatemeh Shams and Fakhr al-Sadat Mohtashami-pour on the other as *the spectacle* – robbed of their agency, autonomy, authority, and defiance. That these two women were two of the most prominent activists in the civil rights movement of their homeland was not part of the manufactured narrative. They were, before our eyes, violently de-subjected. But what was even more troubling was the aggressive transmutation of those letters into their opposite: they were now not the narrative traces of two women's agential autonomy, but instead the ethnographic evidence of their voiceless passivity.

For the rest of the piece – now an unwatchable ethnographic game of power between the voice of the narrator and the demeanor of the professor on the one side and the two Muslim women on the other – BBC Persian Television continued to alienate and distance the two 'Muslim women' and authenticate the academic expert as the facilitator authorized to psychoanalyze the two provided samples. The two 'Muslim women' were thus effectively de-authorized, their agential autonomy as the authors of their own letters and masters of their own lives taken away from them and handed over to the evidently 'not-Muslim' professor to elucidate. As the negational denominator of the 'Islamic Republic,' and as the bugbear of Western European and North American Islamophobia, 'Islam' was thus the not-so-hidden force of this divide. Completely hidden now was the substance, the bodily disposition, of these letters, and with it the hearts and minds of those who had written them. Ethnography could scarcely be more demeaning, anthropology more de-subjecting, Orientalism more efficient at robbing a people of their ability to represent themselves. What was being misrepresented was no mere account of two women writing love letters to their respective husbands, but the narrative evidence of a bodily awareness that was, and remains, definitive of the Green Movement.

The effective (and affective) subjection of the professorial voice and the simultaneous de-subjection (indeed catalytic objectification) of the two Muslim women (thus frozen in this identity by the BBC piece) suddenly placed the gaze of the BBC camera and the voice-over of the reporter at the service of the unveiled professor providing expository ethnographic commentary about things happening inside Iran – *behind the veil*, as it were. This distancing power of the gaze, this positing and positioning of an *inside* space in need of explanation by an *outsider* – reinforced by the face-off between two inarticulate natives and a loquacious expert; a mute text and a verbose interpreter; two Muslim women and a modern-looking interpreter (evidently non-Muslim, for Muslims cannot be modern, as Bernard Lewis has decreed); the two objects veiled and the person authorized to interpret them unveiled – flew in the face of the report itself, which was undoing itself as it unfolded. For here were two eloquent writers of their own lives and loves being turned into the anthropological objects of curiosity in need of explanation. Fatemeh Shams and Fakhr al-Sadat Mohtashami-pour spoke an infinitely superior Persian, when they were allowed to speak, and wrote with a poetic sensibility far beyond that evidenced by their interpreter; and yet here they were turned upside down and made to look like silenced Oriental curiosities needing to be explained – interpreted – by the professor and her learning. The 'extra-textual' fact (omitted from the BBC piece) that Fatemeh Shams is a published poet, a prominent blogger, an accomplished prose stylist, a doctoral student at Oxford University, writing a D.Phil. thesis on contemporary Persian poetry, or that Fakhr al-Sadat Mohtashami-pour is the deputy director of the Reformist Women's Organization (Na'ib Ra'is Majma' Zanan Eslah-talab), or that these women are two of the most prominent civil rights activists of their generation, are factors that never entered the equation. The BBC Persian piece was the negation of itself: it concealed what it was addressing. With every sentence and every second of the piece, the phenomenon staring the audience in the face – the rise of a poetics of the body revealing itself in epistolary prose form – was buried ever more deeply.

Qeshr-e Sonnati

Within minutes of the broadcast, the blogosphere and Facebook were filling with praise and sympathy for the two Iranian women, along with comments critical of BBC Persian Television. One particular phrase the professor had used was especially irksome to the bloggers and Facebook 'friends.' She had said that the letters were particularly 'interesting' for having been written by representatives of *Qeshr-e Sonnati*/'the traditional layer,' thus emphatically identifying the women as pious and practicing Muslim, and as such 'traditional.' The condescending phrasing of *Qeshr-e Sonnati*, which betrays a pronounced bourgeois disdain for Muslim piety, laid bare the attitude, and the obvious politics, of the professor. Yet in revealing that attitude – and here is the rub – the phrase *Qeshr-e Sonnati* covered spoke of something far more important: namely, what the letters revealed, notwithstanding the professorial commentary.

What accounts for this immediate and vociferous negative response? Two radically opposed readings of Iranian society, predicated on divergent readings of people's lives, and the youth in particular, were in play at the time of this broadcast. While the professor was anchoring her argument in the 'traditional' nature of the culture that produced these letters, uppermost in the minds of the television audience was precisely the contrary proposition: that young Iranian men and women were in fact engaged in promiscuous sexual behaviour, including nocturnal orgies, by way of social protest – an argument put forward by the US-trained and California-based anthropologist Pardis Mahdavi. Just weeks before the Green Movement erupted, Mahdavi published a book, *Passionate Uprisings: Iran's Sexual Revolution* (2009), in which she argued that, in the absence of any option for overt political dissent, young people have become part of a self-proclaimed revolution in which they are using their bodies to make social and political statements. Sex has become both a source of freedom and an act of political rebellion.

A year into the Green Movement, by far the largest and most dramatic act of political dissent since the 1979 revolution, and with young men and women at its forefront, the publication of this book was embarrassingly ill-timed. Its argument – that by engaging in sexual escapades young Iranians were expressing their political dissent, when all else was barred to them[2] – not only disregarded the sustained course of political activism and engagement taken over the last thirty years by young and old Iranians alike, but interpreted the natural and healthy sexual activity prevalent in any society as the sole sign of radical political activism. The population of Iran at the time of the 1979 revolution was about 40 million; when Pardis Mahdavi took her summer vacation in Iran and turned her own family and friends into objects of ethnographic curiosity in the first decade of the twenty-first century the population had risen to some 75 million. So obviously Iranians enjoy having sex as much as anyone else. But was that all they did by way of political protest? The space between the portrayal of Iran as a land of Oriental harems enabling sexual excess, on the one hand, and the strange phenomenon of 'traditional women' writing love letters to their husbands, on the other, is where a society ought to be allowed – by historians of the nineteenth century and twenty-first-century anthropologists alike – to sustain the variety of its social behaviour, political activity, and of course erotic mores, without being overinterpreted in one way or another.

Barring both extremes – sexual sensationalism and asexual traditionalism – the beautiful, elegant, and at once politically and erotically charged love letters of Fatemeh Shams and Fakhr al-Sadat

Mohtashami-pour to their husbands mark a particularly poignant transmutation of *public* and *private* domains, the political and the erotic, in contemporary Iranian literary and political culture – a crucial development whose full impact is yet to be assayed beyond the clichéd binary of *tradition versus modernity*, which is quite unable to account for what we are witnessing. The letters need far more sensitive and genealogical analysis within the contemporary Iranian context before we are able to assess their significance in the process of retrieval of cosmopolitan culture. To be able openly and affectionately to talk about one's love for one's spouse is predicated on a full and robust conception of the body as the physical site and sign of a cosmopolitan culture that overshadows and trespasses on all the ideological and metaphysical alienations contingent upon it. It is this bodily evidence that we need to recognize, historicize, and lay bare before we conclude anything worldly or wise about the first and final site of the Green Movement.

One of the best-known texts from the previous generation of Iranian women literati, which might serve as point of reference here, is the powerful and endearing narrative of Simin Daneshvar (b. 1921), a leading literary figure, about her husband, the prominent Iranian public intellectual Jalal Al-e Ahmad (1923–1969). The two texts *Shoharam Jalal/My Husband Jalal* and *Ghorub Jalal/The Sunset of Jalal* were groundbreaking in their time, not so much because the author expressed public affection for her husband but because she used the occasion both to reflect publicly on her famous husband's character and to expand this reflection into a wider discussion of social issues.[3]

Mirroring Simin Daneshvar, though far more provocatively and in poetic diction, Forough Farrokhzad (1935–1967) is now legendary among Iranians for her open and elegiac expression of love for Ebrahim Golestan, the prominent Iranian filmmaker and literary figure, particularly in two famous poems, *Tavallodi*

Digar/'Another Birth' and *Asheqaneh*/'Lovingly'. In these and all her other poems, Farrokhzad's expression of love is obviously in the introverted form of poetic disguise – dedicating her *Tavallodi Digar* to 'alef/gaf' (A/E. G., the initials of Ebrahim Golestan in Persian) being the only signal she gave that she meant Ebrahim Golestan.[4] After Forough Farrokhzad, any Iranian woman might quote a poem of hers by way of expressing her affection for the man she loved – that is, that expression had become a socially coded reference to a poetically encoded expression of love, effectively a disguise in a disguise.

Beyond prose and poetry, the popular music scene has also witnessed a very strong antecedent and preparatory stage for what now the prose of Fatemeh Shams and Fakhr al-Sadat Mohtashami-pour represents. Women pop artists – from Qamar al-Moluk Vaziri and Moluk Zarrabi early in the twentieth century, down to Marziyeh and Delkash mid-century, to Googoosh and Ramesh just before the Islamic Revolution, and then Hayedeh and Mahasti, who enjoyed their popularity long after the revolution – represent another lyrical and musical form of female expression of love for a male object of desire; though in this case most of the song lyrics were in fact composed by men for women singers, with the odd and inadvertent homoerotic undertone of women singers' object of affection, when they sang these songs, being the female features of their beloved! Be that as it may, a woman pop singer expressing in public her love for an object of her desire was a crucial stepping stone to what would come to maturity decades into the Islamic Revolution, even though the Revolution did all it could to silence this voice. In the course of the Green Movement this retrieval of the *corpus eroticus* represents a clear indication of an enduring synergy underlying the body politic.

In the modernist Persian novel, as well as in cinema and drama, we are witness to a few memorable female figures perfectly capable of publicly expressing their feelings for the men they love. The character of Maral in Mahmoud Dolatabadi's novel *Klidar* (1963–1978) is perhaps the perfect example in modern Persian literature of a valiant woman in love. The fact that in the whole of contemporary Iranian cinema or drama one can only think of a handful of memorable women in love is itself an indication of the scarcity of the phenomenon in public. It is precisely for that reason that the roots of this eventual development, for a woman to write a public love letter to the man she loves (and especially, as in Fatemeh Shams's case, with a palpable erotic undertone), in fact run much deeper than contemporary history allows. Legendary figures like Shirin in Nezami's (1141–1209) 'Khosrow and Shirin' story in *Khamseh*, or Tahmineh in Ferdowsi's (935–1020) 'Rostam and Sohrab' story in *Shahnameh*, or even the transgressive love of Sudabeh for Seyavash in their story in *Shahnameh*, are crucial but nevertheless limited examples of prominent women who exercise agential autonomy in their expression of love and who are conscious, proud, and determined in their pursuit of the man they love.[5] The social body, as the *locus classicus* of a defiant politics, is where the public displaying of a physical (not metaphorical) love letter becomes a critical event.

Historically, women, with few exceptions in literature or elsewhere in history (such as in the legendary case of the mid-nineteenth-century Babi revolutionary poet and activist Tahereh Qorrat al-Ayn, 1814–1852), have been the *objects* of affection (*Ma'shuq*), and not its *subject* (*Asheq*).[6] Leaving aside for the moment the fact that in Persian poetry *Ma'shuq* is not gender-specific (for Persian has no gender-specific pronouns; *dustash daram* can signify both 'I love her' or 'I love him,' as both are uttered mostly by a male poet), *Asheq* is a male and definitively masculinist category. In classical Persian literature, only men are cast in the active role of *Asheq*; while women are invariably relegated to the passive position of being Ma'shuq. The word Ma'shuqeh in Persian is in fact doubly feminized, and thus close to the English word 'Mistress.' It was not until the aftermath of the Islamic Revolution that, in a singular act of cinematic liberation, his film Gabbeh (1996), Mohsen Makhmalbaf turned this literary trope around visually by constructing all the close-ups of the leading woman protagonist as her looking at the long shots of the man she loves! These close-ups of the young woman, Gabbeh/Shaghayeh Djodat, served to turn her visually into an Asheq, and the long shots of the man she loved made him a Ma'shuq – an entirely revolution- ary moment in the Persian literary and visual imagination.[7] Without careful attention being paid to such cultural detail, the significance of the public love letters that have surfaced during the rise of the Green Movement will not be recognized – that is, as both amorous and erotic act, and as bearers of political significance.

Those historical, literary, poetic, and cinematic overtures that anticipate the prose and poetry that Fatemeh Shams and Fakhr al-Sadat Mohtashami-pour now write grew far from Santa Barbara, California and in the bone marrow of a social body within the Is- lamic Republic. From the trials and tribulations of ordinary people living in extraordinary times the pain and joy of a purposeful life, and indeed from the erotic disposition of Shi'ism itself, for more than three decades Iranian filmmakers, artists, photographers, bloggers, and feminist activists (the real ones, not those that grow parasitically in American military and foreign-policy circles) have been at work fusing the erotic and the political in the fictive borderlines of the private and the public. In the hidden heart of public space, in cyberspace, the defiant prose of the bloggers (young women in particular) has been chiefly responsible for this public and open expression of love. As crosscurrent forces, the poetic and the erotic moved forward under the tyranny of the

Islamic Republic in art, literature, drama, and cinema. Together they conspired to beguile the anthropologist who, on summer vacation in Tehran, turned her friends and family into 'the subjects' of her fieldwork, describing a 'passionate uprising,' in the words of one, and who saw fit to observe that the religious sensibilities of prominent women like Zahra Rahnavard, now a leading member of the Green Movement, indicated a psychological defect in their character, which could be readily diagnosed with the aid of a quotation or two from Erich Fromm. This kind of prevalent commentary, which secures tenure and sustains academic careers, conceals, distorts, and above all betrays the factual evidence of a people's terms of emancipation.

It remains only to reverse the angle of the analytical gaze that BBC Persian Television had focused on Fatemeh Shams and Fakhr al-Sadat Mohtashami-pour, for to do so reveals the transmutation of the public and the private that has occurred inside Iran, on the battlefields of history, and not on North American university campuses, where academic analysts have a hard time catching up with the world – their tired vocabularies and Orientalized imaginations lagging behind, or occasionally running ahead of, the fast pace of their former homeland, the loss of which has failed to produce a moral commitment to any other cause, with the exception of their own careers. The letters that the two women write to the men they love are infinitely more powerful than any poem that even the great Forough Farrokhzad wrote, for these letters are the natural outgrowth of the abstract lyrics of Hafez – naked prose, deeply personal, potently political, with the fragile face of humanity written over its confident cadences.[8] It is of course impossible to imagine the rise of this prose without the poetry of master lyricists like Forough Farrokhzad and Ahmad Shamlou. But this prose rises emotively much higher than anything we have witnessed before – and the good professor from Santa Barbara sent

BBC Persian viewers on a wild goose chase when she attributed them to the *Qeshr-e Sonnati*.

In Iran things have moved beyond the false and falsifying binary of modernity/tradition (*Sonnat/Tajaddod*), though both the theocratic fanaticism that rules Iran and the expatriate secular fanaticism of bourgeois feminists who oppose it are still very much trapped within their own hateful oppositional stance towards each other. The prose that Fatemeh Shams and Fakhr al-Sadat Mohtashami-pour write is that which has informed a politics beyond violence, whereas the expatriate bourgeois feminism that denigrates it as belonging to *Qeshr-e Sonnati* still speaks the language of an analytic of violence. Those thus designated have long since escaped this violence, as well as the violence that caused an outdated feminism to exile itself in the nearest university campus. The two women, then, are representatives of a generation whose emancipatory prose is changing the very grammar of a political culture, while those who seek to pigeonhole them according to their own analytical framework have yet to fathom what they are about.

What the condescending reference to *Qeshr-e Sonnati* fails to note is that the people who are presented as 'the subjects' of someone else's observations have long since left such clichés behind. What is needed instead is a new set of analytical parameters based on empathy, so that we may in fact learn from a people's struggles (rather than presume to teach them), and understand what animates and agitates them, or else what makes them happy. Their poetry, their art, their cinema, their drama, their daily blogs, and their aspirations are where the roots of these love letters lie. When Mostafa Tajzadeh, a prominent reformist and the husband of Fakhr al-Sadat Mohtashami-pour, was momentarily freed from jail, days before the Persian New Year, Facebook was abuzz with pictures of Mir Hossein Mousavi and Zahra Rahnavard and other prominent reformists visiting his home. Mohammad Reza Jalaipour, husband of Fatemeh Shams, was another of these visitors. One needs to view these pictures and witness Facebook 'walls' dancing with joy in order to comprehend what has happened in Iran. That involves leaving behind the frozen nineteenth-century frame of reference and its isomorphic idea of 'tradition versus modern,' and taking the trouble to inhabit the twenty-first century. Against the grain of militant Islamism, the body has not become political; the body has retrieved its erotic overtone in the prose of these love letters. This is where the Islamic Republic is facing its most enduring challenge – the challenge that will be its undoing. Under the veneer of false modernity, the flawed analytic of *Qeshr-e Sonnati*/'this traditional class' doubly covers that zone, precisely where it has historically revealed itself. The 'modern' interpreter is far more prudishly veiled and veiling than the interpreted 'traditional.'

Fatemeh Shams was a gifted poet long before the cruel separa-tion from her husband made the young couple suffer the hardship of being apart and created the conditions in which her letters were written. Her letters to her husband have nothing to do with this thing called *Qeshr-e Sonnati*. Secular fundamentalists see a scarf and run for cover, as it were. You must have a heart (from where love letters are written) to be able to see and feel the joy of this generation (regardless of their being 'religious' or not), and have the power of empathy in order to understand the meaning and significance of these letters, before you can have an idea what has happened in Iran since the nineteenth century. Central to the formation of this social phenomenon, for example, has been the rise of what the bloggers call *tan-neveshteh*/'body-writings' – a sustained and provocative flow of prose that young women bloggers, in particular, have been writing about their own bodily (erotic) experiences.[9] Related to these *tan-neveshteh-ha* has been *del-neveshteh*/'heart-writing' – writing about one's love and affection, again practiced mostly by young women.[10] The narrative fusion of

tan/body and *del*/heart, particularly in the remissive space of the
blog, defines the metaphorical realm in which this prose form is
incubated. Something has happened in Iran over the last thirty
years that defies augury. What it is must be learned, not taught.

The Retrieval of a Cosmopolitan Culture
on the Site of the Social Body

As we know well from the poetry of Forough Farrokhzad and
Ahmad Shamlou in the previous generation, the erotic body is
politicized in the course of dramatic social uprisings. The false
binary *tradition/modernity* covers and distorts this body, either
concealing its sexuality or else scandalizing it, precisely at a time
when a resurgent cosmopolitan culture is in fact revealing it to
be beyond any such binary. The tradition/modernity binary was
the product of a colonial and colonized imagination and has long
since lost its epistemic force and operative currency. The public
love letters that Fatemeh Shams and Fakhr al-Sadadt Mohtashami-
pour, among others, have written to their husbands are the signs
of a quite different mode of socialization (hitherto denied and
violently repressed), which the manufactured binary *religious/secular*
has successfully concealed. These letters are not a development
that surprises because they come from a retrograde *Qeshr-e Sonnati*,
or traditional class; rather, they are perfectly joyous and normal
expressions, the signs of a healthy retrieval of the social body[11]
that has naturally grown in the body politic of a nation. As such
they require renewed modes of understanding that are in tune
with reality. The public fusion of the political and the erotic is
the defining moment of this resurgent social body as it retrieves
and defines its emancipated cosmopolitan disposition. What we
thus see in this robust and life-affirming prose is not a retrograde
traditionalism (a conception that in fact betrays the retrograde

secularism of the analyst) but its precise opposite: the retrieval of a cosmopolitan culture all but destroyed by the Islamic Republic, all but invisible to fanatical secularism. Islam is integral to that cosmopolitan worldliness but not definitive of it – as indeed is the dual delusion of secularism. To see that fact, of course, you must start treating a human being like a human being, rather than calling the European modernity police the instant you see a woman in a scarf.

The retrieval of this social body is the most hopeful sign of a fundamental change in the politics of the region. Today 'the Middle East' spells a politics of despair, a phantasm trapped inside a culture of violent defeatism. Most of the states in the region, from Morocco to Syria, are ruled by undemocratic potentates. Of the only two states that have a semblance of democratic institutions, one (the Jewish State of Israel) is a colonial settlement built on the broken back of another people's homeland, and the other (the Islamic Republic of Iran) is an abusive theocratic garrison state (to borrow Harold Lasswell's 1941 conception of the United States) seething with discontent. What the desperate geopolitics of the region manages to conceal is the far richer and enduring legacy of each and every individual nation-state in their prolonged history of struggle for self-governance, democratic institutions, social justice, and civil liberties. Today the Green Movement in Iran marks the return of the repressed, the retrieval of the cosmopolitan culture that thirty years of Islamic Republic has failed to suppress; and the public disposition of the erotically mapped social body is the first and final site of its political potency, that which will undo the Islamic Republic. This cosmopolitanism stands against not just the parochialism of the Islamic Republic but also against the tribalism of the Jewish State and Christian imperialism. The desire for total revolution was a product of European modernity, as Bernard Yack has ably demonstrated,[12] and at the colonial end of the selfsame modernity the desire was doubly urgent. European modernity overcame its Christian obstacles via a total revolution. As Fanon demonstrated, on the colonial side, too, a total revolution was needed. Thus, some two hundred years into colonial modernity what we are witnessing in Iran is the end of colonially mitigated modernity, whereby the subaltern can finally speak a language that the colonizer can understand, namely by changing the interlocutor and not speaking to him (it is always 'him'). In these terms the Green Movement is the first postmodern uprising, the occasion for the first postcolonial postulation of liberty no longer in self-defeating oppositional relation to (and determined by) 'the West.'

What the Green Movement also reveals is the historical role of Islam in the making of multiple cosmopolitan cultures, a fact now entirely hidden under the immediacy of unfolding events. A major point of contention in understanding contemporary Muslims and the modern Islamic world is the false binary opposition that tends to be maintained between Islam and the West. In this essentialist distinction, which holds not just in the public domain but also in much contemporary critical thinking, 'Islam' is usually posited as a quintessential, monolithic, and entirely ahistorical proposition, while 'the West' is presumed in equally categorical and definitive terms. The very suggestion of this binary opposition cross-essentializes two otherwise multifaceted historical phenomena. As prominent a contemporary philosopher and public intellectual as Jürgen Habermas is comfortable with categorizing the predicament of Iraq in the aftermath of the First Gulf War (1990–91) as one singularly afflicted by 'Shi'i fundamentalism,' or with positing an uncompromising question such as: 'Are the principles of international law so intertwined with the standards of Western rationality – a rationality built, as it were, to Western culture – that such principles are of no use for the nonpartisan adjudication of international conflicts?' or with the equally ahistorical pronouncement: 'the understandable disposition of the masses to win back for their Islamic world a measure of self-respect against a Western world that is still perceived as colonialist.'[13]

From such ahistorical and conceptually flawed tropes defining the critical vocabulary of one of the most prominent European philosophers to the public pronouncements of former US president George W. Bush, former UK prime minster Tony Blair, or even Pope Benedict XVI – namely the most powerful and influential figures who form public opinion and shape the nature of our civic discourse – a binary opposition between an essentialized 'Islam' and an equally ahistorical 'West' has determined the language and disposition of almost everything that is publicly held and politically consequential about a manufactured and transhistorical encounter between two major (thus separated) components of humanity. With the rise of the civil rights movement in Iran, this binary is finally overcome: the body politic is exposing its erotogenic zones, assuming its rightful public place, demanding and exacting constitutional recognition. This is what those colorful rallies of the Green Movement, with singing and dancing in the streets and highways, public squares and around (phallic) social symbols like Borj-e Azadi/'Freedom Tower' in Tehran, mean.

Preventing a full recognition of the Green Movement in its own terms are the enduring thick walls dividing the world along colonially manufactured and analytically sustained barriers – barriers that reveal more about the colonized minds that speak them than anything they wish to interpret. The more vacationing anthropologists spend their summers in beauty salons in Tehran and come back with a book to secure their tenure in a North American university, the more people around the world are robbed of their agency precisely at the moment that they are remaking their history. Once posited in terms of these false binary oppositions,

Islam and Muslims lose all their internal dynamics, geographical expansiveness, cultural dispositions, doctrinal variations, thematic tendencies, sectarian proclivities, and perhaps above all their prolonged historical developments. In the very same vein, 'the West,' and people who live in Western Europe and North Africa, become a catatonic condition of authenticity, a moral and normative measure beyond cultures and conditions, a civilizational term outside the fold of world history, ready for the trope that represents them to be as much cherished and celebrated by some as demonized and denounced by others.

Facing the fallacious fabrication of a dangerous liaison and a perilous binary between 'Islam and the West,' and altering the terms of public conversation about Islam and Muslims in their immediate, regional, and global contexts so that we are able to come to terms with what an uprising such as the Green Movement in Iran might mean, we can begin with one simple proposition: that throughout their long and venerable history, Muslims have always been in creative, critical, or even combatant conversation with a variety of political, moral, or intellectual interlocutors. This historical fact has given Islam a quintessentially dialogical disposition. In combative battles and skirmishes with Sassanid and Byzantine imperial institutions, imaginaries, and practices, the first Islamic dynasties of the Umayyads (651–750) and then the Abbasids (750–1258) were formed. In a long, productive conversation with Greek philosophy, the vast and multifaceted aspects of Islamic philosophy were formed. In both hidden and manifest exchanges with Jewish theology, various schools of Islamic theology took shape. In similar dialogues with Christian asceticism, Hindu and Buddhist Gnosticism, and Neoplatonic philosophy, Islamic mysticism took shape. In eventual conversation with Pahlavi and Sanskrit literatures, Arabic (as well as Persian, Turkish, and Urdu) literary humanism emerged. Following exposure to Greek, Indian, and Chinese sciences, various disciplines of Islamic science developed. And then ultimately, and most immediately evident in contemporary terms, following Muslim encounters with European colonialism and Enlightenment modernity, a diverse range of ideological movements and political thought came to preoccupy Muslim thinkers and define the modern Islamic world – always in dialogical and progressively unfolding terms. Cosmopolitan worldliness is defining of Muslim identity, as Islam is integral to that worldliness but not constitutive of it. The Green Movement is a manifestation of that cosmopolitanism: the return of what the Islamic Republic had spent thirty violent years trying to repress.

Working from this proposition – that the history of Islam is a history of productive dialogue – we can begin to see the cosmopolitan culture of medieval Islam by way of a preliminary outline of how that dialogical disposition was conducive to the eventual creation of a multifaceted, syncretic, and polyfocal civilization. The rise of literary humanism (*Adab*) in its Arabic, Persian, Turkish, and Urdu contexts is central to this cosmopolitanism, as is the major multicultural urbanism in Muslim lands – in Damascus, Baghdad, Cairo, Istanbul, Cordoba, Isfahan, and Delhi in particular. The territorial and material basis of Islamic civilization, as well as the discursive formation of the symbolics and institutions of higher learning, are the *locus classicus* of this worldly cosmopolitanism. Without first and foremost coming to terms with this worldliness, we will never come close to what is lurking under the thin skin of fear and fanaticism in postcolonial Muslim societies, through which massive uprisings like the Green Movement emerge.

The internal dynamics of Islam itself has historically broken it down into its discursive, institutional, and symbolic forms (or, if preferred, its doctrinal, ritual, and communal formations) – all complementing or competing with each other, and contributing to make Islam a constitutionally multifaceted and cosmopolitan culture, and thus dialectically denying any one component to assume a dominant or exclusionary status. *Polyfocal* has always been the discursive disposition of Islam, just as the languages and cultures in which it speaks have been *polyvocal*, and the geographical domains and domesticities of its historical manifestations *polylocal*. The polyfocality of the Islamic epistemic cultures has spoken and written itself in conflicting *nomocentric* (the law-centered Sharia), *logocentric* (the reason-centered Falsafah), and *homocentric* (the human-centered Tasawwuf or Irfan) languages and lexicons. The centrality of Arabic language in various expressions of Islamic thought has had to contend with an equally powerful tradition in the Persian, Turkish, and Urdu (and now one might even add English) languages – thus giving a distinctly polyvocal disposition to Islamic discourses, all mapped out in a geographical polylocality that has profoundly impacted upon where and when a Muslim speaks a particularly powerful scholastic diction. Only under dire political circumstances does one of these discourses (the nomocentricity of the Islamic law in particular) assume an overriding claim over the entirety of Islam, and always at the heavy expense of repressing, denying, and thus distorting, the factual cosmopolitanism of the Islamic historical experience. In the unfolding of this lived experience of Islamic moral and imaginative history, Islamic cosmopolitanism has wedded its characteristic multifaceted disposition to a rapidly globalized world that has hitherto assigned either a retrograde or a violent disposition to Islam. Today, there is an urgency in the outlining of this historically anchored cosmopolitanism for a large global audience given the rapid globalization of a conception of Islam that is negotiated between two modes of extremism – one systematically demonizing it, the other categorically reducing it to a militant juridicalism. The Green Movement in Iran has arisen from the worldly disposition of that cosmopolitanism that has historically included Islam but has never been limited to it. Militant secularists simply mirror their militant Muslim counterparts, and thereby they mutually collaborate (whilst believing they are opposing each other) in concealing this historical fact about Islam and Muslims, and above all about the world they have inhabited.

The Green Movement is breaking through the cycle of violence that is predicated on a monolithic reading of the binary Islam/the West. Contrary to the enduring assumptions of that binary, the defining disposition of Islam in its encounter with European colonial modernity has been its instrumental presence in a succession of cosmopolitan cultures that embrace and include Islam in its varied forms and doctrinal expressions, but that are not reducible to Islamic religious principles in general or juridical doctrines in particular. Here one must make a distinction between 'Islam' in its doctrinal foundations in the Qur'an and its juridical character in Islamic law (Sharia), on the one hand, and 'Islam' as a cultural category and communal identity that covers a vast body of symbolic, discursive, institutional, and communal domains, on the other. The characterization of a society, thus, as 'Islamic' certainly includes the fundamental beliefs and practices of its inhabitants as Muslims but is by no means limited, and might in fact be contrary, to such doctrinal principles and practices. There are Muslims who are Marxists, and there are Muslims who are anti-colonial nationalists – and these are not contradictory designations; they are perfectly plausible, even logical, for 'Muslim' here is a communal not a doctrinal or ritual designation. We – Muslims and non-Muslims – must expand our conception of Islam and of Muslims if we are to make sense of social uprisings like the Green Movement, which would otherwise defy our abiding categories.

'Islamic societies,' if we are now to characterize them thus, are the *locus classicus* of a vast and diversified body of cosmopolitan mores and practices ranging from the sacred to the profane, and as such not reducible to Islamic or anti-Islamic, religious or anti-religious, sacred or secular, Western or anti-Western identities. Both demographically and culturally, the existence of Jewish, Christian, Hindu, and Buddhist communities alongside Muslims has not been incidental to 'Islamic societies' but in fact a vital factor in their metamorphosis. This view of Islamic civilization is informed by much more than a recognition of Islamic doctrinal beliefs. Positing Islam as a cosmopolitan civilizational category, and doing so in such a way that will have a categorical impact on the way we ordinarily think of the terms 'Islam' or 'Islamic,' particularly in the all-too-important domain of the public construction of knowledge, is a critical epistemic shift in how we view Muslims in their contemporary life. It poses a fundamental challenge to the very division of the world on the basis of an East–West axis – an axis that historically has served more to distort a free and democratic reading of world history than to facilitate any such aspiration. This argument runs contrary to the current fashionable call for 'Islamic reformation' (Tariq Ramadan, Abdolkarim Soroush, Reza Aslan), an entirely unexamined assumption that disregards the integral history of Islam itself. What Muslims need to enable their full participation in global citizenship (notwithstanding the force of political demonization from outside and fanatical reductionism from within), and indeed what the Green Movement is now seeking to achieve, is not 'reformation' but the *restoration* of their own enduring historical cosmopolitanism. The Green Movement is the harbinger of that restoration, where and when Islam has yielded to its worldliness, the world that has always embraced and defined it. It is no accident that the militant Muslims who rule Iran and the militant secularists who oppose them share a suspicion and distrust of the Green Movement.

In specifically ideological terms, the almost simultaneous formation of anti-colonial *nationalism*, transnational *socialism*, and militant

Islamism over the last two hundred years is the clear indication of a multifaceted political culture that is at once domestic to Islamic societies and yet deeply influenced by global factors and forces, the worldliness of Iranians as all other Muslims. The formation of these dominant and profoundly powerful ideological currents over the last two centuries and throughout the Muslim world has been the clear indication that the cosmopolitan disposition of Islamic societies is *ipso facto* irreducible to either 'Western' (modern) or 'anti-Western' (traditional) factors and forces. This mistaken view posits such societies in categorical opposition to the binary 'tradition and modernity,' or 'Islam and the West.' The alternative reading of Islam and Muslims as a mode of cosmopolitan worldliness – in terms of both lived experience and normative disposition – is integral to a liberating humanism that embraces the worldliness of Muslims not despite themselves but precisely because of who they are. That condition transcends any mode of tendentious tribalism, 'Islamic tribalism' in particular. 'Tradition' (from which 'this *Qeshr-e Sonnati*' is derived) in this context will thus reveal itself as in fact the most potent invention of 'modernity,' a binary opposition that grants the universalist claims of European modernity far greater metaphysical weight than is warranted. European Enlightenment modernity has historically withered and been wasted on its colonial edges; the world at large (Europe included) will achieve a renewed momentum and potency from a creative conversation with Islamic cosmopolitanism. The unfolding Green Movement is the most powerful manifestation of the latter.

The natural habitat of Islam, as evident in its long and pervasive history, in both its medieval and its modern phases, is a cosmopolitan setting. Thus by definition an exclusionary, monolithic, and politically overweening Islam is in fact a historical and epistemic aberration, which becomes ideologically contentious

only under pressure of severe political circumstances, effectively
when it is in a combative mode and confronting a colonial or
imperial adversary. One can thus trace the effective mutation of a
cosmopolitan Islam into a militant Islamism back to its historical
encounter with European colonial modernity, when Islam was
systematically reduced, largely by its own leading ideologues and
public intellectuals (from Jamal al-Din al-Afghani and Muhammad
Abdu, through Sir Seyyed Ahmad Khan and Rashid Rida, down to
Mawlana Mawdudi and Ali Shari'ati), into a singular site of ideological resistance to European colonialism. By disengaging from
'Islam and the West,' social uprisings such as the Green Movement
restore to both Muslims and the world they inhabit their otherwise
repressed cosmopolitan self, which while not reducible to any one
religion, nevertheless acknowledges the enduring significance of
multiple religions and ideologies in a polyfocal cultural pluralism.
In this reading of Islam, world history becomes to a level playing
field of fair and open dialogue, in tune with the lived collective
experience of people, and categorically removed from entrenched
ideological and overtly political tribalism of one sort ('Islam') or
another ('The West').

It is imperative that we see the rise of the Green Movement not
as an anathema to Islam in general or Muslims in particular, but
instead as a normative retrieval of the cosmopolitan worldliness
of Iranians as agents of their own history. This caveat is necessary
because, as a world religion, Islam has now been recoded as a
sign and signifier of unbridled and vicious violence. Millennia of
original sources in science and philosophy, literary humanism and
scholastic learning, along with a whole tradition of sustained commentary, plus generations of scholarship in a variety of languages,
have now all been eclipsed, displaced from the public domain
by a socially manufactured notion of Islam entirely synonymous
with the most wanton disregard for universal norms of civility,

nobility, and decency. Notwithstanding that fact that militant Iranian secularists have joined forces with European and American racists in demonizing Islam and Muslims, there is no value in pointing the finger of blame in this state of affairs, and yet at the same time no one can be exempted from the responsibility to restore historical depth and moral imagination to the term 'Islam.' We have reached a stage whereby it is now hard even to imagine, let alone convince, an ordinary citizen in North America or Western Europe that Islam was once the name and designation of a world civilization and today represents the pious parameters of decency and self-respect for millions of people around the globe. Restoring to contemporary Islam its historical cosmopolitanism as a world religion, and to Muslims their self-perception as agents of that history, in a widely accessible and yet historically anchored language, and thus documenting the religion's inherent pluralism and hybridity, is not merely an act of intellectual duty but also one of great urgency. What the Green Movement as a non-violent civil rights uprising has done is to make that cosmopolitan worldliness politically potent, socially evident, and epistemically viable.

Islam has always been a dialogical proposition. The Shi'i clerical claim to absolutist authority (evident in the very constitution of the Islamic Republic) has its roots in both medieval and modern history; its self-referential juridical reasoning has preempted (because it has distrusted) the formation of a public reason. The current uprising bidding to retrieve an Iranian cosmopolitan culture in which Islam will have its fair and natural place and significance but no legitimate claim to absolutism is a historical force that the Islamic Republic will be unable to prevent. That historical inevitability, and the social body contingent on it, has been long in the making. A new generation is now recovering a culture that has been violently repressed and imprisoned within the false binary of *tradition and modernity*, which militant secularists and the clerical clique ruling the Islamic Republic alike continue to uphold despite their occupying apparently opposing poles.

La Vita Nuda: Anarchic versus Erotic Bodies

The cosmopolitan disposition of Islam is now integral to the worldly cosmopolitanism that informs the Green Movement. What today threatens that cosmopolitan worldliness is the state-sponsored constitution and the exposure of atomized individuals and a sustained course of desperate governmentality that seeks to subject the *bare life* of its preempted citizens to the absolutist sovereignty of the state. That *bare life* – the citizen stripped of civil liberties and reduced to naked nullity, as Giorgio Agamben has described it – is now the condition of the globalized world, and thus worldliness is its only pharmakon, the only means we have to oppose it (the medicine that cures and/or the poison that kills), which is the task now incumbent upon the Green Movement. To retrieve that worldliness is the *conditio sine qua non* of fighting back against that totalitarian drive to expose and control the *naked life*. That retrieval of the worldly body is also the condition of cultivating horizontal solidarity against the vertical imposition of tyrannical (Islamic Republic), imperial (US), and colonial (Israel) power.

The writing of public love letters at this juncture in Iranian social history is the healthy sign that the corporeal body is now the site of a robust contestation between *Homo anarchicus* and *Homo eroticus* as the two contending forces in the formation of the social body. As *Homo anarchicus* defies the sovereign state by denying it its site of violence, *Homo eroticus* binds and units these bodies in their formation of a worldly disposition that must survive both that anarchy and the state violence it seeks to defy. The active formation of the social body is the cumulative effect of that confrontation between two contending corporeal forces. The unitary basis of that corporality, in either *anarchic* or *erotic* direction, is the naked life that from Hannah Arendt to Michel Foucault to Giorgio Agamben has been exposed to the mercy of the totalitarian state – and yet it remains resolutely resistant to and defiant against it.

The combined dialectic of *anarchic* and *erotic* bodies (the two competing on one site) now faces the systematicity of the absolutist state (ruled by a Supreme Jurist of the Body – *Vali-ye faqih*) committed to reducing its citizens to their 'naked life,' ready for martyrdom at a moment's notice, or in effect already martyred. Like other totalitarian states, the Islamic Republic has been hard at work for over thirty years trying to reduce its citizens to atomized individuals, men and women stripped of citizenship rights, reduced to the status of what in Iran is termed *Sarbazan-e Gomnam Imam Zaman/'Anonymous Soldiers of the Hidden Imam,'* a cynical reference to the doctrinal belief of Shi'i Muslims in their Twelfth (returning) Mahdi. The anonymity of these 'soldiers' has now become the template for the ideal (absented, nameless, faceless) body that occupies the body-politic of the Islamic Republic.

The constitution of this anonymity is of course not peculiar to the Islamic Republic; all totalitarian regimes have known, used and abused it. Both Leo Löwenthal (1900–1993), in his 'Crisis of the Individual: Terror's Atomization of Man' (1946), and Hannah Arendt (1906–1975) in her *The Origins of Totalitarianism* (1951), fully cognizant of Nazi Germany and the Stalinist Soviet Union, came to grips with and theorized this atomization of the individual as the precondition of totalitarianism. Harold Lasswell's notion of the 'garrison state' (1941) might also be considered a precursor of this transmutation of the state into absolutist bureaucracy and its citizens into what Agamben would later call *bare life*. That *bare life*, in the case of the Islamic Republic, is the Islamized conception of 'the martyr,' which is the ideal case of an Islamist citizenship, a walking-dead person who has already committed his/her life to the state and its self-sanctified appeal to the hereafter.

The systematic transmutation of the Islamic Republic into an absolutist state and its citizens into their *naked (martyred) life* are written into the modus operandi of its heavily militarized security apparatus. The theoretical antecedents of this Islamist development are entirely global and useful in shedding light on its nature and disposition. The origin of Lasswell's insight into the 'garrison state' might be traced back to Max Weber's notion of 'sultanism,' which he of course (as the term implies) derived mainly from and for non-European societies but theorized into a more general ideal-type. While Lasswell was concerned mainly with the United States, and Löwenthal and Arendt, for their part, had Nazi Germany and the Soviet Union in mind, the alternative term for Weberian sultanism, namely 'Bonapartism,' describing a strong and centralized state, was predicated on populist support for a potentate and as such refers to France under Napoleon. This genealogy is important because prominent Iranian intellectuals like Said Hajjarian and Akbar Ganji have long (since the 1980s) debated the terms of this distinction between sultanism, Bonapartism, and the garrison state.[14] While Hajjarian has insisted on the identification of the Islamic Republic as a garrison state and Ganji has preferred the description sultanism, what they share is a diagnosis of the systematic transmutation of the state into an Islamist despotism.[15]

But hidden to the sight of these debates among the leading intellectuals of the Islamic Republic concerning the nature of its state apparatus, the dialectic of *anarchic* and *erotic* bodies was facing a far more insidious operation of Foucauldian governmentality, which the Islamic Republic had set fully in motion in accordance with its ideological and totalitarian disposition. In the normative mode of

that governmentality the Islamic Republic had in fact already sur-
passed all the stages of a garrison state or sultanism, for now power
was no longer directed from one source and was disseminated to
the *body of bare life*. For Foucault, governmentality is far more subtle
and insidious than the practice of any absolutist government,
sultanism or otherwise, and has been elevated to the status of
a mental graft on the body. Biopower is the modus operandi of
governmentality, whereby the body of the citizen has transmuted
into the carrier of the dominant power and internalized its external
means (Weber's terms). Through biopower the vertical relation
of governmental power has become horizontal governmentality.
Schools, hospitals, factories, and above all the body of the citizen
itself – those are the active sites of governmentality. But biopower
has above all reproduced itself discursively, in the manner of
knowledge production. On body and mind, governmentality posits
'a strategic field of power relations in their mobility, transform-
ability, and reversibility,' as Foucault puts it, and as such it posits
the 'relation of self to self.'[16] Until the rise of the Green Movement,
even 'opposition' to the Islamic Republic expressed itself in terms
intrinsic to the Islamic Republic.

With Giorgio's Agamben theorization of 'bare life,' the condition of the atomized individual (and the dialectic of *anarchic* and
erotic bodies it entails) comes full circle, becomes the ground zero
of the globalized state, and the Islamic Republic and the United
States of America become identical in their positing of a *state of
exception*.[17] Nicholas Mirzoeff then took up Guy Debord's conception
and showed how the renewed and more advanced 'society of
the spectacle' had crafted an 'empire of camps,' and Agamben's
naked life had in fact become a depleted subject of a globalized
state of exception.[18] In Alfonso Cuarón's dystopian science-fiction
film *Children of Men* (2006) we received the visual evidence of this
empire of camps in the not so distant future.

Limits of Governmentality: Multiple
Consciousness and Parabolic Interactionism

What about cyberspace? Does the rise of Internet-based social networking (mobile phones, SMS, Facebook, Skype, Twitter, YouTube, etc.) help or hinder, advance or set back, the pervasive reach of governmentality, of the state writing itself on the naked body of its subjects. Does it preempt the possibility of any social uprising, any political revolt, any act of emancipation, like the Green Movement? Is that possible? Does social networking reduce or expand the parameters of governmentality, exacerbate the conditions of the absolutist state and naked life? To answer these questions we need to look at the cyberspace opening up of the world to Iranians as an extension of their *worldliness*, and as a strengthening of their *multiple consciousnesses* as a guarantor of resistance to widespread governmentality. As an extension of W.E.B. DuBois's notion of 'double consciousness,' or Frantz Fanon's 'dual consciousness,' we might speak of 'multiple consciousness' in Iran, though not as a fragmented and schizophrenic state but rather as something entirely harmonious and conducive to the formation of a defiant subject with ample room for creative maneuverability mobilized against repressive governmentality. There is an embedded structural functionalism in theories of the naked life – from Arendt to Foucault to Agamben – whereas in conditions of multiple consciousness there is plenty of space for the formation of a defiant subject, always predicated not on a will to power but on a *will to resist power*.

One glance at the daily calendar used by Iranians use to organize their lives shows that there are in fact three different set of dates that remind them where and when in the world they are – Iranian, Islamic, and the globalized Christian calendar. This triple calendar is the place where Iranian *multiple consciousness* is most palpably evident. The Iranian calendar is solar and has survived from the pre-Islamic period, with distinct pre-Islamic Persian names for the months (Farvardin, Ordibehesht, Khordad, etc.). The seasons have logical and natural divisions, and again all have distinctly Persian names (Bahar, Tabestan, Pa'iz, Zemestan). The single most important event on this calendar is the two-week-long celebration of Noruz (New Year), which runs from the last Wednesday of the year, *Chahr-shanbeh Suri*/'Festive Wednesday,' to *Sizdah Bedar*/'Picnicking Thirteenth,' a day of outings with family and friends, which usually coincides with April Fool's Day.

The second calendar is the Islamic calendar, which is lunar and marks the number of years from the migration of Prophet Muhammad from Mecca to Medina. As such it is punctuated at regular intervals with historic events, birthdays, and mourning days of Muslim saints and Shi'i Imams. If the first calendar marks the *national* aspect of Iranians, the second specifies their *Islamic* identity. At times these two calendars might be in tension with each other, but mostly they dovetail perfectly well.

The third calendar is the globalized Christian calendar, which itself has a dual dimension. The first is its colonial and Christian identity, thus marked as 'Western'. The second identity, on the other hand, signals the connectedness of Iranians with the world at large – not just the Christian world, or that of Western Europe and North America, but also the worlds of Latin America, Africa, and Asia. As such, then, the globalized 'Western' calendar is, paradoxically, both colonial and anticolonial.

This *multiple consciousness*, embedded in this polyfocal calendar, is the space where the creative subject could always find room for political defiance, social maneuverability, mental meandering, symbolic altercations, national identity, pious practices, global adjustments, and so on. Consider the distance between *Chahar-Shanbeh*

Suri/Festive Wednesday and *Sizdah Bedar*/Picnicking Thirteenth on the Iranian calendar year of 1388/2009–10, when the Green Movement was particularly abuzz with excitement and led many observers to conclude that Iranians were, after all, Iranians first and foremost, and their Islamic identity was something artificial and imposed on them. Not so fast!

Let's step back for a moment and take a longer view. In the early annals of the Iranian Revolution of 1977–79, the *Tasu'a-Ashura* Shi'i commemorations of 1978 are now remembered as a major breakthrough, perhaps even the defining moment of the unfolding revolutionary events, when the fate of the *ancien régime* seemed to have been sealed. *Tasu'a* is the 9th and Ashura the 10th of Muharram on the Islamic calendar. On these two days in the year 61 of the Islamic calendar (1–2 October 680 on the Christian calendar), a major battle raged in Karbala in Iraq between Imam Hossein, a grandson of Prophet Muhammad, and the Third Infallible Shi'i Imam on one side, and Yazid, the reigning caliph, on the other. Imam Hossein lost the Battle of Karbala and, along with his most loyal companions, was killed. Ever since that fateful battle, Shi'i Muslims have commemorated it with various forms of self-flagellation.

On 10 and 11 December 1978, or 19–20 Azar 1356, or, more importantly, 9–10 Muharram 1399, an estimated 17 million people marched peacefully to mark the anniversary of *Tasu'a-Ashura*, significantly using the occasion to demand the end of the Pahlavi monarchy and the return from exile of Ayatollah Khomeini. It was on this occasion that a historic resolution declared Khomeini leader of the Iranian people. A little over a month after this major rally, on 16 January, Mohammad Reza Shah and his family left Iran; less than two weeks later, on 1 February, Ayatollah Khomeini returned to Iran and an estimated 5 million people poured onto the streets to welcome him and put an end to the Pahlavi dynasty.

Now let's revisit the end of the Iranian calendar year of 1388, or 2009–10. In the last week of the year, Iranians were celebrating their ancient ritual of jumping over fire in joyous celebration of Festive Wednesday. This happy and jubilant occasion was the culmination of nine months of uninterrupted revolt against the tyranny of the Islamic Republic.[19] Now suddenly the blogosphere was inundated with overeager analysis that read the event as a sign that Iranians were more truly Iranian than they were seriously Muslim or Arab – thus equating Arabs and Muslims and dismissing both as non-Iranian.

So what does this mean? Were these not the same people? Did they not turn to their Islamic calendar to topple a Persian monarchy, and then subsequently to their Iranian calendar to challenge an Islamic Republic? Let's complicate the matter further by reaching for the full texture of the *multiple consciousness* that can *ipso facto* challenge any mode of governmentality, Aryan or Islamic. Come 1 May of the same or any other year on the globalized Christian calendar, the very same people would instantly forget about both Iranian and Islamic calendars and turn to their more worldly, pro-labor, anti-colonial, disposition in order to mark International Labor Day, to challenge the labor abuses of the Islamic Republic, in the same way that decades earlier they challenged the Pahlavi monarchy. Now what?

The systematic, self-conscious, and violent over-Islamization of the Iranian Revolution of 1339/1977–79 can arguably be traced back to the *Tasu'a-Ashura* rally of that year, which marked a key moment in the reading of the event as 'Islamic'; whereas the events between *Chahar-Shanbeh Suri*/Festive Wednesday to *Sizdah Bedar*/Picnicking Thirteenth in the Iranian calendar year of 1388/2009–10 are now used to support exactly the opposite reading. But the fact of the matter is that violent over-Islamization of the Iranian multiple consciousness early in the course of the Islamic Revolution was as forced and flawed in its own terms as the careless and incautious over-Iranization is today in the other direction. Iranians are at once Iranian and Muslim (albeit with significant non-Muslim minorities, including non-believing, non-practicing 'Muslims') and therefore nationalist and Islamic identities are integral to their sense of worldly cosmopolitanism. What unites these calendric occasions – at the commencement and at what has the potential to be the concluding phase of the Islamic Republic – is the creative use of a multiple consciousness to express defiance of and opposition to a mode of governmentality that insists on one identity and disregards the other. The Shah's imposition of a purely 'Aryan' identity on his people's history went so far as changing the Iranian calendar altogether, from its point of origin in the migration of Prophet Muhammad from Mecca to Medina in 622 CE to the presumed coronation of Cyrus the Great some two thousands years ago. In consequence, one fine morning Iranians woke up, took a look at their daily diary and had no clue how old they were. For the last thirty years, the Islamic Republic has done exactly the opposite, suppressing and denying people's Iranian identity and overemphasizing their Islamic heritage, while trying to 'Islamize' International Labor Day! If appealing to an Islamic calendar of events constituted revolt thirty years ago, identifying with the Iranian calendar today serves the same function. Both are at the disposal of a people to maneuver their mode of compliance or defiance beyond the reach of government control.

The reason that the creative constitution of this multiple consciousness is more enabling than fragmenting has to do with the societal formation of meaning in any given social act. The meaning of a social action is embedded in and cultivated by the open-ended hermeneutics of narratives, stories, parables, and symbols that people invest in it. Symbolic interactionism, as a sociological perspective, places emphasis on the fact that people act toward things based on the meaning those things have or that they attribute to them *in the course of* their social action.[20] These meanings are derived from social interaction and modified through interpretation. While symbolic interactionism, a sociological frame of reference that developed in the United States, operates on a single plane of interpretative analyses, one might posit multiple planes of symbolic interaction, which one might in fact call *parabolic interactionism*, in two interrelated senses: (1) related to a set of *parables*, which in this case might be termed Iranian, Islamic, and global; and (2) moving along a *parabola*, or a motion on a parabolic curve, which is a plane curve generated by a point moving so that its distance from a fixed point is equal to its distance from a fixed line.

I suggest *parabolic* instead of *symbolic* interactionism in order to shift the surface level of interpretative grid from one to multiple planes – with the intended consequence of a people's creativity shifting from one gear to another to challenge the authority of the powers that be by destabilizing their dominant symbolic modus operandi – whatever it is. In Iran, there are at least three interrelated planes of symbolic interaction, which shift their calendric base depending on the mode of resistance active in society at large. The creative combination of these planes offers infinite opportunity to play with and subvert the strategems that a garrison state may wish to deploy and thereby persuade itself that it is unassailable in its fictive fortress.

The Defiant Corpus Eroticus

Cyberspace has expanded the cosmopolitan worldliness of Iranian culture, further intensifying its multiple consciousness as a guarantor of resistance to any mode of governmentality that comes its way. Through the sustained course of parabolic interactionism this multiple consciousness and the cosmopolitan worldliness it entails define the limits of governmentality and restore to naked life its erotic disposition. The mechanism that best sets multiple parabolic interactionism to work is the dialectic of legitimating an opposition between the state and rising resistance to its domination. There is nothing inherently Islamic or Iranian or global about Iranian society. These are all symbolic registers and parabolic narratives used by people in order to express their defiance. If the dominant mode is Iranian, they opt for Islamic; now that it is Islamic, they opt for Iranian or even (to thumb their nose at the government) 'Western.'

Perhaps the most significant consequence of coming to terms with multiple consciousness is the fact that it does away with habitual entrapment in the binary opposition of secular and religious. The particulars of this multiple consciousness and the worldliness that sustains it reveal the social dynamics of a people as a living organism that both revives and creates its own varied symbolic registers, not just to make sense of its present and past but in fact to alter its future. So socialization is always in a double bind and counter-governmentality written into the emotive alphabet of Iranian political culture – a fact that always preempts absolutism of one sort or another. The body of evidence staring us in the face – the body itself – is the first and final testimony to the return of the repressed in the *Corpus eroticus* that brought us into this world in the first place!

CONCLUSION

People and Their Parables

THE STORY OF THE aging Lion King, the conniving Fox, and the gullible Ass from *Kelilah and Dimnah* retrieves an ancient wisdom and a mode of political thinking now all but forgotten under the thin veneer of an urgency that politics habitually posits. By invoking this ancient story I have sought to retrieve a political idiomaticity that allows us to think through and beyond our contemporary world with a renewed set of metaphoric lenses. I have proposed the aging, defeated, and cliché-ridden policies of the United States as being tantamount to that ailing Lion that has all the appearance of power but not the visionary wherewithal of the world he now inhabits and wishes to rule. The Islamic Republic, the wily Fox, meanwhile has managed to manipulate the geopolitics of the region, codenamed the Middle East (the Ass of our story) in a manner such that its heart and ears end up on a plate. But, I have concluded, even the Fox has proven to be too smart for his own good, and has just turned around to see that his tail is on fire.

There is of course a limit to this, as to any other, fable as a metaphor and how far it can go to explain the status quo. Be that as it may, the domestic situation in the Islamic Republic prior to the rise of the Green Movement was such that the Islamist faction had successfully managed (by hook or by crook and over the course of some thirty years) to outmaneuver all its political and ideological alternatives and was now ruling Iran with an iron fist – massive popular discontent notwithstanding. To consolidate that power, the Islamist regime had in the meantime cornered for itself a lucrative niche in regional politics, so much so that when President Obama assumed office in January 2009 he would have strengthened it if he sat down to talk to Mahmoud Ahmadinejad about the myriad problems the newly elected president faced and for which he needed help, and it would have been further strengthened had Obama opted to tighten economic sanctions and move towards a military strike. President Obama, not Mr Ahmadinejad, was caught between Iraq and a hard place.

In a dramatic turnaround the Green Movement put an end to that balance of power, undid the paradox by which the Islamic Republic sustained itself by posing a new paradoxical dilemma for the warlike state, and suddenly ushered in a national political agenda to tip the balance towards radical change of the status quo. The Islamic Republic was no longer standing tall watching Afghanistan and Iraq fall to the might of US imperial adventurism. While it was cunningly negotiating the geopolitics of its regional power, it was not watching its back, its *Salus populi*, the well-being of its own people – the *raison d'être* of its being, and that of any state, Islamic or otherwise. The Green Movement – launched by the younger generation from within society, yet led by aging revolutionaries of the Islamist regime itself – now presented the Islamic Republic with the same paradox that the Islamic Republic had presented to the United States and its regional allies. Whatever the Islamic Republic did with the Green Movement – violently suppress or judiciously allow it to unfold – would make it stronger.

The Islamic Republic was being administered its own medicine, by its own people. These people – Iranians – meanwhile, were busy, day by day, becoming a nation in the creative business of rebuilding itself.

The fortuitous rise of the Green Movement, I have sought to argue in this book, has been long in the making. In a significant and enduring way it represented the return of the Islamic Republic's repressed, what it violently sought to deny, denigrate, dismiss and denounce: the cosmopolitan worldliness of a political culture that had brought about the 1977–79 revolution in the first place, before the more violently Islamist faction outmaneuvered the others and claimed the whole thing for itself. The more violently the Islamic Republic denied that multifaceted and polyvocal culture (which included many aspects of Islam but was never limited to them), the more forcefully it had now returned. As the retrieval of Iranian cosmopolitan culture, the Green Movement finally overcame the impasse of the Islamic Republic, exposed its epistemic exhaustion, and with one simple question, 'Where is my vote?', stripped it naked and revealed its brute force. As the Islamic Republic was instantly exposed as a garrison state (mirroring Israel as the first modern garrison state in the region – replicating the Massada Complex), Iranian political culture flexed its cosmopolitan muscles: in liberatory art and underground music, poetry and literature, street demonstrations and color symbolism, weblogs and websites, defiant intellectuals and creative artists, expansive philosophers and progressive theologians, exposed an avalanche of alternative think-ing, feeling, being, and activism. In order to see the nature and disposition of the Green Movement, however, people needed – just like Kardanah – to lift their point of view and see things from an entirely different perspective, on a slightly elevated plane.

The cosmopolitan worldliness that has been pouring into Iran's streets and alleys, into public squares and onto apartment rooftops, and written on weblogs and Facebook pages of Iranians around the globe, has registered a powerful reminder to a world under dire threat of belligerent tribalism. It is not just the clerical clique ruling Iran that is practicing that tribalism and is afraid of that worldliness. The face-off between an Islamic republic and a Jewish state, under the watchful eye of a Christian empire, and in the region of an equally violent Hindu fundamentalism, is the clearest and most present danger that the world at large now faces, with the nightmare of a nuclear holocaust threatening the very life of an already fragile planet at the mercy of ecological ruin and global warming. The Green Movement in Iran has hidden in its fragile unfolding the seeds of a potentially global liberation from such fears and fanaticism.

At stake is not just the life and liberty of one people in one country, but an alternative way of thinking and practicing politics – the exposing and dismantling of a politics of despair that masquerades as realpolitik. Trapped inside that realpolitik, the world is breaking under the burden of old and tiresome clichés – East versus West, Islam versus the West, tradition versus modernity, religious versus secular, religion versus laicism, the clash of or else dialogue among civilizations. The heated debate in the UK around the publication of Richard Dawkins's *The God Delusion* (2006) is one such clamorous instance of misplaced concreteness given to metaphors. All these grand illusions – religion on one side, secularism on another – sit upon the world, suffocating its breathing pores, where life and literature, hope and poetry, happiness and art, curiosity and drama, joy and liberty dance to entirely different, more innocent and enabling, tunes. What a waste it is not to see the infinite possibilities embedded in a short story that tells an alternative history of the world. How foolish it is to gloss over the widening narrative roads of knowing and being in the world – possibilities that embrace the old binaries and reread them in an open-ended hermeneutics of liberation, wherein life, literature, art, cinema, and poetry are so full of alternative ways of seeing and being in the world. The possibilities of a democratic state, of confessional pluralism, are as much threatened by religious absolutism as they are by equally fanatical secularism, denying and denigrating, or else epistemically barring, people's moments of sacred certitude. In the name of what? Terms such as 'post-Islamism' or 'post-secularism,' indicate attempts to find a way out of this impasse of 'religion versus secularism,' but to no avail, for the manufactured binary is where the trouble lies. The world is far richer than such grossly reductive narrative tropes suggest. If anything, the Green Movement in Iran is the harbinger of a retrieval of the world's hidden and denied stories, embedded in a nation's collective memory, at the expense of the old and tired clichés that still pass for History.

The cosmopolitan worldliness that has awakened in Iran after more than three decades of brutal repression, where the world can see its best hopes and perhaps even its forgotten aspirations, is as much a political act as it is an act of aesthetic emancipation, of literary and poetic imagination. Look at the country's art, listen to its music, and try to appreciate the multiple consciousness that has produced it. The best of a nation is at work here – playing itself once again against its cruel fate, gruesome history, troubled geography. The parabolic interactionism at work in Iranian political culture, and the rise of ever new literary and poetic idiomaticity, have mobilized a whole set of invigorated metaphors, geared towards an open-ended hermeneutics, which will not stop, which cannot stop, and which no Basiji, Pasdar, policeman, soldier or any other uniformed officer of tyranny and terror will scare away. In the making of that cosmopolitan worldliness, everyone is who and what one is, or is becoming, and yet in the divergent trails of one's destiny there emerges a consorted harmony, a map and topography of the best that might have been and is still possible. This is like the story of the friendship among the Pigeon, the Crow, the Mouse, the Tortoise, and the Deer in *Kelilah and Dimnah*.

ONCE UPON A TIME, they say, and what a splendid time it was, on a beautiful prairie in Kashmir, a group of pigeons were caught inside a trap. High upon a tree there was a crow watching this. He thought to himself there must be a lesson in this trap for him too, so as the pigeons were discussing how to free themselves from their predicament, he concluded that... Well, I may tell you that story some other time.

Notes

PROLOGUE

1. This is my free and playful adaptation of a famous story in *Kalilah and Dimnah*, an initially Pahlavi (Middle Persian), then Arabic, and then Persian (among other) translation and adaptation from the original Indian text of *Panchatantra*, a collection of animal fables that dates back to least the third century BCE. From the Pahlavi it was translated into Arabic by Ibn al-Muqaffa' in 750, and from that transmitted to Greece in the eleventh and Spain in the thirteenth century, and from there it traveled to the rest of the European continent. In 1121 Abu al-Ma'ali Nasrollah Monshi prepared a superb Persian translation of the text based on Ibn al-Muqaffa's Arabic version. My translation is based on the critical edition of Abu al-Ma'ali Nasrollah Monshi's text, as critically edited by Mojtaba Minovi in 1964 (Tehran: Tehran University Press, 1964: 253–7). These stories subsequently entered an oral register, and parents and grandparents tell them to their children and grandchildren without much attention to their textual origin. I heard this story for the first time from my maternal grandmother, Bibi Mar Vali, at a very young age. I believe the political tropes of these stories reside in our emotional universe from such time, on an almost unconscious plane.

ONE

1. As quoted by Michael Mann in his *Incoherent Empire* (London: Verso, 2003): vii.

TWO

1. This part of the chapter is based on a talk I delivered at Harvard Law School on 17 March 2008, commemorating the fifth anniversary of the US-led invasion of Iraq. An earlier draft of the talk was published in *Unbound: Harvard Journal of the Legal Left*, vol. 4, no. 82, 2008: 82–95.

2. For the most recent edition of Richard Hofstadter's classic study, see *Anti-Intellectualism in American Life* (New York: Vintage, 1964).

3. For the most recent edition, see Alexis de Tocqueville, *Democracy in America* (London: Penguin, 2003).

4. For my review of this film, see Hamid Dabashi, 'The 300 strokes,' *al-Ahram Weekly*, 2–8 August 2007.

5. See 'Clintons' earnings exceed $100m,' BBC News, 5 April 2008.

6. For more on Robert Bellah's notion of 'civil religion,' see Robert Bellah, 'Civil religion in America,' *Journal of the American Academy of Arts and Sciences* vol. 96, no. 1, Winter 1967: 1–21. See also Robert N. Bellah, *Beyond Belief: Essays on Religion in a Post-Traditionalist World* (Berkeley, CA: University of California Press, 1991).

7. For more on this exchange, see John M. Broder and Elizabeth Bumiller, 'McCain and Obama trade jabs on Iraq,' *New York Times*, 28 February 2008.

8. For an example of such theories, see James H. Fetzer (ed.), *The 9/11 Conspiracy* (Chicago: Open Court, 2007).

9. See Amy Kaplan, *The Anarchy of Empire in the Making of US Culture* (Cambridge, MA: Harvard University Press, 2005).

10. See Richard Falk, 'Defining a Just War,' *The Nation*, 11 October 2001. 'I have never,' Richard Falk writes in this essay exactly a month after 9/11/01, 'since my childhood supported a shooting war in which the United States was involved, although in retrospect I think the NATO war in Kosovo achieved beneficial results. The war in Afghanistan against apocalyptic terrorism qualifies in my understanding as the first truly just war since World War II.' This is a sign of sheer historical blindness to the overriding imperial design of American military involvements, even in Kosovo.

11. For more on my reading of the relationship between the Iranian revolution of 1977–79 and the seismic changes in the region, see the new Introduction to my *Theology of Discontent: The Ideological Foundations of the Islamic Revolution in Iran* (2nd edn, New Brunswick, NJ: Transaction Publishers, 2006).

12. I have developed this theme extensively in my *Islamic Liberation Theology: Resisting the Empire* (London: Routledge, 2008).

13. To learn more about the Project for the New American Century (claiming the entirety of a century exclusively for Americans) visit their website, www.newamericacentury.org

14. For an example, see 'US biggest global peace threat,' BBC News, 14 June 2006. 'People in European and Muslim countries,' the report suggests, 'see US policy in Iraq as a bigger threat to world peace than Iran's nuclear programme.'

15. To learn more about Christian Zionism, see Stephen Sizer, *Christian Zionism: Road-Map to Armageddon?* (Westmont, IL: Intervarsity Press, 2005).

16. See Antonio Negri and Michael Hardt, *Empire* (Cambridge, MA: Harvard University Press, 2000).

17. Chalmers Johnson's *Blowback* trilogy began with his *Blowback: The Costs and Consequences of American Empire* (New York: Henry Holt, 2000), and after the events of 9/11 continued first with *The Sorrows of Empire: Militarism, Secrecy, and the End of the Republic* (New York: Henry Holt, 2004), and finally with *Nemesis: The Last Days of the American Republic* (New York: Henry Holt, 2006).

18. See Niall Ferguson's *Colossus: The Price of America's Empire* (New York: Penguin, 2004).

19. For the most recent edition of V.G. Kiernan's classic, see *America: The New Imperialism* (London: Verso, 2005). This edition has an excellent new preface by Eric Hobsbawm that updates Kiernan's observations to the aftermath of 9/11 events.

20. See Michael Mann's *Incoherent Empire* (London: Verso, 2003).

21. See Heinrich Meier, *Carl Schmidt and Leo Strauss: The Hidden Dialogue* (Chicago: University of Chicago Press, [1988] 1995).

22. See Anne Norton, *Leo Strauss and the Politics of American Empire* (New Haven, CT: Yale University Press, 2005).

23. See Earl Shorris, 'Ignoble liars: Leo Strauss, George Bush, and the philosophy of mass deception,' *Harper's*, January 2004.

24. See Naomi Wolf's extraordinary text, *The End of America: Letter of Warning to a Young Patriot – A Citizen's Call to Action* (White River Junction, VT: Chelsea Green Publishing, 2007).

25. Ibid.: back cover.

26. See Solomon Hughes, *War on Terror, Inc.: Corporate Profiteering from the Politics of Fear* (London: Verso, 2007).

27. Psy-Ops (Psychological Operations) is military terminology referring to various techniques used to influence the emotive and interpretative presumptions of a targeted audience.

28. For more on these characters, see my 'Thinking beyond the US invasion of Iran,' *al-Ahram Weekly*, 8–14 February 2007, and 'Native informers and the making of the American empire,' *al-Ahram Weekly*, 1–7 June 2006.

29. For further details, see Chris Hedges, *American Fascists: The Christian Right and the War on America* (New York: Free Press, 2006).

30. For details, see Richard Allen Greene, 'Evangelical Christians plead for Israel,' BBC News, 19 July 2006, at http://news.bbc.co.uk/2/hi/americas/5193092.stm; accessed 5 June 2010.

31. For this and other John Hagee comments, see Richard Allen Greene's article, 'Evangelical Christians plead for Israel,' BBC News, 19 July 2006. See also Nick Miles's article in the same vein, 'Pro-Israel pressure strong in US,' BBC News, 11 August 2006.

32. See Kevin Philips, *American Theocracy: The Perils and Politics of Radical Religion, Oil, and Borrowed Money in the 21st Century* (New York: Viking, 2006).

33. See Thomas P.M. Barnett, 'The Man Between War and Peace,' *Esquire*, 11 March 2008.

34. See Giorgio Agamben, *State of Exception*, trans. Kevin Attell (Chicago: University of Chicago Press, [2003] 2005): 2.

THREE

1. See 'Clinton frets over Chinese, Iranian inroads in Americas,' AFP, 1 May 2009, at www.google.com/hostednews/afp/article/ALeqM5h2Qjbvaekp-jOTRbiPVzymzL61d2A.

2. For the official take of the Islamic Republic on Ahmadinejad's visit to Latin America, see 'Ahmadinejad's Brazil visit startles Washington,' Press TV, 23 November 2009, at www.presstv.ir/detail.aspx?id=93300&sectionid=351020101; accessed 8 February 2010.

3. For more on Ahmadinejad's visit to Gambia and Brazil, see 'Lula takes risk in welcoming Ahmadinejad to Brazil,' *LA Times*, 23 November 2009, at http://articles.latimes.com/2009/nov/23/world/la-fg-brazil-iran23–2009nov23; accessed 8 February 2010.

4. For more details on these developments, see my *Iran: A People Interrupted* (New York: New Press, 2007): ch. 5.

5. For more on the Reagan Doctrine and its context and consequences, see Mark P. Lagon, *The Reagan Doctrine: Sources of American Conduct in the Cold War's Last Chapter* (New York: Praeger, 1994).

6. For an introduction to Abdolkarim Soroush's ideas, see Mahmoud Sadri and Ahmad Sadri (eds), *Reason, Freedom, and Democracy in Islam: Essential Writings of Abdolkarim Soroush* (Oxford: Oxford University Press, 2002).

7. For more details on Khatami's election to the presidency, see my *Iran: A People Interrupted*: ch. 6.

8. For a comparison between Khatami and Gorbachev, see Zhand Shakibi, *Khatami and Gorbachev: Politics of Change in the Islamic Republic of Iran and the USSR* (London: I.B. Tauris, 2010).

9. Most of Najafi's songs are available on YouTube. For 'Taraf-e Ma,' see www.youtube.com/watch?v=_ckQPLV6csQ (accessed 8 February 2010). 'Taraf-e Ma' is a deliberately ambiguous title. It means both 'Our Side' and 'Our Opponent' or 'Our Interlocutor.'

10. The notion of 'the end of ideology' was first articulated by Daniel Bell in the 1950s and then published by him in 1960 in *The End of Ideology:*

On the Exhaustion of Political Ideas in the Fifties (Cambridge, MA: Harvard University Press, 2000). I first extended Bell's argument to an Islamic context in my 'The end of Islamic ideology,' Social Research, vol. 67, no. 2, Summer 2000: 475–518. I subsequently expanded that argument in my Islamic Liberation Theology: Resisting the Empire (London: Routledge, 2008). My use of the term 'post-ideological' generation is predicated on that set of arguments.

11. That the Islamic Republic abuses the memory of the CIA-engineered coup of 1953 does not mean that some corners of the US foreign policy establishment have abandoned the idea of covert operations in Iran. For an exposé of such designs, with the collaboration of Iranian native informers, see my 'A tale of two cities,' al-Ahram, 20–26 August 2009.

12. The original letter was published on Saham News, the official website of Mehdi Karroubi's Etemad Melli Party, on 8 August 2009 at www.etemademelli. ir/published/0/00/65/6571; accessed 8 August 2009. For a reliable English translation, see: http://enduringamerica.com/2009/08/10/iran-the-kar-roubi-letter-to-rafsanjani-on-abuse-of-detainees/. For a New York Times report of this letter, see 'Iran tries to suppress rape allegations,' at www. nytimes.com/2009/08/15/world/middleeast/15iran.html. For a New York Times editorial on these rape charges, see 'Shame on Iran' at www.nytimes. com/2009/08/28/opinion/28fri2.html?_r=1&adxnnl=1&ref=global-home&adxnnlx=1251454080-9+nzy+AIqjK2uhSxa6+UUw; accessed 28 August 2009. For my initial reflections on this letter, see 'Iran confronts rape, torture allegations,' CNN commentary, 22 August 2009, at www. cnn.com/2009/WORLD/meast/08/22/dabashi.iran.morality/index.html; accessed 7 September 2009.

13. For my earliest reflections on the Green Movement as a civil rights movement, see 'Looking for their Martin Luther King, Jr,' New York Times, 23 June 2009, at http://roomfordebate.blogs.nytimes.com/2009/06/23/behind-the-protests-social-upheaval-in-iran/; accessed 9 February 2010.

14. See Abbas Barzegar, 'Revolution halted in Iran,' Guardian, 12 December 2009.

15. For a more extended argument of this point, see my 'An Epistemic Shift in Iran,' The Brooklyn Rail, July–August 2009, at www.brooklynrail. org/2009/07/express/an-epistemic-shift-in-iran; accessed 9 February 2010.

16. For a more detailed argument of this point, see my 'White moderates and Greens,' al-Ahram Weekly, 21–27 January 2010, at http://weekly.ahram. org.eg/2010/982/op8.htm; accessed 9 February 2010.

17. See Homa Katouzian, 'Wither Iran?,' Iranian, 12 August 2009, at www. iranian.com/main/2009/aug/wither-iran; accessed 18 December 2009. For a more elaborate version of the same unfortunate and condescending

argument, see Homa Katouzian, *The Persians: Ancient, Mediaeval and Modern Iran* (New Haven, CT: Yale University Press, 2009). At the dawn of the twenty-first century, one might have hoped that blatant forms of self-Orientalization would cease to be the cause of such frankly embarrassing utterances. But evidently not. Even worse than these comments, indeed an outright pathologization of Iran and Iranians, are those in the interview that Fatemeh Shams conducted with Homa Katouzian (in Persian), '*Asib-shenasi Kholq va Kho-ye Iranian*/'The pathology of Iranian mentalities and habits,' at www.rahesabz.net/story/12631/; accessed 25 March 2010.

18. The Jim Crow laws were state and local laws enacted between 1876 and 1965 in the United States, effectively mandating racial segregation in all public facilities.

19. For more details, see Aldon D. Morris, *Origins of the Civil Rights Movements* (New York: Free Press, 1986).

20. For more details on these initial charges of fraud, see 'Angry Mousavi says Iran vote result a fix,' *Reuters*, 13 June 2009, at http://in.reuters.com/article/worldNews/idINIndia-40300620090613.

21. For more on the atrocities committed at Kahrizak, see Muhammad Sahimi, 'The mysterious death of a Kahrizak doctor,' PBS, 25 November 2009, at www.pbs.org/wgbh/pages/frontline/tehranbureau/2009/11/the-mysterious-death-of-the-kahrizak-doctor.html.

22. For more details on this sermon on 19 June 2009, see 'Iran protests: live,' *Guardian* contemporaneous blogging; at www.guardian.co.uk/news/blog/2009/jun/19/iran-unrest.

23. For more on my notion of 'anticolonial modernity,' see *Iran: A People Interrupted*: Epilogue.

FOUR

1. 'A former Afghan prime minister called for an inquiry after Al Jazeera broadcast footage showing Christian US soldiers appearing to be preparing to try and convert Muslims in Afghanistan.' For details, see http://english.aljazeera.net/news/asia/2009/05/20095485025169646.html; accessed 5 June 2010.

2. See 'US army 'does not promote religion,' Aljazeera, 5 May 2009, at http://english.aljazeera.net/news/asia/2009/05/2009542250178146.html.

3. Ibid.

4. Ibid.

5. For details of Muslim reactions to the remarks of the Pope about Prophet Muhammad, see BBC News, 14 September 2006, at http://news.bbc.co.uk/2/hi/5346480.stm; accessed 20 February 2010.

6. For more on Hamas, see Zaki Chehab, *Inside Hamas: The Untold Story of the Militant Islamic Movement* (New York: Nation Books, 2008).

7. See 'Cyprus searches 'Gaza arms' ship,' BBC News, at http://news.bbc.co.uk/go/pr/fr/-/2/hi/middle_east/7868726.stm, posted 2009/02/03 23:29:24 GMT.

8. See Michael Howard, 'Mahdi army commanders withdraw to Iran to lie low during security crackdown,' *Guardian*, at www.guardian.co.uk/world/2007/feb/15/iraq.iran/print; posted 15 February 2007.

9. Ibid.

10. Ibid.

11. Ibid.

12. See 'Ahmadinejad in historic Iraq visit,' BBC News, 2 March 2008, at http://news.bbc.co.uk/2/hi/middle_east/7273284.stm.

13. For a first hand account of Muqtada al-Sadr and the Mahdi Army, see Patrick Cockburn, *Muqtada: Muqtada al-Sadr, the Shia Revival, and the Struggle for Iraq* (New York: Scribner, 2008).

14. For an excellent account of the rise of Hezbollah, see Hala Jaber, *Hezbollah* (New York: Columbia University Press, 1997).

15. The term 'diabolic genious' is used by Scott Conroy in 'Iran denies Iraq weapons charges,' CBS News, 12 February 2007. See www.cbsnews.com/stories/2007/02/12/iraq/main2460938.shtml; accessed 5 June 2010.

16. See Bruce Hoffman, 'Al-Qaeda has a new strategy. Obama needs one, too,' *Washington Post*, 10 January 2010, at www.washingtonpost.com/wp-dyn/content/article/2010/01/08/AR2010010803555.html; accessed 22 February 2010.

17. Ibid.

18. For an account of Tony Blair's defiant insistence in the course of his appearance at the Chilcot Inquiry that he would do it again — go to war in Iraq — see 'Iraq inquiry hears defiant Blair say: I'd do it again,' BBC News, 29 January 2010, at http://news.bbc.co.uk/2/hi/uk_news/politics/8485694.stm; accessed 20 February 2010.

19. See Marwan Bishara, 'Iran's unambiguous ambiguity,' Aljazeera, 17 February 2010, at http://blogs.aljazeera.net/imperium/2010/02/17/irans-unambiguous-ambiguity; accessed 20 February 2010.

20. Ibid.

21. See 'Sunni party to boycott Iraqi elections,' CNN, 20 February 2010, at www.cnn.com/2010/WORLD/meast/02/20/iraq.election.boycott.call/; accessed on 23 February 2010.

22. See Robert Dreyfuss, 'The Chalabi factor in Iraq,' *The Nation*, 18 February 2010, at www.thenation.com/blogs/dreyfuss/531390/the_chalabi_factor_in_iraq; accessed 23 February 2010.

23. Ibid.

24. See 'Yemen declares truce with rebels,' BBC News, 11 February 2010, at http://news.bbc.co.uk/2/hi/8511705.stm; accessed 23 February 2010.

25. See 'Dubai knows Hamas man's killers,' BBC News, 29 January 2010, at http://news.bbc.co.uk/go/pr/fr/-/2/hi/middle_east/8487967.stm; accessed 26 February 2010.

26. Ibid.

27. See 'EU signals displeasure with Israel,' *Financial Times*, 22 February 2010, at www.ft.com/cms/s/0/d3283f5c-1fbd-11df-8975-00144feab49a.html?nclick_check=1; accessed 26 February 2010.

28. For details, see 'Israeli politician Livni hails Dubai Hamas killing,' BBC News, 23 February 2010, at http://news.bbc.co.uk/2/hi/middle_east/8532009.stm; accessed 1 March 2010.

29. See M.J. Rosenberg, 'Is Harvard Prof advocating Palestinian genocide?,' *The Huffington Post*, 22 February 2010, at www.huffingtonpost.com/mj-rosenberg/harvard-prof-urges-popula_b_472191.html; accessed 8 March 2010.

30. For the details of Ahmadinejad's theological foreign policy, see the report (in Persian) of his appearance in Birjand at www.mardomak.mx/news/Ahmadinejad_12th_Imam_US/; accessed 1 March 2010.

FIVE

1. For an excellent study of the origin of US–Saudi relations, see Parker T. Hart, *Saudi Arabia and the United States: Birth of a Security Partnership* (Bloomington, IN: Indiana University Press, 1999).

2. For more details, see Seyyed Vali Reza Nasr, *Shia Revival: How Conflicts within Islam Will Shape the Future* (New York: W.W. Norton, 2006).

3. Seyyed Vali Reza Nasr was competing in providing this service with the not-to-be-left behind Fouad Ajami, who sought to provide similar explanations in his *The Foreigner's Gift: The Americans, the Arabs, and the Iraqis in Iraq* (New York: Free Press, 2007). But judging by the success of their respective books, Seyyed Vali Reza Nasr seems to have replaced his Lebanese role model over the last decade or so.

4. 'The Arab street' is a common journalistic expression in the North American and Western European press, referring to presumed pubic opinion in the Arab world regarding a critical issue.

5. For more on the Christian disposition of American empire, see Kevin P. Phillips, *American Theocracy: The Peril and Politics of Radical Religion, Oil, and Borrowed Money in the 21st Century* (New York: Viking, 2006).

6. In June 2010, the Israeli army's attack on Freedom Flotilla taking humanitarian aid to Gaza and the killing of at least nine activists onboard ignited global anger against the continued Israeli blockade.

7. For more details on the CIA-sponsored coup of 1953, see Stephen Kinzer,

All the Shah's Men: An American Coup and the Roots of Middle East Terror (New York: Wiley, 2008).

8. For more on Amir Naderi and the social context of his cinema, see the chapter on him in my *Masters and Masterpieces of Iranian Cinema* (Washington, DC: Mage Publishers, 2007).

9. For a critical review of the Public Prosecutor's indictment, see the opposition party Jebheh Mosharekat's response, at www.mowjcamp.com/article/id/22014; accessed 4 March 2010.

10. For a critical review of this history and the eventual dawn of the Islamic theocracy, see Said Amir Arjomand's *Turban for the Crown: The Islamic Revolution in Iran* (Oxford: Oxford University Press, 1989).

11. For Zbigniew Brzezinski's own reflections in this period, see his *Power and Principle: Memoirs of the National Security Advisor 1977–1981* (New York: Farrar, Straus & Giroux, 1985)

12. For an account of the American hostage crisis, see Mark Bowden, *Guests of the Ayatollah: The Iran Hostage Crisis: The First Battle in America's War with Militant Islam* (New York: Grove Press, 2007).

13. For an account of the Operation Eagle Claw, see Mark Bowden, 'The Desert One debacle,' *The Atlantic*, May 2006, at www.theatlantic.com/magazine/archive/2006/05/the-desert-one-debacle/4803/; accessed 4 March 2010.

14. For an account of the Iran–Iraq war, see Farhang Rajaee, *The Iran–Iraq War: The Politics of Aggression* (Gainesville, FL: University of Florida Press, 1993).

15. For the complete text of the 'Letter from a Birmingham Jail,' see the archive at African Studies Center, University of Pennsylvania, at www.africa.upenn.edu/Articles_Gen/Letter_Birmingham.html; accessed 4 March 2010.

16. See Flynt Leverett and Hillary Leverett, 'Another Iranian revolution? Not likely,' *New York Times*, 5 January 2010, at www.nytimes.com/2010/01/06/opinion/06leverett.html; accessed 4 March 2010.

17. See Flynt Leverett and Hillary Leverett, 'Ahmadinejad won. Get over it,' *Politico*, 15 June 2009, at www.politico.com/news/stories/0609/23745.html; accessed 4 March 2010.

18. For more details on the Leveretts' courageous standing up to the Bush administration's politicization of intelligence, see Steve Clemons, 'Flynt Leverett blasts White House National Security Council censorship of former White House officials critical of Bush policies,' *The Washington Note*, 16 December 2006, at www.thewashingtonnote.com/archives/2006/12/post_7/; accessed 4 March 2010.

19. Leverett and Leverett, 'Another Iranian Revolution? Not Likely.'

20. For the central role of Abbas Milani in lobbying the US Congress to push for 'crippling sanctions' on Iran, see my 'A tale of two cities,' *Al-Ahram*

Weekly, 20–26 August 2009, at http://weekly.ahram.org.eg/2009/961/op51.htm; accessed 4 March 2010.

21. See Marwan Bishara, 'It is time for Obama to meet Ahmadinejad,' Aljazeera, 27 February 2010, at http://blogs.aljazeera.net/imperium/2010/02/27/it-time-obama-meet-ahmadinejad; accessed 5 March 2010.

22. Ibid.

23. Ibid.

24. Ibid.

25. See www.politico.com/news/stories/0609/23745.html; accessed 6 March 2009.

26. Here I am not referring just to the rise of asymmetric warfare in the region where Hezbollah and Hamas become stronger every time Israel pounds Lebanon and Gaza. I am also referring to the rise of antiwar films in Israeli cinema and thus among Israelis themselves. For more detail, see my essay on antiwar Israeli cinema, 'A deadly cinematic subconscious,' *al-Ahram Weekly*, 19–25 November, 2010, at http://weekly.ahram.org.eg/2009/973/op5.htm; accessed 6 March 2010.

27. See 'World reacts to Iran violence,' BBC News, 28 December 2009, at http://news.bbc.co.uk/2/hi/middle_east/8432884.stm; accessed 6 March 2010.

SIX

1. Abu al-Ma'ali Nasrollah Monshi's, *Kalilah and Dimnah*: 253–257.

2. At the time of writing this chapter both the UN and the United States have condemned Israeli aggression in Gaza and the simultaneous expansion of their colonial settlements on the West Bank. But Israel defies both the international community and their principal superpower patron with total impunity and continues aggressively on both fronts. For the most recent UN condemnation of Israel, see 'UN humanitarian chief criticizes Israel over Gaza,' BBC News, 12 March 2010, at http://news.bbc.co.uk/2/hi/middle_east/8563569.stm; accessed 12 March 2010; and for US denouncing of Israeli settlement expansions in the West Bank, see 'Joe Biden attacks Israeli plan for East Jerusalem homes,' BBC News, 10 March 2010, at http://news.bbc.co.uk/2/hi/middle_east/8558850.stm.

3. For an informed account of the genealogy of this cabal, see Anne Norton's *Leo Strauss and the Politics of American Empire* (New Haven, CT: Yale University Press, 2004).

4. See my 'Why Obama deserves the prize,' CNN, 9 October 2009, at www.cnn.com/2009/WORLD/meast/10/09/dabashi.obama.nobel.prize/; accessed 12 March 2010).

5. See my 'Does Obama compromise too much?,' CNN, 22 December 2009,

at www.cnn.com/2009/OPINION/12/22/dabashi.obama.copenhagen. leadership/index.html; accessed 12 March 2010.

6. For the most recent iteration of a bold and visionary assessment of such a possibility for a one-state solution to the Israeli–Palestinian conflict, see Ali Abunimah, *One Country: A Bold Proposal to End the Israeli–Palestinian Impasse* (New York: Picador, 2007).

7. See Ralf Dahrendorf, 'In praise of Thrasymachus,' in *Essays in the Theory of Society* (Stanford, CA: Stanford University Press, 1968): 129.

8. Ibid.: 129.

9. Ibid.: 130.

10. Ibid.: 133.

11. Ibid.: 137.

12. Ibid.: 141.

13. Ibid.: 144.

14. Ibid.: 138.

15. Ibid.: 150.

16. Ibid.: 150.

17. See Majid Mohammadi, *Az Rabbani-salari beh Obash-salari: Tahavvol Sakhtar-e Qodrat dar Jomhuri Islami*/'From theocracy to thugocracy: the transformation of the structure of power in the Islamic Republic,' Radio Farda, 19 Esfand 1388/10 March 2010, at www.radiofarda.com/content/f35_Development_IRI_Soc_Base_Com_MM/1979164.html; accessed 10 March 2010.

18. Mohammadi, 'From theocracy to thugocracy'; my translation of the Persian original.

19. For an account of an attack by a band of these plainclothes vigilantes on the home of Mehdi Karroubi, a leading opposition figure, intimidating him, his family, and his neighbors, see the eyewitness account given by Mr Karroubi wife, Ms Fatemeh Karroubi, at the official site of Mr Karroubi's political party, www.sahamnews.org/?p=1332; accessed 16 March 2010.

20. For Mir Hossein Mousavi's original letter, dated 21 Shahrivar 1388/12 September 2009, and Ayatollah Montazeri's response, dated 31 Shahrivar 1388/22 September 2009, see http://amontazeri.com/farsi/topic.asp?TOPIC_ID=223&FORUM_ID=2&CAT_ID=2&Forum_Title=%26%231582%3B%26%231576%3B%26%231585%3B%26%231606%3B%26%231575%3B%26%231605%3B%26%231607%3B&Topic_Title=%26%231662%3B%26%231575%3B%26%231587%3B%26%231582%3B+%26%231576%3; accessed 23 September 2009.

21. For more details of the early history of mass communication in Iran, see my *Iran: A People Interrupted*: chs 3 and 4, inter alia.

22. I have provided a number of expositions (in both Persian and English) detailing why I read this uprising as a 'civil rights movement' and not

a revolution. See, for example, 'An Epistemic Shift in Iran,' *The Brooklyn Rail*, July–August 2009, and 'People Power,' *al-Ahram Weekly*, 25 June–1 July 2009.

SEVEN

1. Flynt Leverett and Hillary Mann Leverett, 'Iran's Green Movement approaches irrelevance: why does Washington continue to gamble on it?' *Foreign Policy* 17, 2010, at http://mideast.foreignpolicy.com/posts/2010/03/17/iran_s_green_movement_approaches_irrelevance_why_does_washington_continue_to_gamble; accessed 6 August 2010.

2. See Jalal Al-e Ahmad, *Occidentosis: A Plague from the West*, trans. R. Campbell (Berkeley, CA: Mizan Press, 1983). This was by far the most influential essay of the 1960s in Iran, and ensured that for a long time the coinage *Gharbzadegi*/'Occidentosis'/'Westoxication' was the most damned term in an entire political culture.

3. See Gideon Levy, 'The unrest in Iran makes me green with envy,' *Haaretz*, 21 July 2009, at www.haaretz.com/hasen/spages/1093876.html; accessed 18 March 2010.

4. For a historical outline of the commencement of this encounter with colonial modernity, see my *Iran: A People Interrupted* (New York: New Press, 2007): ch. 2.

5. See Firoozeh Kashani-Sabet, *Frontier Fictions* (Princeton, NJ: Princeton University Press, 2000).

6. For details, see Haqverdi Naseri, *Zir Derakht-e Nastaran* [Under the Wild Rose Tree] (Tehran: Sephr Publications, 1355/1976).

7. Afshin Matin-Asgari, in his *Iranian Student Opposition to the Shah* (Costa Mesa, CA: Mazda Publishers, 2001), is particularly attentive to this dialectic in his assessment of the role of expatriate students in revolutionary uprisings in Iran.

8. For more on Mirza Habib Isfahani, see Ja'far Modarres Sadeqi's Introduction to his critical edition of Mirza Habib Isfahani's translation of James Morier's *Adventures of Hajji Baba of Ispahan* (Tehran: Markaz Publications, 1379/2000).

9. For these and other references to James Morier's text and a more detailed critical analysis, see my *Iran: A People Interrupted*: ch. 2.

10. For more on the significance of Mirza Saleh Shirazi see my *Iran: A People Interrupted*: ch. 1.

11. For more details, see Mirza Ali Khan Amin al-Dowlah, *Khaterat-e Siyasi* [Political Memoir] ed. Hafez Farmanfarmaian (Tehran: Amir Kabir, 1341/1962).

12. For more details on the history of this novel, see Mohammad Reza Fashahi, *Gozareshi Kutah az Tahavollat-e Fekri va Ejtema'i Jame'eh Feodali-ye Iran* [A

Short Account of the Social and Intellectual Developments of the Feudal Society of Iran] (Tehran: Gutenberg Publishers, 1354/1975): 302–21. For further details about the author and the text, see Yahya Aryanpour, *Az Saba ta Nima/From Saba ta Nima*, 3 vols (Tehran: Zavvar Publications, 1350/1971), vol. 1: 304–13. For an English translation of the first volume of the novel, see Zayn ol-'Abedin Maraghe'i, *The Travel Diary of Ebrahim Beg*, trans. James D. Clark. (Costa Mesa, CA: Mazda Publishers, 2006).

13. See Fashahi, *Gozareshi Kutah az Tahavollat-e Fekri va Ejtema'i Jame'eh Feodali-ye Iran* [A Short Account of the Social and Intellectual Developments of the Feudal Society of Iran]: 314.

14. For a critical essay on this issue, see my 'Left is wrong on Iran,' *al-Ahram Weekly* 16–22 July, 2009, at http://weekly.ahram.org.eg/2009/956/op5. htm; accessed 7 April 2010.

15. See Gayatri Chakravorty Spivak, 'Can the subaltern speak?' in Cary Nelson and Lawrence Grossberg (eds), *Marxism and the Interpretation of Culture* (Urbana, IL: University of Illinois Press, 1988): 271–313.

16. For more on my reading of Atom Egoyan's *Ararat*, see my 'Visions impossible: Atom Egoyan's *Ararat*,' in Marc Nichanian et al. (eds), 'Art and Testimony,' *Armenian Review*, vol. 49, no. 1–4, 2004–05.

17. Also known as Interactionists or the 'Chicago School,' Symbolic Inter-actionists were a major sociological force in the 1960s and 1970s in the United States. For a comprehensive and critical narrative, see Bernice M. Fisher and Anselm L. Strauss, 'Interactionism,' in Tom Bottomore and Robert Nisbet (eds), *A History of Sociological Analysis* (New York: Basic Books, 1978): 457–98.

EIGHT

1. See *'Asheqaneh-ha-ye Evin: Nameh-negari-ye Hamsaran Zendanian Siasi Iran/*'Evin love letters: the letter-writings of the spouses of Iranian political prisoners,' BBC Persian, 27 February 2010, at www.bbc.co.uk/persian/iran/2010/02/100227_l12_evin_love_letters.shtml; accessed 11 April 2010.

2. See Pardis Mahdavi, *Passionate Uprising: Iran's Sexual Revolution* (Stanford, CA: Stanford University Press, 2009): 299–302.

3. See Simin Daneshvar, *Ghorub-e Jalal* [Jalal's Sunset] and *Shoharam Jalal* [My Husband Jalal] (Tehran: Ravaq Publishers, 1360/1981).

4. For a discussion of Forough Farrokhzad's taboo-breaking poetry, see my 'Forough Farrokhzad and the formative forces of Iranian culture,' in Michael C. Hillmann (ed.), 'Forough Farrokhzad: A Quarter Century Later,' *Literature East and West*, 1988.

5. The late Ali Akbar Sa'idi Sirjani has done a comparative study of active

and passive women in love, comparing Shirin and Leili in Nezami's *Khamseh*, in his *Sima-ye Do Zan* [Portrait of Two Women] (Tehran: Nashr-e No, 1367/1988).

6. It is crucial not to make these considerations culture-specific or to Orientalize them – and thus lend legitimacy to the nonsense of 'tradition versus modernity' or 'Islam versus the West' – and always to have a comparative context in mind. In the American context, the cinema of the two legendary Western filmmakers John Ford and Howard Hawks can be divided according to their leading women's roles. Ford's women are mostly homely, stately, the pillar of the family, the definition of a solid life; in Hawks women are independent loners, agential to the point of aggressively pursuing the men they love. Compare the repressed Martha Edwards/Dorothy Jordan in Ford's *Searchers* (1956) with the rambunctious Tess Millay/Joanne Dru in Howard Hawks's *Red River* (1948).

7. For more on these and other aspects of Makhmalbaf's cinema, see my *Makhmalbaf at Large: The Making of a Rebel Filmmaker* (London: I.B. Tauris, 2008).

8. In her *Khaterat Zendan* [Prison Memoir] (Spånga, Sweden: Nashr-e Baran, 1996), Shahrnoush Parsipour pays occasional attention to the erotic aspects of her body while in prison.

9. For a sample of these *tan-neveshteh-ha*, see the following blog: http://naan-va-sharab.blogspot.com/2008/09/blog-post_11.html (accessed 12 April 2010). 'From the very beginning I knew,' the latest entry on this blog reads in Persian (my translation), 'no one makes love ['makes love' is written in English but using the Persian alphabet) like you do, not just because of your calmness, which was different from others', and made me more horny' ['horny' is written in English but using the Persian alphabet].

10. For a sample of these *del-neveshteh*/'heart-writing,' see http://balatarin.com/topic/2010/3/30/1004717. Here we should also note that these love letters are not only written by married women to their husbands. A young woman only known as 'Lebkhand' ('Smile') was the girlfriend/fiancée of Amir Javadi-far, a young man who was arrested by the security forces of the Islamic Republic, viciously beaten, and murdered while in custody after one of the rallies in support of the Green Movement in Iran. Labkhand has written some of the most beautiful love letters of her generation to the memory of the man she loved and so cruelly lost. Neither the reformist Iranian press, nor the international media, nor BBC Persian for that matter, ever paid any attention to people like Labkhand and their pain, because they were not officially married. This is a site (in Persian) with a rare interview with Labkhand: http://www.rhairan.us/archives/17372, accessed 8 September 2010. I am grateful to Mina Khanlarzadeh for alerting me to Labkhand's letters. All these letters

are crucial to our renewed conception of the Iranian social body. In *Making a Social Body: British Cultural Formation, 1830–1864* (Chicago: University of Chicago Press, 1995), Mary Poovey has examined the development of a mass culture in Victorian Britain via the representation of the society as a body-social, a social body.

12. See Bernard Yack, *The Longing for Total Revolution: Philosophic Sources of Social Discontent from Rousseau to Marx and Nietzsche* (Princeton, NJ: Princeton University Press, 1986). Equally relevant is another excellent work of Bernard Yack, *The Fetishism of Modernities: Epochal Self-Consciousness in Contemporary Social and Political Thought* (Notre Dame, IA: University of Notre Dame Press, 1997).

13. Jürgen Habermas, *The Past as Future* (Lincoln, NB: University of Nebraska Press, 1994): 16–20.

14. For more details, see Akbar Ganji, *Manifest-e Jomhuri-khahi* [A Manifesto of Republicanism] (Tehran: 2002) – Ganji wrote this book while in jail; in English, see his 'The Latter-Day Sultan,' *Foreign Affairs*, November–December 2008, at www.foreignaffairs.com/articles/64606/akbar-ganji/the-latter-day-sultan; accessed 11 April 2010.

15. For more on Said Hajjarian's positions, see his *Jomhuriyyat: Afsun-zedai az Qodrat* [Republicanism: Demystifying Power] (Tehran: Tarh-e No, 2000)

16. Michel Foucault, *The Hermeneutic of the Subject: Lectures at the Collège de France 1981–1982* (New York: Palgrave, 2001): 252.

17. See Giorgio Agamben, *State of Exception* (Chicago: University of Chicago Press, 2005).

18. Nicholas Mirzoeff, *Watching Babylon: The War in Iraq and Global Visual Culture* (London: Routledge, 2005)

19. For an excellent article on Chahar-Shanbeh Suri festivities of 1388/2010 during the course of the Green Movement, see Asef Bayat, 'Iran: torch of fire, politics of fun,' *Open Democracy*, 24 March 2010,' at www.opendemocracy.net/asef-bayat/iran-torch-of-fire-politics-of-fun; accessed 30 March 2010).

20. For more on the history of this sociological perspective and its prominent theorists, see Bernice M. Fischer and Anselm L. Strauss, 'Interactionism,' in Tom Bottomore and Robert Nisbet (eds), *A History of Sociological Analysis* (New York: Basic Books, 1978): 457–98.

Index